Children Sing
His Praise

Contributors

Paul Bouman, Helen Kemp,
Carlos Messerli, Ronald Nelson,
Donald Rotermund, David S. Walker

Children Sing His Praise

A Handbook for Children's Choir Directors

Edited by Donald Rotermund

Concordia
Publishing House
St. Louis

Copyright © 1985 Concordia Publishing House
3558 S. Jefferson Avenue, St. Louis, MO 63118-3968
Manufactured in the United States of America.

Library of Congress Cataloging in Publication Data
Main entry under title:

Children sing His praise.

    Includes indexes.
    Contents: Discovering the heritage of children's choirs / Carlos R. Messerli — Involving the children's choir in worship / Carlos R. Messerli — Directing the children / Ronald A. Nelson — [etc.]
    1. Choral singing, Juvenile—Instruction and study.
2. Choirboy training. I. Title.
MT915.C45 1985   784.9'62   85-7699
ISBN: 0-570-01333-X

1 2 3 4 5 6 7 8 9 10 MAL 94 93 92 91 90 89 88 87 86 85

Contents

7. Nonmusic Resources (with annotations) 116
Donald Rotermund

8. Music Repertoire Resources (with annotations) 133
Donald Rotermund

Acknowledgments

As the Christian delights to sing His praise, it is the delight of the editor to sing the praises of those whose contributions compose a significant part of this book. These include the five coauthors:

Paul Bouman, former teacher and highly successful leader of children's choirs;

Helen Kemp, experienced clinician and motivator of choral directors and young singers;

Carlos Messerli, respected musicologist and specialist in church music;

Ronald Nelson, creative music educator and skillful children's choir director; and

David S. Walker, innovative professor of music education and specialist in integrating accompanimental instruments with young voices.

Further praises are gratefully sung for the staff of Concordia Publishing House, who proposed and nurtured this project throughout its development and produced the accompanying video cassettes, and to the members of its Music Editorial Advisory Committee.

My coda of praise is sung for a quartet whose assistance was of immeasurable value: Carole Fisher, for typing a considerable portion of the final manuscript, which freed the editor's hands for doing other aspects of the project; and my three Ds—Doris, Debbie, and David—who relinquished many hours of family time.

Preface

Several years ago an interesting fact was shared by an Anglican priest as he spoke informally to a small group visiting one of the great cathedrals in England. Having been asked about the future of the choir boys after their rich musical training and regular participation in public worship, he replied that one important statistic that can be documented is the fact that over 90 percent of the Anglican clergy were former choir boys!

Another example that demonstrates the lasting effect of a substantive musical experience for children is from the early Lutheran church. The development of that church in a manner that led to its reputation as a "singing church" was not a coincidence. The roots for this are found in Luther's early exposure to good music as a child. Like the apple that falls near the tree that produced it, the musical heritage that the Lutheran church developed was largely determined by its leader, whose early training equipped him with the appreciation he showed as an adult.

It is encouraging to witness the increasing interest many contemporary churches show in fostering strong choral programs for the children under their care. As with Luther and the Anglican clergy, so it will be with many children in the future who have had the advantage of similar training. As adults they will reflect supportive attitudes toward and experience a more meaningful participation in the worship life of the church.

As a resource for children's choir directors, especially for those who serve in Christian congregations, one of the major objectives of *Children Sing His Praise* is to help them in their ministry of music as they nurture young singers to offer their finest sacrifice of praise to God. The reader will be enriched by the insights, philosophy, skills, and methods that the various authors have found to be effective in their own music ministries. The practical information will also help children's choir directors in their selection and use of quality music that will complement the rich worship themes accented in the church year.

One of the unique contributions of *Children Sing His Praise* is a valuable chapter reviewing the illustrious history of the use of children's voices in the Western Church. Here the reader will find in composite form information that heretofore has only been available in fragmentary form.

The reader will also recognize that each author supports the concept that the more carefully the music is prepared and integrated into the fabric of the service as a voice of proclamation, prayer, and praise, the stronger will be its contribution to a cooperative ministry related to Word and Sacrament. From this perspective, the book supports an increasing number of denominational hymnals and worship books, including the recently published *Lutheran Worship* and *Lutheran Book of Worship*.

A historic perception of choral ministry, which *Children Sing His Praise* strongly affirms, is that the singing of the choir serves best when it becomes a "living voice of the Gospel," the *viva vox evangelii,* as Luther commended well-ordered church music. With understanding guidance, children's choirs can function as vital voices of the proclamation of the Word, a function more and more congregations come to appreciate as they experience the results of meaningful planning and participation.

Since experience demonstrates that no one person or group has all the answers to the variety of challenges that arise with children's choirs, the need for leaders to grow by being exposed to resourceful people, new ideas, and additional skills and materials is ongoing. It is from this perspective that *Children Sing His Praise* has developed. We hope it will prove to be a constructive resource for those dedicated to the ministry of children's choirs, particularly the directors and singers.

"Glory to God in the highest" was the song of the heavenly angelic choir centuries ago, and it is an overarching focus of this book. Indeed, heaven has taught us who is to be central in our singing. Preparing earthly choirs to join in the grand chorus that rejoices to sing to its Savior-King is the ultimate purpose for training young choristers. Fortunate is the church and the choir whose director upholds this focus in both precept and practice.

If you have been entrusted with the noble work of guiding young angelic voices to offer their finest musical praises to the Son of David, Mary's Son, Christ the Lord, cherish that role with gratitude. Remember that what is sown makes possible what will later be the harvest. As you help children learn beautiful melodies, strong harmonies, and meaningful texts, help them also to treasure the ministry they have of echoing the angelic song in word and with a loving heart: "Glory to God in the Highest!"

Gloria in excelsis Deo!

Christmastide 1983   DONALD ROTERMUND
Dallas, Texas

"The history of children's musical participation in worship begins in the early centuries of the church. . . . Today, the church . . . could profit from a review of the history of choirs that included children."

Chapter One

Discovering the Heritage of Children's Choirs

Carlos Messerli

A Musical Treasure

In 20th-century America children seldom perform in the forefront of the musical scene. Unless they are prodigies, children are rarely seen today performing serious music professionally.

It was not always so. Throughout the history of the Western world, particularly from the 15th through the 18th centuries, children were key members of musical ensembles that were considered the best of their kind in the world. The chiefly choral ensembles to which the children belonged performed complex works by the foremost masters of the age and sang them to perfection for admiring audiences of considerable sophistication. The sponsors of these choirs were usually associated in some way with the church.

Today the church, along with society in general, could profit from a review of the history of choirs that included children and from the potential beauty that is a part of such choral ensembles.

The place that children have occupied in choral performance has varied from age to age and from country to country, but certain features have remained constant: (1) Girls were generally excluded from choral membership until the 18th century, reflecting thereby a male-dominated clergy and society. (2) Most often, boys participated in choirs of adults by singing the highest voice or voices, while men sang the lower parts. (3) The choral training of children often took place in residential institutions that provided comprehensive academic education along with sophisticated musical instruction. (4) The great choirs of men and boys have been associated with important churches, cathedrals, monasteries, royal court chapels, or municipalities. While the quality of instruction and the performance level of the choirs varied widely, the largest, wealthiest, or most prestigious institutions provided the best leaders and attracted the most talented singers. The choral schools maintained by these institutions held a virtual monopoly on musical instruction of high quality through the 15th century. Nearly every recognized musician of that time received training in a choir school. From the 16th through the 18th centuries most of the leading musicians of Europe were either trained in or associated with choir schools. Even later many eminent musicians began their careers as choir boys.

The musical training received by choristers prepared them for the extensive liturgical responsibilities demanded by their role. In earlier ages Gregorian Chant was the basic musical language of the choir. Later, polyphonic music at first supplemented the repertoire of chant and then gradually dominated the literature. In the 17th century concerted music and in the 18th and 19th centuries symphonic music assumed a leading role. Whatever the medium or style of music, choir boys, especially those of the cathedrals and royal chapels, belonged to the finest choirs of the land and participated as fully professional singers, performing a difficult repertoire before patrons who were at once demanding and appreciative.

The choir schools accepted as apprentices only the brightest and most promising candidates. Children with outstanding voices were scouted by recruiters and even bribed or spirited away to join rival organizations. Those chosen to receive the special education of the choral school were sometimes children of the nobility and the wealthy families or, after the Reformation, children of the clergy. In 18th-century Italy especially but also elsewhere, the most talented orphans were chosen for special musical education in *ospedali* or *conservatories,* institutions that developed highly acclaimed choral and instrumental ensembles.

Highlights of the History of the Treasure

The Early Church

The history of children's musical participation in worship begins in the early centuries of the church. Various chronicles tell of the singing of Christians at worship in the lands dominated by Roman rule up to the first quarter of the fourth century after Christ. Although Christian gatherings were not officially tolerated during the early centuries, especially in the Italian peninsula, documents refer in numerous instances to the singing of Christians at worship. Psalms in alternation and with refrains, hymns for the people, and acclamations were all reportedly sung by men and women or choirs and soloists, but hardly any specific references are made to the special singing of children. That development seems to have awaited the legitimization of the Christian church by the Edict of Milan in A.D. 313 and the subsequent official approval of Christian worship. As basilicas and other structures for worship were opened, the liturgy became more elaborate, and institutions were founded to support the church's expanding liturgical and musical life. In the early church, boys often were trained as lectors or readers of lessons in special schools. Since the sacred lessons were always sung, the training given the boys had to be vocal instruction. Boys receiving such training often became members of the clergy; some even became ecclesiastical officials.

Music instruction in the Middle Ages. Cantor and class of choristers before a large choir-book

The emerging church of the fourth century also saw the rise of monasticism, a development of separate male and female communities in which worship and song became very important. The modern medieval scholar Higini Anglès asserts that these communities "vied with each other in devotion to the chant."

Abbess Etheria of Spain, on a pilgrimage to Jerusalem in about A.D. 385, carefully described the many liturgical practices that she observed, including the fully developed Divine Office (with Morning Prayer and Evening Prayer) and the beginning of a church year cycle. She attended Vespers, in which the singing of the Kyrie eleison was specifically reserved for boy choristers.

In the fourth century the Synod of Laodicea (360—81) established a singing school. Later Pope Celestine I (422—32) established a model *Schola cantorum* in Rome. But the foundation for (or, more likely, the reorganization of) the *Schola cantorum* on what was to be a permanent basis awaited the influence of Pope Gregory (590—604). With a great interest in liturgy and worship, he stimulated the establishment of a permanent *Schola* in Rome and propagated the spread of such institutions to other parts of Europe through the commission of foreign missionaries and teachers of music.

Monasticism and the Expanding Church

Meanwhile, in about 530 St. Benedict (died ca. 543) established a full liturgy for the offices of the church year as part of his monastic rule. The Benedictine order, which ascribed to music a place of great prominence, was to proliferate across the continent to such an extent that the period between the sixth and ninth centuries is sometimes called the "Benedictine Era."

Medieval schoolboys' choir at an evening serenade

In 596, only one year after he had assumed the papal throne, Gregory the Great sent Augustine, first archbishop of Canterbury, to England, and by 630 a flourishing school of chant had been established. And already in the fifth century the *maitrise* (choir school) of the Chartres Cathedral in France had been founded.

In the seventh and eighth centuries, schools were founded in France and in Germanic lands—for example, those at St. Gall (in modern Switzerland) and Metz. In the ninth century schools were established in Reichenau, Mainz, Fulda, Soissons, Rouen, Tours, Reims, St. Martial, and Paris (both at Notre Dame and Sainte Chapelle). In England there were schools of singing at York, Exeter, Herford, and Lincoln. These regional efforts to provide trained liturgical leadership coincided to some extent with the efforts of Charlemagne (ruled 768—814), who attempted to unify the northern lands in part through the encouragement of a common liturgical and musical practice.

The songs performed in the singing schools and monasteries were those of the immense repertoire of Gregorian Chant to which the texts of the developing Mass (Eucharist, Holy Communion) and Divine Office were set. The singing was communal, i.e., for all members of the congregation of monks, priests, students, and those of lesser religious orders, except for those assigned positions of special leadership. The performance was direct (by the entire community), responsorial (by the cantor and the congregation in alternation), or occasionally antiphonal (between two nearly equal segments of the community). Special music, such as the settings of the Introit, Gradual Psalmody, Offertory, and Communion of the Mass and the Responsory, antiphons, and certain other chants of the Office were assigned in part or entirely to soloists and to the choir, including the singers of the *Schola*.

With the emergence of polyphony in Western music, beginning in the 10th century, and its proliferation in the three centuries thereafter, there arose an increasing need for treble voices in the choirs of the church. Although the polyphony was at first soloistic (and thus would probably have required the skill of experienced adult singers), from the 14th century onward choral performance of polyphonic music became the accepted province of choirs. Since polyphony required the simultaneous singing of high and low voices, and since women were not admitted into choirs with men, the position of boys as treble singers became even more secure.

Western Europe

In the 14th century the exile of the papacy to southern France (1309—77) led to the development of a second *Schola* at Avignon. Elsewhere in France *maitrises* were attached to important cathedrals and monasteries. Nearly all of the famous musicians of France and the lowlands were trained in or were associated with such schools. In the 14th century, kings and princes used the prestige that would accrue to them as patrons of court chapels to impress their supporters and rivals. The dukes of Burgundy and Dijon developed chapels with choirs of men and boys that accompanied their royal entourages on journeys and diplomatic missions as symbols of wealth and power. Probably the most prestigious of the French chapels was the royal Sainte Chapelle of Paris, founded in 1299. The 15th century Flemish and Netherlandish cities advertised their prosperity and stability through maintenance of choir schools such as those at Antwerp, Bruges, Liège, Hainout, and Cambrai.

The size of the choirs was not as important a factor in their organization as was the quality of membership. Cambrai had only 10 men and 6 boys but maintained a quality of performance that led Philip of Luxembourg to exclaim in 1428 that the cathedral "surpasses all others and may well serve them as a model, with the beauty of its chant."

During the musical period called the Renaissance, choirs that included children flourished all across Europe. In Spain many musical centers developed, especially in Toledo, Seville, Málaga, and the monastery of Montserrat near Barcelona with its famous *Escorial* choir. The royal chapel at Palermo was noteworthy in Sicily. In Italy the cathedrals of nearly all of the major musical centers maintained choir schools patterned after that of the papacy of Rome.

Vienna

In 1498 Emperor Maximilian I founded the famous *Hofburg Kapelle* that was to grace his court with such distinction in Vienna. The *Kapelle* had been preceded in that city by other choral and instrumental groups that served Archduke Sigmund in Innsbruck in the Tirol between 1446 and 1490. The emperor brought these musicians together to form one royal *Kapelle* led by Heinrich Isaac (ca. 1450—1517), the composer, and Paul Hofhaimer (1459—1537), the organist. With the endowment of this choral school he established an institution that was to include a large number of renowned musicians ranging from Ludwig Senfl (ca. 1486—1543) to Franz Schubert (1749—1859) and Franz Joseph Haydn (1732—1809). The *Hofburg Kapelle* exists today as a treasure of the city of Vienna, where it performs weekly settings of the Mass by major composers, especially those of the classic period. It is often assisted in performance by instrumentalists of the Vienna Philharmonic.

Germany

Another renowned choir that has continued a strong tradition in Germany from the 15th century to the present is the *Kreuzchor* of Dresden (now East Germany), of which Richard Wagner (1813—

Courtesy ICM Artists, Ltd.

83) was once a member. Other significant choirs of the German tradition are those in Innsbruck, Weimar, Halle, Lüneberg, Berlin, and Regensburg. Courtly and ecclesiastical chapel choirs of the Renaissance in Germany were called *Kantoreien*. One of the most famous of these chapels was located at Torgau, where it rose to prominence as the *Urkantorei* (first or original *Kantorei*) of the religious Reformation. Its leader was Johann Walter (1496—1570), Martin Luther's musical adviser. After 1526, when the Torgau court moved to Dresden, Luther successfully encouraged the citizens to assume responsibility for the *Kantorei* as a municipal project. The *Kantorei* consisted of schoolboys and men of the school, church, or community who sang both chant and polyphonic styles of music in a repertoire that included the best of the old Roman Catholic and the new Lutheran compositions. Responsibilities of the *Kantorei* included providing music for all services and special music for weddings and funerals.

Another famous German choir of men and boys is the *Thomanerchor* (choir of St. Thomas Church) of Leipzig in Saxony. The monastery and choir school of St. Thomas was founded in 1212. Through the centuries the school curriculum provided training in all subjects, but especially in music and singing so that the choir could lead in daily worship. The choir director also taught Latin and religion. Over the course of its 700-year history St. Thomas has been blessed with outstanding cantors. One was Georg Rhau (1488—1548), who led his choir in singing a 12-voice Mass of his own composition at the famous 1519 debate between Martin Luther and Johann Eck (1486—1543) and who later became the chief musical publisher of the early Reformation. Other St. Thomas cantors were Sethus Calvisius (1556—1615), an eminent musical theorist; Johann Hermann Schein (1586—1630), a leading Lutheran composer of the early Baroque period; and the great Johann Sebastian Bach (1685—1750). Bach was cantor of St. Thomas from 1723 to 1750, during which time the choir sang many of his choral works, including his great Passions, parts of the *Mass in B Minor,* and dozens of his cantatas.

The size of the choir that was needed by Bach was not great. The minimum number of singers for a good choir according to Bach's specifications was 16 and included a disposition of four to each part (soprano, alto, tenor, bass). Actually, Bach had to settle for 12 singers, three men or boys assigned to each section, and at times not all of the three singers for each part were available.

Since the time of Bach the choir has maintained its position of excellence under such leaders as Gustav Schreck (1849—1918) and Karl Straube (1873—1950), although in recent years its traditional Lutheran liturgical emphasis has been diluted by the secular sponsorship of the (East) German Democratic Republic.

Concert in the Thomaskirche under Karl Straube

HIGHLIGHTS OF THE HISTORY
21

England

The record of participation by children in the church music of England forms a remarkable history, not only because of its longevity but also because of its quality and intensity. Children have sung in English choirs in a nearly unbroken line since the end of the sixth century when Gregory the Great sent Augustine from Rome to England with about 40 singers to teach the proper (i.e., Gregorian) form of the liturgy and method of singing. The Canterbury *Schola cantorum* was founded by Augustine in 597. Other choir schools, such as York, Lincoln, St. Paul's in London, and the famous King's College and St. John's College at Cambridge University, were established subsequently.

Probably the foremost choral organization throughout England's history has been the Chapel Royal, which has a lineage that can be traced to the 12th century. As with similar choirs on the Continent, in some periods of its history its quality was maintained by kidnapping and pressing into service boys with outstanding voices from various other choirs throughout the country.

English cathedrals and monasteries continued this type of training until the advent of choral polyphony. When polyphony was introduced, the value of the boys' unchanged voices for the singing of treble parts was recognized by assigning the upper parts to them. However, in contrast to the Continental practice in which boys are more often given the two highest parts, for example, the alto and soprano of four-part music, the English most often elect to assign only the topmost part to unchanged boys' voices and to leave the second highest voice to adult male altos. The lower voice parts were, of course, sung by adult males.

Although its continuity over so many centuries is indeed noteworthy, the marvel of English choral music practice today is the vitality and beauty of the more than 20 cathedral and collegiate choirs that perform a liturgical (and in some cases also a concert) repertoire of chants, motets, and anthems from the masterworks of the past and present.

The Reformation of the 16th century did not deal English choral institutions a mortal blow. Instead, it resulted in a reorganization of the supporting ecclesiastical structure that adjusted to the change from the Latin language to English and from the Roman Catholic to Anglican liturgical practice without seriously affecting the quality of the resulting performance.

Latin America

Choral singing by children spread across the Atlantic following the discovery and Christianization of the New World. The colonization of Latin America by the Spanish and Portuguese soldiers and missionaries that began in the 16th century resulted in an amazing development that included children as part of the choirs of natives participating in the service of the newly established mission churches. When the European conquerors of Mexico and Peru in particular (and to a lesser extent Venezuela, Argentina, and Brazil) invaded these lands, they found highly developed civilizations that had fostered a love for music among the people. Thus when the Catholic missionaries accompanying the soldiers sought to convert the natives to the new faith, they discovered that music proved to be a helpful ally in communicating with and influencing their talented converts.

The natives were strongly attracted to both chant and polyphony and proved to be apt pupils. Some learned the techniques of song and composition so rapidly that within one generation native choirs could chant liturgical pieces and sing polyphonic compositions at Mass. Just like their European counterparts, the native boys were taught music in singing schools and performed the treble parts of polyphony in choirs in which men also participated.

One example will illustrate the accomplishments of the natives. In 1560, only 39 years after the arrival of the Spaniards, an elaborate commemorative pageant with a vigil and Mass was held in Mexico City to commemorate the memory of Charles V, who had just died. Two antiphonal choirs of native performers sang settings of the Invitatory and the Psalmody by the renowned Spanish master Cristóbal Morales (ca. 1500—63) with boys singing the treble parts. A choir of boys also sang polyphonic psalm settings in alternation with the chanting of adults.

North America

Children's voices are commonly found in two types of choral organizations in North America: a small number of choirs of men and boys that perpetuate the historic European tradition and choirs of children's voices alone. The traditional all-male choir receives sponsorship from one of two sources: churches and church-related organizations or communities and independent bodies. The repertoire of the male choirs, which often achieve professional or semi-professional status, depends on their sponsorship. Those affiliated with the church focus on "classic" liturgical or general sacred works and only occasionally explore secular music. Community-based or independent choirs usually sing a smaller religious repertoire and devote more attention to secular or even popular music.

The emergence of choirs of boys and girls is a relatively recent phenomenon. Most of these groups in America consist of children of a single parish. Those with the greatest longevity are usually associated with large congregations. The groups commonly focus on the preparation of service music, some of it liturgical, some topical, some merely entertaining. The most successful church children's choirs are usually part of a multiple-choir program under the lead-

Photo by Robert Reicher

The choir of St. Thomas Church, New York, New York, Gerre Hancock, Organist and Master of Choristers.

ership of a professional musician. A few such groups also exist as community-based programs, often located in urban centers in America. The mixed children's choir usually consists of children between the ages of 9 or 10 and 14 or 15.

In recent years interest has developed in the formation of parish choir schools that offer weekly musical and religious instruction in a graded program that extends over several years. Such schools have been most successful in attracting sufficient participants when the sponsoring congregation has been able to provide adequate financial resources for inspired professional leadership and when the parish boundaries have not been so distant as to create serious transportation and schedule problems.

A Checklist of Representative Composers Who Sang in Choirs as Children

John Blow (ca. 1648/49—1708), Chapel Royal
William Boyce (1711—79), St. Paul's Cathedral
John Bull (ca. 1562—1628), Chapel Royal
Jeremiah Clark (ca. 1673—1707), Chapel Royal
Josquin Deprès (ca. 1440—1521), Collegiate Church, St. Quentin
Guillaume Dufay (ca. 1400—74), Cambrai Cathedral
Carl H. Graun (1704—59), Kreuzchor, Dresden
Orlando di Lasso (1532—94), St. Nicolas, Mons
Leonhard Lechner (ca. 1553—1606), Hofkapelle, Landshut
Luca Marenzio (1553—99), Brescia Cathedral
Claudio Monteverdi (1567—1643), Cremona Cathedral
Cristóbal Morales (ca. 1500—53), Seville Cathedral
Leopold Mozart (1719—87), Augsburg Gymnasium
Johannes Ockeghem (ca. 1420—96), Antwerp Cathedral
Giovanni da Palestrina (ca. 1525—94), S. Maria Maggiore, Rome
Peter Philips (1561—1628), St. Paul's Cathedral, London
Giuseppe Pitoni (1657—1743), S. Giovanni des Fiorentini, Rome
Michael Praetorius (1571—1621), Kantorei, Torgau
Henry Purcell (ca. 1659—95), Chapel Royal
Balthasar Resinarius (ca. 1486—1544), Hofburgkapelle, Vienna
Johann H. Schein (1586—1630), Electoral Chapel, Dresden
Franz Schubert (1797—1828), Hofburgkapelle, Vienna
Heinrich Schütz (1585—1672), Collegium Mauritianum, Kassel
Ludwig Senfl (ca. 1486—1543), Hofburgkapelle, Augsburg and Vienna

Antonio Soler (1729—83), Montserrat monastery
Tomás L. de Victoria (ca. 1549—1611), Avila Cathedral
Richard Wagner (1813—83), Kreuzchor, Dresden
Johann Walter (1496—1570), Electoral Chapel, Saxony
William Walton (b. 1902), Christ Church Cathedral, Oxford

"To fulfill its most noble and uplifting potential the Christian children's choir must be approached as an activity that focuses on the worship of almighty God as revealed in the person of Jesus Christ."

Chapter Two

Involving the Children's Choir in Worship

Carlos Messerli

Children as Leaders of Worship, Not Performers

Of all acts of corporate worship probably none is more inspiring than the singing of a well-trained, well-disciplined choir of children. To hear the pure voices of children produce freely floating tones in perfect unison or in harmony is one of the most uplifting of musical experiences. An even more spiritually profound impression is made if the song is an integral part of the theme of the day and if the singers actively participate in worship by listening, singing, and praying as full partners in the worshiping community.

And yet singing and worship leadership of this kind are rare in the modern church. Children are often trained to participate in worship by singing only a single anthem with a "catchy" or "cute" setting of a childishly repetitive text. The accompaniment of the song may consist of "snappy" rhythms provided by piano, bells, or guitars. When the choir is not singing the anthem, the children often appear uninvolved in the actions related to worship and instead talk, doodle, fidget, or simply daydream. Hymns, lessons, congregational liturgy, Holy Baptism, or Holy Communion pass unobserved and thus are quite meaningless to the children.

The difference between the noble ideal of the first instance cited and the pathetic reality of the second is for many congregations primarily a matter of will. In the first example leadership of the

congregation has determined that children are important members of God's family, that their work in worship is significant, that they can make a worthy contribution to corporate worship, and that children are worthy of fine training. In the second instance children, perhaps by default, have been led to believe that they are not ready for active participation and that, while they may entertain adults at worship, more serious activity must wait for another time in their lives.

In order to understand how it is possible for children to worship actively in what some falsely view as an adult liturgy, it may be helpful to examine the theological relationships involved in children's participation in worship.

The spiritual foundation for the work of the children's choir consists of several components. The components are rooted in worship, for the primary task of the choir of children singing in church is to worship. Without the high purpose of worship, the choir is simply an organized activity for children that is educationally worthy and aesthetically satisfying or, at a more mundane level, merely enjoyable for the participants and their parents and entertaining for the other listeners. While there is nothing improper about either enjoyment or entertainment, both of these activities pale in ultimate worth when compared with the divine imperative of worship.

To fulfill its most noble and uplifting potential, the Christian children's choir must be approached as an activity that focuses on the worship of almighty God as revealed in the person of Jesus Christ. This activity is conducted within the community of the faithful commonly called the congregation.

Evelyn Underhill, in her classic treatise *Worship,* begins with the illuminating premise that there is a sense in which "we may think of the whole life of the universe, seen and unseen, conscious and unconscious as an act of worship, glorifying its Origin, Sustainer, and End."[1] Anyone who has meditated at length on the psalms must be convinced of the legitimacy of Underhill's premise, for above all the psalms develop the thought that all creation—earth, stars, vegetation, animals, and all other objects—praises the Lord.

And yet in the Christian understanding this worship is incomplete. Underhill continues by defining Christian worship as "the total adoring response of many to the one Eternal God self-revealed in time."[2] George Hoyer comments that "Christian worship is the response of faith to the Blessed Trinity who has revealed himself as he is and does through the life, death, resurrection of his Son Jesus Christ."[3]

Stated another way, it is our chief purpose to glorify God. Our human creatureliness requires that we worship our Creator. Such a relationship presumes that humans—in this case, children—first appreciate the fact that they have been made by a Creator and that this Creator has revealed Himself to humanity in the person of Jesus

Christ as recorded in Holy Scripture. Once they have heard this marvelously good news, people (children) must learn to appreciate that of which God-pleasing worship consists.

In some areas Christians have assumed that if the nature of God has been communicated intellectually to children (insofar as that is possible) and if the children believe what they have been told, then the child's relationship to God the Creator and Jesus Christ His Son is complete. In communities where worship education is taken seriously, it is sometimes assumed that if children are told about worship activities such as prayer, posture, song, meditation, celebration, and Word and Sacraments, somehow they will begin to worship properly.

Both assumptions are false, for they do not consider the fact that children learn far more by example than they do by lecture and that they learn most of all by their own activity. Thus, while it is very important for adults to tell children about the nature of God and of worship, it is far more important for adults themselves to act out (fulfill) the precepts of worship faithfully and consistently in front of children, so that they may see how (and also to some extent why) it is done at all.

With this background, the work of children's choirs begins to come more clearly into focus, for it is in the regular and faithful worship by the choir in rehearsal and in weekly services with adults that children learn most about worship. In the regular exercise of worship activities, children learn by doing, communicate to other children, and communicate with adults. And in the process of doing and communicating, the children themselves adopt the true posture of worship and lay a foundation for an ever more faithful and meaningful attitude of true worship.

Thus far we have suggested that worship is a response of the creature to the Creator and that the nature of worship is best communicated to children not by lecture but by example and involvement. Now let us look at some specific themes or points of contact that relate to children who are to worship as members of the choir.

Themes of Worship

In "The Child in Christian Worship"[4] George Hoyer outlines six areas in which God's Word, that is, God Himself in action, is revealed in worship. It is in these six interrelated and overlapping areas that the child—or for our purpose, the children's choir—responds in worship to the working of God.

God's Word in God's Words

In the Bible God reveals Himself and His plan of salvation for us in words meant to be heard and believed. The children's choir at worship listens to, absorbs, and often sings the Biblical words. Some of the most significant settings of Scripture are those assigned to the choir: Versicles, Introits, Psalms, Verses, Offertories. As specified by the liturgy for various Sundays and festivals of the church year, these short (one could almost say "child-sized") fragments illuminate the larger readings, the Old Testament, Epistle, and Gospel, and comment directly on the larger theme of the day or festival. In addition, if the musical settings of these short texts are of high quality, their meaning is illuminated in a special and significant way.

Children in the choir learn God's words by singing God's words. They learn of His Son (God's Word) by focusing on the relationship of the various aspects of the liturgy and the church year in which the choir is immersed.

God's Word in Water

The washing of Baptism is the Christian rite that seems most easily to captivate children. They respond naturally to the special attention given to young children and to water. From the point of this natural fascination it is not far to draw their attention to the true meaning and rich symbolism of Baptism for their own lives. Through regular attendance at church and active participation in song at baptismal rites, children in choirs have the opportunity not only to recall their own baptism but also to contribute to the appreciation of the entire community for this basic rite of initiation. Especially from the festival of the Baptism of Our Lord through Transfiguration, Lent, and Holy Week, to the Vigil of Easter, the Resurrection of Our Lord, and the full Easter season, the liturgy and the meaning of God's Word in water can be made to come alive for children.

God's Word in Relationships

Hoyer says that "by our relationship with our children we begin to teach them the love of God." One of the fundamental contributions of worship to the life of the individual of any age, but particularly to the child, is to teach the relationship of the individual to the community. In worship we are members of one body. "We believe in one God." We sing together. We pray together. We stand together.

The child in the choir learns to use and to value his or her own voice, but the child also learns to blend voice, will, and actions into those of the community—first in the child's small section of voices, then in the choir, then in the worshiping congregation, and finally in the entire community of believers on earth or the body of saints here on earth and in heaven.

In worship, then, each individual is important, for Christ died for each personally, but also in worship the child is led beyond this egocentric salvation history to an appreciation of the fellowship of all the saints—a fellowship in which each child in the worshiping community holds treasured membership.

God's Word in the Church's Fellowship

This area extends the relationships of the previous section deep into the life of the church. Boys and girls are redeemed children of God and members of the church's fellowship no less than are adults. The needs, activities, and maturation levels of children may be different from those of adults, but everything should be done to incorporate children into worship with adults while recognizing the differences between them.

In most cases children can participate fully in adult worship as a sign of their role in the church, but they must be prepared for the experience by caring adults, and they must see the consistent example of worshiping Christians who thereby communicate that which is important in their own lives.

In the church's fellowship children have the opportunity to associate with those who are "little Christs" to their fellow Christians. Children no less than others can lead a "Christ-like" life that can reveal God's love to others. One of the greatest joys of working with children in worship is to observe how these "little Christs" can subtly influence behavior and effect change for the better within the choir.

God's Word in the Act of Worship

Christ's promise that wherever two or three are gathered in His name He will be present is valid even if one or two (or three) of those gathered are children.

The point here is not that Christ watches us to see that our worship is genuine but that we can be assured of His powerful presence when our worship is heartfelt. And when Christ is present things happen. Thoughts are redirected, and lives are changed. Hoyer asserts the truth that "among growing children, as well as among adults, in the very act of worshiping, a child is making the most direct and personal application of the word to him or herself. Worship is a *means* for the means of Grace."

God's Word in the Eucharist

As the chief liturgy of the church, the Eucharist or Holy Communion, that continuation of the meal instituted by our Lord, is of prime importance to children and adults. When it is celebrated, Christ is present in a *special* way that demands the attention of those who say that they belong to Him. Although the age at which young children partake of the bread and wine may vary from congregation to congregation, the Lord is undeniably present in the liturgy of the Supper. Children of the choir, no less than adults, can feel the presence of the Lord that is so effectively communicated in most congregations by word, song, vestments, and above all ceremony. Of course, the mystery that surrounds the Sacrament can be fully understood by no one, not even by adults. But children can share in the awe at the mystery and in the spirit of celebration that is also a part of the Sacrament as they participate in the liturgy, particularly with their song.

The Repertoire of the Children's Choir

Principles of Selection of Music

The repertoire of the children's choir can consist of music drawn from many traditions and countries and composed over many centuries. The array of music available from publishers today is staggering in quantity and variety. The director needs to give careful thought to music selection, for except for the vocal and choral techniques to be taught, the selection of music is the most critical aspect of the director's work. Three criteria for the selection of music must be established if the children's choir is to fulfill its role in worship effectively:

First, the music of the children's Choir must be textually worthy. It may be simple or complex, depending on the requirements of the occasion, but it must possess textual merit. The text of a worthy children's choir composition should also be rooted in Holy Scripture. Finally, it may consist of direct quotations from the Bible, or it may take the form of prose or poetic commentary on Biblical truths, but it should follow high standards of literary composition.

Next, the music of a worthy composition for children should display excellence. Not all of the compositions sung by the children's choir need to have been written by the great masters, but each piece should reveal high standards of craftsmanship of melody, rhythm, harmony, and text underlay. The music need not be difficult, for some of the most effective pieces for children are quite simple. On the other hand, it must not be trite, for to assume that children, even preschool children, can only sing repetitive "ditties" is to insult their intelligence and to deny them the opportunity to grow musically.

Last, the music to be sung in church by a children's choir is strongest when it serves a clear thematic or topical function in the service. The most effective choral music in worship is that which fits appropriately into the prescribed liturgical order and is not arbitrarily added to it.

To summarize, the music for children's choirs is selected on the same basis as that for any other choir: musical quality, textual suitability, and appropriateness for the specific occasion. To paraphrase Scripture, the music sung is "a sweet-sounding sacrifice" to the Lord and therefore must be the finest that can be offered.

The Choir and the Propers of the Day

Throughout the history of the church, wherever there has been corporate worship, certain individuals or groups have been assigned the task of performing special musical functions. Because of their ability and training, these choirs performed in the stead of the community. The choir usually sang those texts specifically assigned to it and led the congregation in its part of the worship.

In the history of the chief service of the church, the Mass of the Holy Communion, the choir usually sang those texts that articulated the theme of the day at significant points in the order. These texts are collectively called the Propers of the Day or simply Propers.

The modern Propers are the Verse (or Tract), the Offertory, and (in some circles) the Introit and the Gradual. The Psalm of the Day[5] may also be placed in this category, although it is often considered a fourth reading from Scripture. As in historic times, modern worship books assign Proper texts to choirs, and it is appropriate for the children's choir of today to strive to carry on the tradition of these historic choirs. When it is not possible for the entire choir to master all of the Proper settings on any given day, effort should be made to have the choir sing at least one of the Propers. The other texts may be sung by a single child (cantor) or a small group of children, by an adult cantor, or by another choir, or the general text from the worship book may be sung by the congregation. On occasion it may even be desirable to have the choir (or the congregation) read the Proper text of the day. This exercise in choral speaking is yet another way to draw attention to the significance of the Proper texts.

The Propers to be sung by the choir depend on the liturgical tradition being observed in a given congregation. The Verse text (Alleluia Verse or Tract in Lent), usually drawn from the Psalms, serves as the introduction to the chief reading of the service, the Gospel of the Day. It thus assumes a prominent position in the order in spite of its brevity.

The traditional Introit, which sounds the theme of the day, is sung before the Kyrie at the beginning of the service or as an optional entrance song. The Introit consists of an antiphon, psalm verse, Gloria Patri, and repeated antiphon.

The historic Gradual (an abbreviated psalm text) or the Gradual Psalm may be sung after the first reading, although the full

Gradual Psalm or Psalm of the Day has replaced the shortened form in some parishes.

The Offertory, a longer text also often drawn from the Psalms, is intended to be sung as the gifts are presented at the altar. It often comments on the relation of the Scripture readings to the Lord's Supper that follows.

All of the Proper texts are available to children's choirs in a variety of published settings. Any of them may also be set to traditional (Gregorian) or modern chant settings. One of the simplest methods is that available in *Lutheran Book of Worship* through the application of the psalm tones (pp. 290—91) described in the *Manual on the Liturgy* (pp. 94—96). The psalm tones of *Lutheran Worship* found at the head of each psalm (pp. 313—68) also serve this purpose.

Psalm of the Day

In recent years much attention has been given to the reintroduction of entire psalms into the service. Placed after the first Scripture reading (which is usually from the Old Testament), the Psalm often comments on that reading and prepares the worshiper for the coming Gospel of the Day. Children should be given the chance to explore the rich spiritual treasury that is the Psalms by singing them in any one of the several methods available. One must not assume that children cannot or will not be able to follow the thought of the Psalms or to chant them. Experience has established that if the task is approached with insight and enthusiasm, children can enjoy this significant contribution to worship.

When it is possible to do so, children should sing all of the psalm text, paying particular attention to the clear articulation of the words. If it is long, perhaps the children could alternate in singing verses with a child or an adult cantor or even with the congregation. The melodies to which the psalms are to be sung may be those of traditional Gregorian chant, the sprung rhythm of the melodies made popular by Father Joseph Gelineau, or one of the other modern methods. A flexible and highly adaptable system of chant is presented in *Lutheran Book of Worship* (pp. 290—91) and further articulated in the *Manual on the Liturgy* (pp. 82—85). The useful psalm tones of *Lutheran Worship* are found at the head of each psalm (pp. 313—68).

In chanted psalmody it is also possible for the children's choir to sing the antiphon refrain after every verse or every few verses if the congregation or a cantor (or the children's choir itself) sings the remainder of the psalm. (An example of a pentatonic antiphon, composed by Helen Kemp, for use with Psalm 113—the appointed Psalm for Epiphany 3/C—can be seen at the beginning of chap. 5, p. 66.) Brief refrain melodies composed by Richard Hillert, which are compatible with the 10 psalm tones of *LBW* are found in the *Manual on the Liturgy* (pp. 144—45). Another convenient source of simple refrain melodies for Psalms is that of Roger Petrich in *Psalm Antiphons for the Church Year* (see chap. 8, p. 149). Melody instruments or handbells are especially effective when played to signal the beginning of the refrain, to accompany the melody in unison, to provide harmonic support, or even to add a second melodic line. (See Psalm Collections, chap. 8, p. 149. Ferguson, *Worship Blueprints: Guide to Planning for Worship Music*, chap. 8, pp. 42—45, 60—66, offers excellent help.)

Many published anthems for children's choirs are based on texts from the Psalms. By consulting the tables of Psalms assigned to each Sunday or festival of the Church Year (*Lutheran Worship*, pp. 10—123; *Lutheran Book of Worship*, pp. 13—41), the choir director can select a given psalm anthem for the appropriate day to sing in place of the Psalm (*Lutheran Worship*, "Propers of the Day," pp. 10—123). One caution must be observed in the selection of anthem substitutes for the singing of full psalm texts: Many anthems for children's choirs present only a truncated version of the full text. Such abbreviation may be acceptable (or even desirable) from a musical point of view, but it is not appropriate from a liturgical standpoint. Each complete psalm or major psalm segment identified in the Proper tables has an integrity and meaning that is necessary to respect and to communicate in worship. If the psalm text is severely abridged, what remains may not truly present the thought or intent of the whole psalm. If the choir sings a shortened psalm version, the congregation must at least be made aware of the original text by means of an announcement in the service folder, so that the people can follow it in the worship book as the choir sings its version. (See chap 8, pp. 141—49, for psalm materials for singing.)

Many metrical hymn paraphrases of the 150 psalms have been written in the past 400 years, largely for use in the churches of the Reformation.[6] While they are of uneven literary merit, some have become beloved hymns, and many of these are still available in modern worship books. For example, "O God, Our Help in Ages Past" is a paraphrase of Psalm 90 by Isaac Watts set to the sturdy *St. Anne* tune of William Croft. Choirs (and congregations) can sing published or hymnal settings of these hymns in place of the Biblical psalm text. British settings of *St. Anne* often assign stanzas or descants to children's voices. (See appendices B and C, pp. 183—208, for lists of metrical psalms in *Lutheran Worship* and *Lutheran Book of Worship*.)

The original purpose of the psalm paraphrase was to permit congregations to sing the entire Scriptural text to a simple, repeated melody. Often the rhymed text sacrifices fidelity to the Hebrew thought and form for the sake of the metrical demands of the poetry. Oftener still, the modern hymnal abbreviates the psalm text so severely that much of the original thought is lost. As in the case of abbreviated psalm anthems, the congregation should be informed of the source of the text when a shortened metrical paraphrase is to be sung.

Hymns

One goal of conscientious musical and pastoral leaders of worship will be to help the congregation develop a repertoire of hymns that embrace the best of the genre. The purpose of striving to attain this goal is to expose the congregation to the theological and poetic insights of great hymns as well as to encourage an appreciation of hymns of high musical quality in order to lead the people to a deeper and more fervent expression of the faith.

In hymn selection, high quality suggests that both text and tune be sturdy and significant. The texts should be carefully crafted, consist of imaginative poetry, and be expressive of a wide range of Scriptural and devotional truths. In general, the strongest hymns often speak of God, His mighty acts and saving love to us in Christ Jesus, and the sanctifying power of the Holy Spirit rather than of human actions, feelings, or intentions. Other subjects that have captured the attention of great hymn writers are the church, Holy Communion, and the themes of the great festivals of the church year.

The most significant hymn melodies seem to exhibit two characteristics: they are rhythmically vigorous and melodically flowing and soaring. One measure of the quality of a hymn is its capacity for embellishment or development by composers. By this standard *Es ist das Heil* ("Salvation unto Us Has Come") rates as a more durable melody than *O store Gud* ("How Great Thou Art"). Such value judgments, of course, are not absolute but indicate directions to follow in selecting hymns for children.

Children's choirs should learn the best hymns not only for choral suitability but also in order to help the congregation develop its repertoire. The program of hymn instruction for the choir could proceed on a systematic basis through the years in which a child is in the choir. Usually, simpler hymns will be learned in early years, and more complex hymns later on. Even the youngest child can memorize the melody and words of a few of the classic hymns.

In the performance of hymns in church, the children's choir may make its most significant contributions by singing hymn stanzas in alternation with the congregation. In this way each group, the congregation and the choir, may hear itself as the partner of the other in singing praises to God, each vying with the other to sing "the most excellent song" to the Lord.

The potential repertoire of hymns in worship books is so great that only the construction of a master plan of hymn singing can achieve the desired goals. It is well for the choir to develop a core of classic hymns on the major themes and seasons of the church year. Many of these are to be found in the traditional Hymn of the Day lists used by congregations to develop a rich practice of hymn singing through selection of the chief hymns of the church year that are strong in both tune and text. Such a traditional list with contemporary adaptations is found in *Lutheran Book of Worship* (pp. 929—31) and *Lutheran Worship* (pp. 976—78). The Hymn of the Day (a complete listing for the church year may be consulted in Appendix D, pp. 209—14) could well become the subject of embellishment and special settings by the children's choir in alternation with the congregation.

Many congregations with excellent singing traditions have discovered that as the singing of worthy hymns became a subject of high priority, congregational song improved, participation in worship increased, and parish life was strengthened.

Another vehicle for encouraging good hymn singing is to establish a list of "core hymns" that are given special attention by choir and congregation. Although each congregation and each children's choir will want to develop its own core list of basic hymns, the following may serve as a suggested list:

Core Hymns for Seasons

Advent	Savior of the Nations, Come	*LBW*	28	*Nun komm, der*
(Hymn of the Day for Advent 1)		*LW*	13	*Heiden*
Christmas	From Heaven Above	*LBW*	51	*Vom Himmel hoch*
(Hymn of the Day for Christmas)		*LW*	37	
Epiphany	O Morning Star	*LBW*	76	*Wie schön leuchtet*
(Hymn of the Day for Epiphany)		*LW*	73	
Lent	My Song Is Love Unknown	*LBW*	94	*Rhosymedre*
(Hymn of the Day for Lent 5)		*LW*	91	*Love unknown*
Easter	Christ the Lord Is Risen Today	*LBW*	130	*Orientis partibus*
		LW	142	
Pentecost	Spirit of God *or*	*LBW*	387	*Donata*
	Holy Spirit, Ever Dwelling	*LBW*	523	*In Babilone*
		LW	164	

Songs of both Holy Baptism and Holy Communion are especially important to children, and hymns on the sacraments should receive the attention of children's choirs:

Core Hymns for the Sacraments

Baptism	Dearest Jesus, We Are Here	*LBW*	187	*Liebster Jesu*
		LW	226	
Baptism	We Know That Christ	*LBW*	189	*Engelberg*
Holy Communion	At the Lamb's High Feast	*LBW*	210	*Sonne der Gerechtigkeit*
		LW	126	
Holy Communion	O Lord, We Praise You	*LBW*	215	*Gott sei gelobet*
		LW	238	

Songs of Praise to the Holy Trinity or Songs of General Praise

God the Father (Psalm 117)	Praise to the Lord, the Almighty	LBW 543 LW 444	*Lobe den Herren*
Christ Jesus	In Thee Is Gladness In You Is Gladness	LBW 552 LW 442	*In dir ist Freude*
Holy Spirit	Holy Spirit, Ever Dwelling	LBW 523 LW 164	*In Babilone*
General Praise	Earth and All Stars	LBW 558 LW 438	*Earth and all stars*
The Trinity	All Glory Be to God on High	LBW 166 LW 215	*Allein Gott in der höh*
Holy Communion	Isaiah in a Vision Did of Old Isaiah, Mighty Seer, in Spirit Soared	LBW 528 LW 214	*Jesaia, dem Propheten*

Ordinary of Holy Communion

Most children take great pleasure in being able to teach adults. At corporate worship, when there presumably is little for children too do but to be quiet, they can realize their importance as members of the body of Christ in a special way if they are given the responsibility to prepare a song that is being introduced to the congregation.

On occasion, the children's choir could sing a different setting of traditional songs of the Ordinary of Holy Communion as a festal alternative to standard practice.

Kyrie eleison	Kyrie! God, Father in Heaven	LBW 168 LW 209	*Kyrie, Gott Vater*
Gloria in excelsis	All Glory Be to God on High	LBW 166 LW 215	*Allein Gott in der höh*
Credo	We All Believe in One True God	LBW 374 LW 213	*Wir glauben all*
Sanctus	Isaiah in a Vision Did of Old Isaiah, Mighty Seer, in Spirit Soared	LBW 528 LW 214	*Jesaia, dem Propheten*
Agnus Dei	O Christ, Thou Lamb of God	LBW 103 LW 7	*Christe, du Lamm Gottes*

Many settings of the entire Holy Communion Ordinary have been created for unison voices by musicians of the distant past as well as by contemporary composers. These settings or parts thereof are often within the range of difficulty of good children's choirs.

Considering that the texts are sung at nearly every Holy Communion service, it would be well for the director of the children's choir to place into the choir repertoire one or more of the settings for performance at festivals or whenever some special emphasis is desired. Two examples of the genre are Jean Langlais, *Missa in simplicitate* (Durand, 1953), and Vincent Persichetti, *Hymns and Responses* (Elkan-Vogel, 1956).

Anthem

Many children's choirs perform anthems as their chief song in the service. Many pleasing anthems have texts of such general applicability as to be of little specific help for worship on any given Sunday or festival. To complicate matters, much attractive music—often conscientiously written with superficial appeal for children—has texts with no serious theological or Scriptural content.

Probably the most beguiling tendency of some contemporary composers is to write "musicals" on Biblical subjects in "pop" style. These musical shows can be very attractive and can even communicate spiritual truths. Yet because they are sung in what primarily amounts to concert performances of music written in a shallow idiom, they do little to enhance corporate Christian worship. It is difficult to condemn such music totally, but there is such a wealth of better choral music available for worship that perhaps the musicals ought to be reserved for congregational socials, dinners, or other programs.

There is a growing body of well-written anthems based on texts assigned to specific Sundays or festivals. When one of these anthems is performed near the text to which it refers, the entire congregation knows immediately that the children's choir has made a direct contribution to worship. For example, Jan Bender's dramatic unison anthem "Begone, Satan!" (see chap. 8, p. 154, Lent 1) is actually a part of the Gospel for the First Sunday in Lent, Series A, and could be sung in place of the reading of that part of the Gospel of the Day. If it cannot be sung there, it should at least be sung in the proximity of the Gospel or the sermon if the sermon is based on the Gospel. (The extensive listing of "Choral Music for the Day," chap. 8, pp. 149—64, contains suggestions similar to the Bender example just mentioned.)

If it is impossible to place an anthem near the text to which it is related, it is best to sing such a number during the gathering of the offerings. In many services this placement would allow the choir more time to perform its selection because of the time taken to gather the offerings.

Other Rehearsal Songs

Many choir directors use vocalises in order to help children

learn to produce good tone and to develop proper breath support and clear diction. These vocalises are important and should always be taken seriously by directors and children alike. The time taken from rehearsal of other songs will ultimately be saved as the children learn to work more efficiently and effectively as a result of the improved vocal technique developed with the vocalises.

Every children's choir needs to relax at times in the course of the important work of preparing music for worship. This is the time when religious songs of a lighter nature or even secular songs could be sung. Rhythmic songs, motion songs, musical games, and rounds are all suitable for this purpose.

Children should not be permitted to lower their vocal or musical standards when singing these "fun" songs. Good singing habits are relatively easy to maintain if encouraged consistently. To sing any songs carelessly is injurious to the individual voices and to work of the choir. All music that is worthy of any attention at all is worthy of being sung well.

Placement and Appearance of the Children's Choir in Church

The work of the choir is made difficult if the children are exposed to the full view of the congregation throughout the service. But whether the children's choir is seated near or in the chancel or is in the rear balcony of the nave, the task of trying to concentrate on one's own worship while leading others takes considerable experience and training. The director must be patient yet firm and encouraging while training a choir to do the right thing at the right time (and for the right reason) in worship.

Robes are very important to the proper appearance and decorum of the choir. They bring dignity to the choir and identify the members as part of a special group. Experiments have clearly established that, while clothes do not make the man, they surely improve the decorum of choristers. The traditional English liturgical garment has been the waist-length white cotta worn over the black cassock. The American desire for simplicity has sometimes abbreviated the cassock to a black ankle-length skirt, usually fitted with elastic at the waist. In recent years many churches have been robing choristers in albs, an appropriate garment for the assisting ministers that the members of the choir become in their role as leaders in worship. These liturgical robes are preferred over academic robes with circular stoles around the neck or collars and large bows, all

of which have the support of no particular liturgical or historical tradition.

No matter where the children's choir sits or what is worn, it is important that the children be instructed in the details of choir decorum in public. Robes are not to be played with or swung about. Folders are to be held high with both hands (if music is used at all) so that the director can be seen at all times. Service folders must be clearly marked before the service so that children will know what they are to do and when they are to do it. Attention must be given to the efficient use of the service book or hymnal; perhaps banded book marks will help children find the several places to which they must refer. Children must learn to stand, sit, and stand again promptly and quietly. Pencils, gum, toys, and puzzles must all be avoided.

Choir parents can help solve problems before they occur by sitting near the choir in the church. No choir composed of normal boys and girls can be expected to exhibit perfect behavior all of the time, but if choir parents and the director set high standards and live up to them themselves, the example of the children will be remarkably effective in leading the congregation.

Worship postures must be taught carefully. Standing is best for singing praise; it is also a good position for prayer. Another traditional posture for prayer is kneeling, which teaches without words much about our relationship to God. Kneeling can be especially difficult for choristers in view of the often poorly designed pew or chair space and the necessity of holding music or hymnals. But with patience and planning, the difficulty of kneeling can be overcome, and the important benefits of assuming the posture can be gained. Teaching children to fold their hands during prayer can also be of great help in developing a spirit of reverence in the singers. The interest of the children in Baptism will also make quite natural the encouragement to mark the sign of the cross on themselves at the appropriate places in the service such as the Invocation prayer termination and Benediction in memory of their own baptisms.

Summary

The achievements of the choir in either music or worship are often limited by the prejudices and preferences of the unenlightened choral director, not by the ability of the children or the time or resources available. The director who merely wants to be liked or who wants children to "enjoy" the experience is unlikely to achieve outstanding results either in music or worship. The choral director who approaches the choir with high musical and spiritual expectations tempered by knowledge of children's ability and characteristics is likely to achieve superior results that will be a lasting blessing to the children and to the congregation they serve in worship.

Notes

1. Evelyn Underhill, *Worship* (New York: Harper and Brothers, Torchbook Edition, 1936), p. 3.
2. Ibid., p. 61.
3. George Hoyer, "The Child in Christian Worship," in *The Child in Christian Worship*, ed. Roland H. A. Seboldt, Sixteenth Yearbook (River Forest, Ill., Lutheran Education Association, 1959).
4. Ibid., pp. 8—20.
5. A convenient index by psalm number appears in *Lutheran Book of Worship: Ministers Desk Edition* (Minneapolis & Philadelphia: Augsburg Publishing House & Board of Publication, Lutheran Church in America, 1978), pp. 505—07.
6. An index in *Lutheran Book of Worship: Ministers Desk Edition,* p. 467, reveals 24 paraphrases of psalms. This listing is also contained in Appendix C, p. 199, of this book. The *Worship Supplement* (St. Louis: Concordia Publishing House, 1969), p. 240, lists 42 metrical paraphrases, mostly from *The Lutheran Hymnal* (Concordia, 1941), and *Lutheran Worship* lists 32 paraphrases (p. 1004). Appendix B, p. 183, in this book shares the paraphrase listing found in *Lutheran Worship.*

"A director whose strength is built only on personality and charisma will soon experience waning respect and disappointing results unless those winning qualities are backed up by solid musical, theological, and liturgical training."

Chapter Three

Directing the Children

Ronald Nelson

Attributes of the Director

In *The Male Singing Voice Ages Eight to Eighteen*,[1] Frederick Swanson wonders if the day will ever come when directors of high school choirs will be "promoted" to the junior high school; his conviction is that more skill and training are required to work with younger children. To whatever extent that may be true, there is no doubt that churches have been guilty of the opposite supposition: the younger the choir, the less it really matters who the director is or how much background and training he or she has. Certainly a paramount qualification must be a love of children and a desire to work with them. But someone who is "really great with the kids" is not enough. A director whose strength is built only on personality and charisma will soon experience waning respect and disappointing results unless those winning qualities are backed up by solid musical, theological, and liturgical training. In fact, a director with a low-key personality, who is quickly seen by the children (and oh, how perceptive they are!) to be qualified in every other way and well prepared for every rehearsal, will gradually win and more easily maintain the cooperation of the group and their enthusiastic response.

This is especially true of the years from middle elementary grades on up. For working with preschool children it is essential to know how to *speak their language* without talking down to them. In my experience this skill is extremely rare among adults. To work successfully with preschoolers requires a real entering into the mind of the child and thinking as he or she thinks. Thus it is only for this age group that musical and theological training may be considered secondary. Even here, however, the children respond much more to a rather low-key and quiet approach than to a whiz-bang "personality plus" individual. And it is extremely important to remember that in terms of quality of repertoire, even at this age—indeed, especially at this age—"only the best is good enough for a child" (Zoltán Kodály). The preschool director with minimal musical training must therefore seek the help and guidance of the trained church musician in the selection of music.

Organization and Scheduling

How should a parish that has no children's choir program begin? How should a parish that has done only minimal work with children set out to expand its program? One of the first hard facts to emerge in exploring possibilities for organization and scheduling is that it is impossible to meet every need and accommodate every family's schedule. There will always be a conflict with some child's ballet lesson or some other child's football practice. One must, however, look forward to the day when those families that cannot be accommodated will realize that it might be possible to adjust the ballet or the football to the choir schedule instead of the other way around. With that realization may also come the understanding that no child can possibly do all the good things that are competing for time and that—just as in adulthood—sometimes choices must be made between two fine activities.

It is impossible in the scope of this chapter to spell out every possibility for choir scheduling. My own experience has been to hang on to Saturday morning as the best time for an extended program for most elementary and lower junior high school ages. But churches just starting a program may meet much resistance to Saturday scheduling. Some parishes are trying to schedule everything on Sundays; others find that impossible because of weekend absences. A midweek "Family Night" with activities for every age group has offered possibilities for some parishes. This can be workable only if there is a different director for each choir and ample rehearsal space for several groups at the same time. The after-school hour is still successful for many. This has seemed especially appropriate for the preschool and early elementary years.

How long a rehearsal can children tolerate? This can range from a very short period (ideally supplemented by home listening to records or tapes) for the preschoolers to a three-hour choir school program on Saturday morning. In the latter program there may be, in addition to records, separate classes in sightsinging, studies in the Bible and worship, creative artwork, and a worship experience to begin or end the session. Each class period may be 40 minutes long, giving children a change to move between class and rehearsal areas as well as a "juice break" in midmorning. Short of a full-blown choir school program, each congregation should consider how and when these other important subjects may be woven into the choir rehearsal itself. The ALLELUIA curriculum now available from Augsburg Publishing House has much to offer in this regard and should be explored by congregations beginning or revising their children's choir program.

Effective Age Groupings

What about age grouping? Much depends on the size of the parish and the number of available children in the parish and the community. But even in the smallest parish it is probably unwise to make the age span of any one choir too large. The older children may become bored with the limitations of repertoire, and the younger ones may become discouraged and lost if the emphasis is on the older. A few generalizations will help:

1. It is best to divide between reading and nonreading singers. Thus first graders who are just beginning to read may best be kept with kindergarten and perhaps other preschoolers. All learning must be done by rote with this group.

2. Starting with second graders we may begin to teach the use of music, especially from the worship book of the congregation. While a children's hymnal may be a first step, even second graders will enjoy the challenge of using the "big book" with the help of knowledgeable third and fourth graders.

3. Students in the lower grades of junior high should best be kept to serve as leaders with the upper elementary singers. This can make possible the use of some of the really great church music that has been written for children's treble voices. Fifth and sixth graders in most parish music programs will be hard pressed to achieve this without the leadership of the more experienced seventh and eighth graders. That leadership may not be so evident in the first few years of a program's existence, but it will become very strong when more seventh and eighth graders have come through the earlier years of training.

"We can't do everything the first year. Where should we begin?" If one age group is to be singled out as most important, it should be the preschoolers. A most logical strategy would be to begin with the youngest age group and simply add one more year each year. In long-range terms, this will provide the surest foundation for the future. In my own parish the participation of the older children grew from about 25 percent to over 50 percent in some grades as those who began as preschoolers came into the upper grades.

Making choir work a part of a preschooler's life-style establishes priorities and values that make choices in favor of church activities easier in later years. Whether one begins at age two, three, or four, psychologists insist that the years before age five are the most important formative years in a human being's life. In fact, a parish doesn't need to wait until age two to encourage acquaintance with the music language of the church. Recordings may be placed in the home when a child is baptized so that even in the crib the child may hear the sounds of the church music and worship that will help it feel at home in Sunday worship right from infancy. (How else will the "language" of worship be taught?)

Motivation and Recruitment

What makes a child want to come to choir? This question assumes that the ideal is a membership based on the child's desire, not the parents' coercion. I would suggest a two-part answer to this question: It is important to get a child involved in the program, but it is also important to hold the child's interest and stimulate the desire to continue on a long-term basis.

To achieve initial membership, we need to convince the child that (1) it will be a "fun" experience; (2) many friends will also be joining; and (3) the choir gives a unique opportunity for an important service to the congregation and for glorifying God. Parents, on the other hand, need to be shown the worthwhile benefits to the child—education, challenge, etc.

Publicity aimed at the children themselves, therefore, will be quite different from that directed at parents. (Examples of sample letters and notes to parents can be found in Appendix A, pp. 171—81.) If the natural leaders of each age group can be given special attention and helped to commit themselves, others will be sure to follow their example. But we underestimate our children if we omit the third point—service. They have too few such opportunities in most congregations and can rise to such a challenge if we give them the chance.

Indeed, it is this third point that will keep them coming long after the initial fun may have worn off. To make this happen, however, requires much care on the part of the director that the choir's work in the leadership of worship is *real* and that the children never see the group as providing only "special music" or added entertainment in the service. Leadership in liturgy and the learning of new hymns and the Propers for the day will need to be stressed at every rehearsal and made to happen when the choir appears in worship. An anthem is selected first and foremost because it fits the readings for the particular Sunday or festival. The children know *why* they are singing it on *that* day.

When the singers catch the spirit of this kind of leadership and are constantly challenged to do more and better work of this kind, they will be most likely to continue with growing enthusiasm the work they may have begun for social reasons.

What about awards? Many children's choirs have successfully used award systems ranging from very simple to very complex. It is hard to make specific recommendations about this, since every situation is unique. But in the long run the biggest reward should be the work itself. If rehearsals and services are neither enjoyable nor exciting, no award system will compensate. In my own experience with a system of pins for good attendance, the children's own interest in the pins waned to the extent that many never bothered either to pick them up or to wear them. Since attendance was basically good anyway, the system was dropped. A cross to wear with choir vestments survives, and that is given only to children who spend extra hours in rehearsal each week to do more advanced work.

Both director and clergy, as well as members of the congregation, should take every opportunity to express appreciation to choir members for the hours of work they devote to serving in that capacity and for the talents they train and dedicate to their Lord. Those thank-yous probably mean more to the children than any award they might get.

A choir camp has provided good motivation for faithful service for some children's choirs when only those children who are faithful are eligible for the camp. And the idea has also served to integrate new members into the group socially and to stimulate interest in the choir.

Other ways of creating initial interest might include a one-time project that could serve as a springboard for a new choir group. Children's musicals abound, but the director who wants a choir to be excited about serving in worship must beware, lest the musical become the one highlight in an otherwise uninteresting choir year. Sunday worship can and should be just as exciting. The other concern about children's musicals is quality—both musical and literary. Remember again Kodály's words: Only the best is good enough for a child.

Rehearsal Strategies

Long before a rehearsal can be planned, of course, the music must have been selected. One sometimes feels that full-time effort would not be enough to find just the right music for each particular group with its own distinctive needs and abilities and for the theme of the particular day on which the group is leading in worship. So many factors need to be weighed: quality of text and music (only the best is good enough for a child), range and tessitura (high enough to demand use of the head tones), and balance of old and new music (solemn and lively, easy and difficult).

When the music has been selected, it must be learned by the director. Children are quick to sense the confidence of a director who knows the music and the lack of it in one who doesn't. Melody, harmony, counterpoint, accompaniment—every part of the piece should be well established in the mind and ear of the director before beginning work with the choir. Potential trouble spots should be identified and a strategy planned to deal with them. A good test for a beginning director would be to ask a friend to play through the piece, deliberately making one rather inconspicuous mistake. Can the director not only hear the mistake but also point out exactly what was wrong and how to correct it? This test could be discouraging to a novice director with little ear training but should be a real incentive for self-improvement in that area. One of the most common failings of inexperienced directors is the inability to hear exactly what is wrong and to correct it immediately. Too often mistakes are practiced week after week until they are learned too well to ever respond to treatment.

Finally it is time to plan a particular rehearsal. (A sample choir rehearsal planning sheet is on p. 65 at the end of chapter 4.) The needs are laid out and a careful schedule is developed with these general guidelines:

1. Plan by the clock. Your vocalizing or opening devotion should begin on the stroke of the hour. After that, your plan should indicate when you expect to begin work on each item, for example:

10:05—Entrance Hymn for next Sunday
10:10—Psalm
10:17—Final memorizing of Alleluia Verse
10:25—Begin work on . . .

Rarely will such a schedule be followed without variation. But as the director glances at the written plan throughout the rehearsal, it is obvious whether the group is on schedule or behind. In the latter case adjustments must be made in the balance of the plan so that nothing crucial is neglected. If some items are not rehearsed at all, careful note must be made so that the next rehearsal will compensate.

2. Include a brief opening prayer or devotion to focus on the choir's mission.

3. Rehearse next Sunday's music (or the next music to be done by this choir) near the beginning of the hour when the group is fresh. A good rule of thumb for any group is to pretend that all music must be done one week earlier than actually scheduled. This develops the

confidence of the group, provides opportunities for some real polishing at the final rehearsal, and makes it possible to proceed with the music that is scheduled even if a rehearsal must be cut short because of a storm or other emergency.

4. Place the newest and most challenging music next on the schedule. To do the newest music at the end gives the rehearsal a downward slope and may send the singers away discouraged if it doesn't go well. Do the hardest work before they are tired.

5. Send them off singing! Place a favorite piece that poses no technical problems at the end of the rehearsal.

"Variety with a Purpose" might be a good slogan in preparing for a rehearsal. In every rehearsal provide a good mix of keys (avoid two pieces in the same key back to back), moods (Lent is always balanced with Easter preparation), easy and difficult (keep one challenging piece in the learning process for the entire year; it will end up being the favorite), amount of time spent on each piece, rehearsal area (use the sanctuary part of the time at some rehearsals), standing and sitting, and seating arrangements.

The most important mix of all may be in the goals for each piece to be rehearsed. First of all, be sure to identify these goals. Aimless running through numbers without the singers being aware of goals will waste precious rehearsal time. Here are some possible goals as examples:

1. Polish the phrasing and the meaning of the words.
2. Practice expressive speech rhythm in chant.
3. Correct the notes in the fourth measure of page 5.
4. Work on articulation of the text.
5. Work backwards; learn the last page first (to build confidence).
6. Speak, clap, sing, count, etc., to correct a difficult rhythm.
7. Listen carefully to intonation in a difficult spot.
8. Balance voice parts with the accompaniment (organ registration).
9. Sing unaccompanied.
10. Beautify tone quality to enhance the text.
11. Work on memorizing.

One suggestion for the last goal is to use the chalkboard. At first the entire page may be written there (or in the case of a nonreading group, pictures may be used as reminders of the text). As the song is repeated, the chalkboard is gradually erased, but even when it is entirely erased, the director continues to point to the place where the words *were*. Children enjoy this process, and it is nearly always effective.

Rehearsal mechanics—attendance, distributing music, etc.—should be handled when possible by an older child with a minimum of fuss and time. Music can be placed on chairs ahead of time or

made available for each choir member to pick up as he or she enters the room.

Under no circumstances should each piece of music be handed in and the next distributed between numbers. Discipline and momentum will fall by the wayside while this happens. A compromise that saves wear and tear on music is to have each row pass a piece of music to the middle or to the end of the row as it is no longer needed. The person on the end or in the middle can then stack it by his or her chair until the end of the rehearsal. But the next piece that is needed should already be in hand so that the rehearsal can proceed even while the previous music is being handed in.

What about choir mothers? Many directors find that choir parents (let's not limit it to mothers!) can be very useful at every rehearsal. Others feel it not necessary to ask parents to come and do little or nothing. This really depends on the director, and a good argument can be advanced for both views. I have found such help necessary for services with groups up to fourth grade level but for rehearsals only with preschoolers.

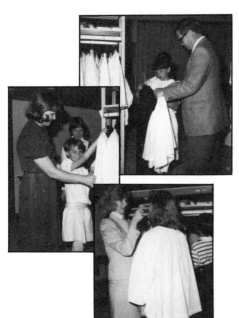

Problem Solving

1. Are high notes a problem? Use the entire vocal range at each rehearsal. Vocalize! This is the "one thing needful" in so many junior choirs. It would solve a multitude of problems of tone and pitch. Exercise the voice—like athletes—but without strain.

2. Are the singers flatting? Use a piano to support pitch until you are *sure* it's no longer needed.

3. Make a careful selection of music. There are dangers of low pitch level in many folk and "pop" hymns.

4. Change key for flatting and intonation problems (usually 1/2 step up—occasionally 1/2 step down).

5. Playing the melody line an octave higher (organ more 4′, less 8′, with well-defined bass) will also help.

6. How much should you talk about flatting? As little as possible unless you know the group can deliberately correct it. Most can't. It will get worse instead of better.

7. Tone quality—make it beautiful! Grow on higher notes; take it easy on low. In starting an upward passage, begin thinking on levels of the top rather than pushing the bottom upwards.

8. Does the sound express the words? Remind the choir often of the meaning of the text.

9. Use "Ferris wheel" energy toward top notes. Think of a big circle. Go forward over the top, not backing away.

10. "Keep the choristers relaxed and in a good humor" (Father

Finn). Can you gracefully make a fool of yourself and laugh with them at yourself?

11. Let them know you love them! (How?)

12. Should there be memorization?

    a. Yes! They will sing better and develop confidence.

    b. No! They need to learn to hold music and watch at the same time.

    c. How should they memorize? The music should be mastered in rehearsals. Extra stanzas may be assigned for home memorization. Testing should be done by choosing reciters at random (from "pin-the-tail-on-the-seating-chart").

13. *Keep them busy!* There will be little time for discipline problems. Don't talk. Sing!

14. Don't do too much rote teaching with juniors, but it is basic to younger groups. The cardinal principle should be to keep the rhythm going between what you sing and what they echo. Also let them *hear* as much as possible before singing a note. Ask questions, sing it again, play a record, etc.

15. Attendance

    a. Keep a strict and accurate record.

    b. Ask members to notify *in advance* of each absence, whether for rehearsal or service. *Keep reminding* them of this; compare it to a pastor who simply doesn't show up on a Sunday or for an appointment. There should be no apologies for stressing responsibility.

    c. Ask for a commitment to this policy from every new member. (See a sample commitment pledge, Appendix A, p. 174).

    d. In a choir school, list reasons for each absence. The secretary should call those not present. Drop children from membership after three absences for insufficient reason with encouragement to join again when they can be regular.

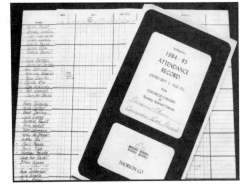

16. If you accompany the rehearsal yourself, be sure to do some unaccompanied singing and get another accompanist frequently so that the members can be trained to follow a conductor's beat. Be sure your conducting is well practiced and follows standard patterns.

Constructive Discipline

Should we discipline children in church choirs as they are (or should be) disciplined in school? Certainly it has been established that children really want the security of good discipline, but an inexperienced director may feel that strict discipline will cause a group to dislike the director. In fact, the opposite is more often true. Most children do not want to waste time at rehearsals listening to the director plead for better behavior. And it is just as bad to do nothing but struggle along hopelessly while the group is completely out of hand. Even the singers who seem to be the worst behavior problems probably like to be well controlled. After all, if we love the children with whom we work, we can insist on good behavior just as truly loving parents do. It is also commanded by God (see Proverbs 3:11-12; Romans 13:1-5; 1 Thessalonians 5:12-13).

If one or two children are disruptive, it may be necessary to give them a warning that they must cooperate or leave the rehearsal room. Then to maintain the respect of the entire group, the director must follow through and excuse the offenders if they do not improve behavior. Empty threats are disastrous! The parents of the children thus dealt with should then be informed of the situation, especially if it happens a second time. Always make it clear that you *want* the children in the group—that you like them but not their bad behavior.

Of course, an ounce of prevention is worth a pound of cure. Some preventive medicine for discipline includes the following:

1. The director is present and ready before the first child arrives.

2. A seating chart is strictly followed as a matter of course and is subject to change at any time. Good friends and classmates may be encouraged to sit together at first if they can handle it well.

3. There is a good, well-balanced rehearsal plan that keeps the children busy every minute having fun in active participation.

4. Services and other appearances are scheduled far in advance.

5. There is good and frequent communication with parents, whether through a regular monthly church newsletter or special mailings.

The Child Voice

Although this subject is dealt with in another chapter, it can hardly be overemphasized. All children should have the right and privilege of discovering the real beauty of the voice that is theirs only through childhood, never to return.

Nearly every child is a soprano and should be helped to realize that fact. In assigning parts to older children it is well to either divide the group into two equal sections and alternate higher and lower parts or divide it according to the best balance for two-part (or three-part) singing. However, make sure that those who sing the lower part in two-part or three-part music also have an opportunity each week to sing some music that takes them to the top of their range in unison with the other voices.

Children's voices work well with many instruments. Their quality may be buried by brass, but a woodwind solo instrument or duet, strings, handbells, and Orff instruments can serve to enhance the vocal beauty. Some directors have found much use for Orff instruments within the rehearsal. Even the youngest children can improvise pentatonic accompaniments for certain songs, and older children can perfect more complex instrumental parts. The danger of getting carried away with the use of these instruments in rehearsal lies in the potential neglect of the voice and of the precious time needed to help it develop to its full beauty. If a choice must be made, I would choose to work with more voices, even to the neglect of the instruments. Time with our church choirs is usually so limited, and the greatest body of our musical heritage usable with children is music for *voices*. In fact, some of the very greatest church music of past and present was written for children's voices and is sung by the best children's choirs throughout the world. Can *church* choirs of children rise to such a challenge? Yes, they can! And the kids will love it!

Note

1. Frederick J. Swanson, *The Male Singing Voice Ages Eight to Eighteen* (1977), paraphrase from p. 6. [Sole distributor: D. M. Phillips, P. O. Box 446, Iowa City, IA 52240.]

Chapter Four

"It has been proven time and again that the more one expects of a group, the more one is likely to get. Goals must be very high!"

Rehearsing Young Choristers

Paul Bouman

The success of nearly any venture is largely due to the amount of time the leader has spent in preparation. The director of a choral organization must have set some well-defined goals in looking ahead to a year's program. For a church-related choir the planning would center around the seasons and festivals of the church year. Immediately a built-in repertoire presents itself in the wealth of material available in psalms, verses and offertories, and the hymns and chorales of our heritage with the many available arrangements for children's voices.

Preparing for Meaningful Participation

The liturgies in the new books of worship should be thoroughly studied and learned so that children, too, can be leaders in worship. Historically, that has been the primary reason for having a choir. The director should also be acquainted with whatever lectionary series is in use, always studying ahead to know what the coming themes are on given Sundays. Obviously, the Good Shepherd theme commonly observed in the Easter season would present an opportunity for children to participate, if only to sing the antiphon for a Gelineau psalm arrangement while a smaller group or soloist sings the text of Psalm 23. Hymns on this theme, such as *Brother James' Air,* would be a time for alternate stanzas to be sung by the children.

In choosing additional music for a service, the director should seek guidelines in developing a musical taste that provides adequate background for the choice of music to be rehearsed. This is admittedly a considerable task but is not as formidable as it may seem.

There are many resources available that can be very helpful to any director, whether experienced or a beginner. Workshops abound to guide the director in the choice of music as well as in the techniques of teaching and performance. Publishers have also given much assistance by providing opportunities for the music teacher to participate in reading sessions where new and old music may be experienced. This is very important, because playing a choral piece on the piano is often not at all convincing, while singing the same number can be of much greater help for a director in deciding whether or not to choose it.

Great care must be used in the choice of music so that the repertoire doesn't develop with "gimmicky" music that may tickle the ears for a season but will have lost its attractiveness or usefulness by the next year. Do not ignore the classics; music that has an enduring quality has proven its worth and presents a challenge to a group. Never underestimate a child's ability! Children are very often more receptive to challenging music of all styles and periods than are adults because they are refreshingly free of prejudices. (See a criteria plan at the conclusion of this chapter.)

Ideally, one could say that *all* choral music is suitable for children's voices, granted, of course, that they have been trained to handle it. European children's choirs (girls and boys) and boy choirs in England as well as on the continent bear this out. A few American children's choirs are examples of this also. It has been proven time and again that the more one *expects* of a group, the more one is likely to *get*. Goals must be very high! Usually directors give up too soon. Play recordings of well-known, excellent children's choirs, and stress the fact that the children singing on those recordings are the same age as your group. If choosing music continues to be a problem, consult people whose judgment you respect.

Assets of an Effective Director

While it is true that directors do not all fall into the same mold, the following general qualities may provide helpful guidelines in the pursuit of this profession:

1. The director should genuinely love children! It may appear strange to list this as a general quality because it seems it should be taken for granted. But, alas, this is not always the case. The love of children is essential, and the director should pause to experience what delightful creatures of God children can be. This realization may grow out of the individual's own personal relationship with God, a relationship in which there is an awareness of one's weaknesses that helps to develop a tolerance and understanding of the limitations of others, in this case the children to be taught.

The director must treat the children with the respect they deserve as created and redeemed children of God, just as he or she wishes to be respected by the children. Too often this appears to be a one-way street; respect is demanded by the leader, but none is given in return. Teachers should never forget that they are an example, good or bad, in *all* situations. This does not imply a soft approach. On the contrary, one should expect and demand the best that it is possible to give, but in a courteous manner. "Friendly, but firm!" is a good motto to follow.

2. The director should be at home in the Scriptures. This is particularly important when choosing music with a nonbiblical text that needs to be evaluated as to its theological integrity. Study the text carefully. Ask yourself how it fits into the particular service that is being planned. A pretty tune isn't enough. Music that is to be performed in a church service *must* have a text worthy of such use!

When it is not possible to match a text in a sacred music selection exactly to the specific readings for a given service, consider those that are generally fitting for the specific season of the church year or that reflect the love of God toward us.

3. The director should have a clear understanding of the worship format of the church for which children's groups are being trained, liturgical or nonliturgical. A concerted effort should be made to explain the rationale behind the various acts in the worship rite. Teaching and directing go hand in hand. Texts themselves, as well as their use at a specific place in the service, must be explained. As has been mentioned before, the singing of psalms and responses to the readings presents an immediate repertoire for the children to learn, thus giving them an opportunity for direct participation in the worship service in a role of proclamation that is functional and meaningful. Sharing this important responsibility with the adult choir gives a far greater significance to their function than the mere presentation of a pretty anthem.

4. A word should be added here about the director's professional growth. As in any profession, it is easy to become mired down in one's own little kingdom with multitudinous demands on one's time and energy. However, stagnation will very readily develop, and this must be avoided at all cost. One can become accustomed to familiar sounds, good or bad, and soon be lulled into thinking that all is well. But the world keeps moving and will soon pass us by if no time was taken to see what is going on "out there."

Therefore, get acquainted in your community! See what is being done in other churches and schools. Attend concerts, workshops, and lectures—occasions that will stimulate the mind. Be interested and, if possible, be active in music groups, such as local chapters of the American Guild of Organists (AGO), the American Choral Directors Association (ACDA), the Hymn Society of America (HSA), or the Choristers Guild (CG). (Addresses of these groups are provided in chapter 7, p. 125.) If you have had limited experience in a choir, join a *good* local choral organization, particularly to give yourself the opportunity to sing the well-known oratorios. You may not have the chance to perform them, but you should know them as part of your professional background. Attendance at symphony concerts, organ recitals, and an occasional opera can broaden the horizon of the director and keep him or her musically alive and healthy. Subscriptions to professional publications (see p. 124 for more information) are helpful because they will give notices of concerts, workshops, new music, critical reviews, etc., as well as articles that are interesting and educational. Often participation in a workshop or the reading of an article can be a reassuring experience, underscoring what one is already doing while giving added information and help for doing it better. Learning and growing are key words for any professional person who wants to pursue a productive and fruitful career.

Selection and Placement of Singers

When the director selects singers for a children's choir, it is advisable to have an audition with *every* child in a grade or unit in order to establish a record of the musical ability (vocal or instrumental) of the school population. This is recommended whether the child will be in the choir or not. Eventually some may be interested in joining or, because of their potential, could be given additional encouragement to participate as a result of this inventory of their voice and musical gifts. Establishing a friendly rapport and a mutual trust is very helpful in conducting an audition, and it would be beneficial if the director or music teacher would visit the various classes involved in order to become acquainted and to rehearse a few simple vocalises (do-mi-sol-do-sol-mi-do) on the syllable "ya" or "loo" and the tune of a well-known hymn (the common doxology, "America," "Glory Be to Jesus," etc.). These could also be sung on the syllable "loo" or with the words of the text. In such a visit, an observant director will soon recognize the more aggressive singer or the open-singing personality, and some of them might be encouraged to sing some phrases alone. This often provides others with the incentive to do likewise and will help to set the stage for the auditions later.

On the day of the audition, the excitement usually runs high, and arrangements must be made with the classroom teacher to excuse two or three children at a time to come to a specified room. Having company at an audition serves to put them at ease. Personalities of children need to be handled carefully and gently to encourage them to perform in such a manner that the audition is of value. All children are interviewed and auditioned. A simple form to help the director remember the quality of the voice is helpful. The following is one way it might be done:

Name	Grade	Instrument	Pitch	Range	Quality of Voice	Choir

1. Hearing a child's speaking voice when giving the name, grade, and instrument played is sometimes a key to the personality behind the face. Some children show their aggressive natures under these circumstances. Timid souls are also observed. A natural charm often presents itself.

2. The mere fact that a child plays an instrument indicates some training in note reading and an acquaintance with musical symbols.

3. The column under pitch should receive a number from 1 to 4 (1 being the best) to indicate the child's sense of pitch. Play a note on the piano, and ask the child to match it. Hearing the child sing a simple hymn tune would also indicate the child's sense of pitch.

4. To determine range, vocalize with the child on a D-major scale. Then play the arpeggio and increase perhaps to high G. If there was already a hint of a voice change in a boy, stop at E and then vocalize down from G above middle C to an octave below and record the extent of the range.

5. In the column marked "Quality," use the same scale as under pitch. A roman I or II could be used to indicate first or second soprano and III or IV to indicate alto. Some voices are easily recognized, while others are not so readily placed.

6. The column marked "Choir" would contain a yes or no in response to the question "Would you like to be in the choir?" Most children in my experience have wanted to be in such an organization, but occasionally someone will say no, and if this is from a person who has influence among classmates, it could be contagious. However, in a choir of fifth and sixth graders one might include all the children so that they all experience the training and gain a musical repertoire. In the case of some of the negatives, the parents often made the decision, and when such a child really had talent, a serious discussion about the use of talents in the praise of God sometimes produced results.

Sometimes the yes may come from a candidate with dubious musical ability, so it should be recorded with a question mark. Indicate this to the child privately, and offer a trial period of about two months. This person should be placed among strong singers. Ninety percent of the time such a child will become aware of the sounds around him or her and develop into an adequate singer.

This writer accepted anyone into the choir who evidenced a

desire to be in it. Sometimes a lovely personality with limited ability is preferred over a real talent with a discipline problem. Very often a singing personality will develop because there has been a poverty of musical experience in the child's previous history. There was a talent that needed to be nurtured and brought into active expression.

Assisting Insecure Voices

A word might be said about the person who has great pitch difficulty. This is someone who needs much attention from the director, but it is not always obviously given. Considerable time should be spent during a rehearsal listening to all singers, keeping an alert ear for the problem singer. Occasionally a few moments can be taken to place a hand on the child's stomach and apply a gentle pressure. Usually a change in pitch will result. Sometimes this may be done in a private session to avoid embarrassment for the child. Periodic discussions with the problem singer may be held to discover, first of all, whether the person is aware that there is a problem. Second, if the child is aware, he or she must realize that in a choir this could become a problem for everyone else as well. Usually a great effort is made by the child to correct the situation, and this could be discussed with the parents. Sometimes real miracles result. This writer will forever hold dear the memory of the charming little fourth grade girl who wanted so desperately to be in the choir but whose sense of pitch was limited at first hearing. However, through sheer determination and much effort she became a leader in the second soprano section by the time she reached grades seven and eight.

If it appears that the case is hopeless—that the nonsinger will remain a nonsinger—a decision will have to be made, particularly if the individual is a detriment to the choral performance. Parents of children in upper grades are usually aware of a child's inability to carry a tune, and in most instances it will come as no surprise when the situation comes under discussion. But it deserves to be discussed, and parents should be notified if there is a thought to terminate a child's choir participation, whether the reason is discipline or the inability to sing.

Having a definite seating plan and sticking to it is an important factor in placing problem singers where they can hear correct singing and also in making sure that potential discipline problems are not all confined to one place. After all children have been auditioned and there is some idea of how many choristers there are in each voice, the seating arrangement can proceed. It is most practical to seat the choir in the same number and length of rows as are in the choir loft of the church. This allows the group to move from rehearsal room to church with a minimum of disorder.

A number of seating plans may be followed, and the best one is the one that works well for the director. However, it may be helpful to suggest at least one plan:

Soprano I	Alto II Alto I
	Soprano II

Just as the first violin section is the largest in an orchestra, so in a choir the first sopranos usually predominate. The second soprano part is often the hardest musically, so care must be taken that that section has some good musicians in it. Altos would divide only rarely, but in case they must be, the suggested arrangement works well. In two-part music all second sopranos and altos sing the second part, so usually the parts are equally divided.

When a seating plan has been arranged, the choristers should always take the same place unless someone is absent or a change is made at the discretion of the director. This may be necessary in case there is an imbalance in the sound from, for example, the second sopranos in relation to the rest of the choir. Perhaps the section is too weak. It would not be out of the question to explain the qualifications necessary to be a good second soprano and to ask if a first soprano might like to try the challenge. Again it should be stressed that it is up to the judgment and discretion of the director to rearrange voice assignments and seating plans until a satisfactory situation has been found. The above may also apply if more altos are needed. It is a good idea to tell the children what the director is trying to accomplish. This serves to build a good rapport between chorister and director, a feeling of mutual trust. It is not unusual to have children in any voice part of the choir who would be able to sing any of the other parts, as far as both range and musical ability are concerned. In the past those who could read music would often automatically sing second soprano or alto, and all others would be put into first soprano. This procedure literally buried potentially excellent sopranos, who developed into raucous altos. It also seriously hindered the development of a strong first soprano section that would not collapse when asked to sing an independent part other than a familiar hymn tune. Descants would be out of the question if they had to be carried by a weak soprano section. Ideally, the entire choir should be able to sing high or low parts, and frequent vocalizing in either direction will keep the range wide and flexible. To hear a strong body of children sing a soaring descant in a festival service is an experience that is hard to surpass.

This writer had the unusual experience of a very talented boy singer who burst into tears at being placed into the first soprano section because he considered it a disgrace to be in that section when he was such a good note reader! Patient explanations finally convinced him that it was precisely because of his musical talent that he was such an asset to the first soprano section.

The Rehearsal Event

The rehearsal for any choir should be treated as a special event, one for which careful preparation has been made so that the time allotted is wisely used. For children the event should be particularly special, requiring the director's thorough planning. The room should be well-ventilated and cheerful. It should be set up as a choir room, allowing for space around chairs for any physical movements that may be called for. The chairs should be sturdy with straight backs and seats on which it is easy to sit forward in an erect position. (Many current offerings on today's chair market are molded to fit the body for comfort but do not support the proper chorister position).

The ideal rehearsal location is a room set aside for that purpose only, with music files and wardrobe facilities close at hand. A folder containing the music to be rehearsed should be laid out on a table for choristers to take as they arrive.

Having a phonograph or tape player on hand is desirable because there are often instances when it is helpful to play a recording to demonstrate tone; this is a wonderful way to develop an idea. Children are born imitators, and hearing the model sounds from the best choirs is a great help.

The conductor would be wise to have another adult or two who could assist with details such as taking attendance, distributing communications to the home, collecting forms requested from the home, and doing a multitude of other things that might arise. The rehearsal room is not a playground, and the conductor must be careful to provide an atmosphere that discourages rowdy or crude behavior.

As the children arrive, recordings could be playing music that is familiar or currently in rehearsal. Or the director might be playing such music at the piano to attract the attention of the children and heighten their interest in the activity at hand. This is also a fine way to forestall potential discipline problems.

Mental, Physical, and Musical Aspects

When everyone has arrived, the rehearsal might begin with

a few physical exercises to relax the body, the singer's instrument. Games can be devised to inject fun into this project:

1. Roll the head around on the neck like an apple on a little stick or on a nail. When the director counts to four, some rhythm is given to this activity.

2. With hands held high, sway from side to side like trees in a wind. Increase and diminish the force of the wind. Have the fingers move rapidly to indicate leaves in a breeze.

3. With hands on hips, rotate the body first in one direction and then in another.

4. Rotate the arms at the shoulders.

Other exercises to relax the body may be supplied by the director, or perhaps a child may think of one.[1] This activity should not last more than a few minutes.

While the children are standing, some vocalizing may begin. This also should take only a few minutes.

These routines are often seized on by some children as a time to be silly. An alert director will watch for the "clown" and divert attention as soon as possible. Do not allow this to disrupt your rehearsal, but deal firmly with such a situation if it is necessary. Constant clowning can be a demoralizing influence for an entire rehearsal, and the instigator may have to be removed; hence, it is wise to have another adult present to accompany the child to another area of the building.

After the vocal and physical warm-up, it is time to get to the music. Beginning with an already familiar hymn or anthem can attract the desired attention and build confidence to attempt new materials to be rehearsed. Be constantly on the alert for proper note values, rests, and dynamics, all of which are gently stressed while the music is being learned. Also listen intently to the way more difficult vowels are treated, and if the resulting sounds are not to your liking, correct them. Invite the children to express their views on the treatment of vowels whose natural sound at a particular range is not pleasant. Some slight manipulation of this vowel may be necessary. Take, for example, the hymn tune *St. Columba* ("The King of Love My Shepherd Is"). In stanza six on the words "Good Shepherd," the vowel in "Shep" will usually sound to rhyme with *lap*—in a broad, "blatty," strained sound with the mouth in a smile position. Try various ways to correct this, beginning by singing the interval on "loo loo." Then sing "Good loo," then "Good Shoo," then with the mouth in the position of "Shoo" change the vowel to "ay" and sing "Shay." Sing "Good Shay" with the *a* having just a touch of long *e*. Try singing "Good Shee" (long *e*) with the mouth in the "oo" (as in *moon*) position. Do this with several vowels. This will direct and focus the tone forward into the head and produce a rounder sound—particularly on an E-flat, which is at the upper limit of the chest tone range.

Good Shep-herd

In stanza one of the same hymn, similar experimenting in the third line will result in a head tone sound infinitely more pleasant than what one usually hears. For example, the average child will pronounce "nothing" to sound "*nah*thing," and the vocal production at that pitch would probably be chest-throat centered rather than head-voice. To correct this, have the children sing "I no" (long *o*) until you hear a clear head sound, watching that as the child is singing this vowel the mouth and lips are puckered in a fish-mouth position.

I   noth - ing

Try this with the words from the other stanzas at that spot. In stanza two the words "and where" may give the most trouble because the short *e* in "where" needs to be tempered. Soon the children will hear this themselves and will submit ideas on correcting unpleasant vowel sounds. It was a fifth grader who suggested how to treat the words "I nothing lack" in stanza one. When asked to demonstrate this to the others, she instinctively manipulated the vowel in order to place the tone in the head thus producing a lovely, clear sound, pure and in tune. When she was asked how she did it, she replied, "I just changed the vowel in 'Nothing' to a long *o*." Needless to say, that kind of reply and understanding brings joy to any director's heart.

The following table may be of help in correcting certain vowel sounds in order to produce a more pleasing tone:

	As seen in	Manipulated to sound like
Long Vowels		
a	praise	prēēze
e	feet	füt
i	high	ha-ē
o	low	lōw
u	lute	loot
Short Vowels		
a	sat	saht
e	let	löt
i	sin	seen
o	lot	laht
u	son	sōn

Troublesome Sounds	As seen in	Manipulated to sound like
aw	walk	wōk
or	Lord	Lōhd
orl	world	wuhld
al	always	ohlwēēze

Benefiting from Careful Organization

Many schools are not fortunate enough to have a special room that can be used solely for rehearsals. In that case a classroom may have to be reorganized to accommodate children coming from other rooms. Movement among children within the room may also be necessary as choristers are shuffling about to get to their assigned choir seats. Extra chairs may have to be set, and all of this activity has the potential of developing into chaos.

The alert director will anticipate this and might take his place at the piano and begin to play a familiar song that attracts and encourages the children to sing along. A suggestion to this effect should be made during a time of orientation when the choir meets for the first time. At that same time, before unproductive habits develop, routines should be established for distributing the music, arranging the room for rehearsal, and returning it again to its original seating plan for classroom use.

As the children are gathering, familiar music played by the director or accompanist will have a quieting effect. If their memory falters, the leader might supply a line of text to keep the song alive. The children's attention has been attracted, and by the end of the song everyone is seated, and music has been distributed by the librarian. This same attention-getting scheme might be used with a recording of a choral number currently being rehearsed. None of this should be done loudly. Noise begets noise, so all these activities should strive for a calming influence. Here it might be mentioned that the director's call for attention should also not border on yelling in order to be noticed.

After the desired climate has been established, a brief time may be taken for announcements, calling attention to future singing commitments and reminding the choristers of their responsibilities.

A few sample announcements to parents of projected plans for the choristers are included in Appendix A to give an idea of the type of communication that is important between the school, the chorister, and the home. It is easy to blame parents when children don't honor commitments, but it is very possible that they were never informed that such an obligation existed. As the signed notes are returned, check the choir roster under the proper heading (date) so that a count of who will be present is readily available. Some inspirational words might follow on the subject of the service for which preparations are being made (Christmas, Lent, Easter, etc.). This should be brief. Too much *talking* in a *singing* period destroys attention. A sensitive director will know when enough has been said.

Posture is stressed, often more by example and gesture than by words. Sitting erect and toward the front of the chair keeps the mind and body alert for the job at hand. (When there are pauses, the choristers may relax and sit back.) Then use a few vocalises, as mentioned earlier. Variations of these procedures are wholesome. While working on a good sound, don't be afraid to inject some humor into the process so the atmosphere does not become tense or rigid but remains enjoyable. Always be sensitive to the endurance of the group. This can vary from rehearsal to rehearsal.

Introducing the New/ Strengthening the Familiar

Now may be the time to introduce a new song or one that has just been begun at the previous rehearsal and still needs attention. Perhaps a musical pattern from one of these songs can be used as a vocalise. Using this technique reviews, strengthens, and tends to produce efficient results, and it is interesting to watch children's reactions as they meet the familiar fragment. Instead of singing from page one at each rehearsal, call attention to a difficult passage and rehearse that. Then back up a few measures and work up to the passage just rehearsed. Follow this procedure until you are at the beginning. Stop occasionally and have the children sing without the piano. Choose a small group to sing certain sections as a demonstration so the rest can listen. Be very careful *never* to pound on the piano when practicing parts. Always play musically with a gentle touch. Again, noise begets noise, and the sounds coming back to you may be correct, but they will reflect your manner and approach. If you don't know whether or not you are playing too loudly, ask a colleague to come in and listen.

If the number being rehearsed is a two-part selection, plunge right into it, giving help with the piano (Watch it! Not too loud!). After a few trial runs, have each section sing alone without the piano. Sometimes have the entire group sing each part. Remember that if you keep them singing, you will have less talking. Keep encouraging them all the time, and compliment them for a good effort. Correct musical difficulties by singing with them or playing lightly on the piano.

Dynamics should be a part of the piece almost immediately, as should explanations and interpretation of the text. Call the children's attention to long held notes, and establish a rule of thumb that those notes should begin softly and increase in volume as the note is held. Use the terms "crescendo" and "swell" interchangeably. Children adapt very easily to this technique.

Throughout the rehearsal reminders about correct posture, vocal suggestions, and general hints about proper choral participation are given. If an excellent recording of children is available to offer as a model, or if a tape recorder of excellent quality is available to record the choir so it can hear itself, consider using these so the children can relate to the results they are striving to attain.

Because of the demands on the singers, a rehearsal time of 30—45 minutes is desirable. The limited attention span of children makes longer rehearsals both unenjoyable and unproductive. Marked differences in the attention spans of younger and older children preclude their being grouped together in choral rehearsals. Primary children should be rehearsed by themselves as a choir, separate from intermediate and junior high children. Groupings of grades one through three, four through six, and seven and eight may be workable in the typical Lutheran elementary school.

At the conclusion of the rehearsal the singing of a familiar round or anthem helps to end in a positive manner and may even serve as a background to the dismissal of the children or the repositioning of the chairs and other furniture. If the director is clearly in control of the rehearsal from warm-up exercises to the conclusion, the results will be seen and heard in the marked progress of the children's choir throughout the season.

Cooperative Planning with Colleagues

Finally, it is assumed that the choir director is in close touch with the parish music director, if they are different individuals, and with the pastor to facilitate proper planning of all worship services involving the children's choir. It is through such close communication that a unity of theme and purpose emerges for each service among pastor, organist, congregation, and children's choir.

Note

1. Numerous additional techniques can be found in W. Ehmann and F. Haasemann, *Voice Building for Choirs* (Hinshaw Music Inc., 1982).

Choir Rehearsal Planning Sheet

_____
date

Prerehearsal preparations/needs
(physical, visual, aural, devotional/spiritual)

Time: from ___ to ___	Selection or Activity	Concentrate on:

Variations/additions: Excused Singers:

Announcements, etc.

Chapter Five

From the ris-ing of the sun to the place where it sets, the name of the Lord is to be praised.

H. Kemp

*"God of all lovely sounds, grant us a share
In Thy great harmonies of earth and air;
Make us Thy choristers, that we may be
Worthy to offer music unto Thee."*

Understanding and Developing the Child's Voice

Helen Kemp

The Many Sounds of Children's Choirs

Today I listened to a Gregorian Chant, a Bach chorale, a cheerful canon, a beautiful Norwegian folk song, and a rhythmic American composition, all sung by a children's choir made up of 18 boys and girls, ages 9 through 12. It was a church choir, and the children, not chosen by audition, rehearsed one hour each week. The choir was made up of several excellent singers, a number of average singers, able to match pitches and sing a light, clear sound, and several (four) children who were inexperienced singers, just beginning to get into the "singing channel." Together they formed a choir, a singing group, capable of participating effectively in the worship service.

In most churches, the children's choirs are made up of average children who are not required to have a high degree of innate musical ability. In fact, given the shrinking pool of children available in many communities, choir directors are busy recruiting—even coaxing—children to become choir members. The purpose of the children's choir in the church goes beyond the vocal aspects or the performance proficiency of the group.

Consider for a moment the purpose of children's choirs as proposed by Choristers Guild:[1]

- to make the choir a religious, educational, artistic, and recreational factor in the lives of its members;
- to develop and foster a sense of worship;
- to encourage a sense of personal responsibility;
- to develop the spirit of cooperation;
- to present worthy music, well prepared;
- to influence as many children as possible with these high ideals.

With these "high ideals" I heartily agree. You will notice that there is no specific mention of singing, song, tone, clarity, accuracy, phrasing, or diction. But when you consider the medium through which these purposes are to be realized, you will agree that singing is at the heart of the action. Yes, choirs are for singing. Good singing happens in good choirs. Church musicians have the responsibility of teaching skills and enabling young singers to strive toward a standard of excellence. God, the Creator of the music of the spheres, must have perfect pitch, and I am sure He appreciates our efforts to honor His laws of sound and song.

But, you ask, how do I go about establishing a standard of excellence with my variety-pack singers? There are no easy, instant-success formulas, but there are proven techniques built on solid vocal information and knowledge of the stages of development of the child voice.It is essential for the children's choir director to have a concept of the kind of sound he wants to achieve. There are varying opinions on what an acceptable singing sound is for children.

Positive Vocal Qualities

Teachers and directors must be able to recognize positive vocal qualities in their choristers. The quality of the voices in any group will be mixed, but here are six attributes of good, acceptable vocal sounds:

1. The tones are clear and free, without harsh nasality or muffled throatiness.

2. Head tones are well developed but not forced.

3. Pitch is secure.

4. Full and free upper tones pass into the lower pitch range with brightness and lightness, and voices do not change gears abruptly or push out on lower tones with an obvious break.

5. Voices have carrying power (projection) because vowels are pure and well focused (centered).

6. Voices keep both "ring" and "roundness" in the singing volume spectrum from *p* to *f*.

The director must also be able to recognize singing production problems such as limited pitch range, insecurity of pitch, unpleasant sounds (guttural, harsh, breathy, over-zealous, inaudible), poor breath control, poor posture habits (caved-in chest, protruding chin), and personal attitudes (indifference, negative behavior).

Concepts Involved in Singing

One of the most hopeful statements for those who work with young singers in unauditioned choirs is that "Singing is a learned behavior." It is true that the ability to sing is more often caught from the environment than taught by a teacher, but it is possible to help a child *discover how* to sing. There are some children who seem to have been born singing, repeating sounds and matching pitches at a very early age and enjoying child chanting and recitative-style singing conversations throughout early childhood. Others come to our choirs with little or no experience at creating a singing sound. It is *not* natural for every child to sing by instinct, but it *is* possible for an inexperienced singer to discover what it feels and sounds like to sing even at the fourth- or fifth-grade level.

To show the different attitudes children have in their subconscious about singing, I quote the response of five-year-old Charles when he was asked: "What is singing?"

> Singing is you kinda hear tunes and beats in your head when you don't listen even; and when you breathe them, they come out. And you can't stop. Well, maybe just for a little while if your daddy or teacher says, "You better STOP!" But right away you forget; and you are still breathing, and they come out again. Sometimes you learn words of songs in Sunday school and sing them with other kids, or you learn television commercials; but sometimes they just come out when you breathe and you never heard them before.[2]

Then there is the poem that expresses the plight of another would-be chorister with a completely different self-image as a singer:

> I'm just a little monotone,
> I'll never learn to sing,
> 'Cause when I listen to a tune
> I hear a different thing.[3]

Even at age five or six, there is more to singing than a vocal technique. Already the child's environment has had its impact. Already a child's personality is part of the singing experience. Many children have "caught" their singing skills; others have to be taught from the very beginning.

When it is necessary to develop the singing abilities of the choristers from scratch, it is essential that the teacher be aware of the transfer and connection from *concept* to *skill*. The following information will help the reader be aware of the connection between mental concepts and the development of skills and abilities.

Concept	**Skill**
1. Singing tone versus speaking tone	1. Ability to sustain a vocal sound
2. Definiteness of pitch	2. Ability to sustain a mental image of pitch
3. Highness and lowness of sound	3. Ability to move from high to low or low to high with the voice
4. Sameness of two pitches (unison)	4. Ability to recognize matching pitches and to match pitches with one's voice
5. The sound and feeling of the act of singing	5. Ability to move from one tone to another with the voice
6. What a melody is	6. Ability to sense the organizational quality which makes a group of sounds a melody
7. What a melody does	7. Ability to reproduce organized melodic patterns with the singing voice
8. A vocabulary of singing skills	8. Ability to reproduce melodic patterns and melodies repeatedly, at will, and with accuracy[4]

Perhaps the most important concept to develop in both teacher and chorister is a positive attitude toward singing. A good attitude is developed by enjoyable singing experiences, even though it requires work and thought, and by developing confidence in the ability to sing. Nothing succeeds like success, so the teacher's challenge is to create success for the singers.

Father William Finn said, "The extraordinary choir is usually made up of ordinary singers," but the discipline of good vocal training is the essential ingredient in the transformation from ordinary to excellent. In training young voice teachers at the college level, this writer often proposes the four "-ations" necessary for them to become effective teachers. They are:

—information, the facts;
—demonstration, the how-to;
—communication, from me to you;
—inspiration, the positive feeling level.

These are also the secrets of success among directors of children's choirs. The first, information, is easiest to write about. The others must be experienced. For this reason, it is recommended that you become acquainted with the *video tapes* that were made to accompany this publication.[5] You can see the principles and information demonstrated and communicated to children. Our aim is that the visual and aural will continue where our written words stop. The next section will deal with vocal information for young singers in third through seventh grades.

Vocal Information and Terminology

It is necessary to establish a terminology so that disagreement on the meaning of terms does not prevent understanding. It has been said in jest that whenever there are two or more voice teachers in the same room, there is bound to be mild to violent disagreement. Since we are addressing children's choir directors who have varying levels of vocal experience, nontechnical language will be used to provide solid vocal information.

Most children are capable of producing and sustaining vocal sounds in two ways:

1. In a sustained speaking or yelling quality that we shall call *chest register*. A register is a group of tones, produced in a similar manner and limited to a certain range. It is important to know the range and volume characteristics of the chest voice in order to identify that production in children's singing.

2. In a sustained singing sound in *head register,* with clearfree tones that result from the pleasant-surprise open throat as part of breath inhalation. The height or space created by the gentle-surprise breath remains in that open throat position to produce head tone singing. It is important to know the reasonable range and volume expectations for the age group with which you are working (see Vocal Range Charts, p. 72).

Let us look at these two registers to establish the main differences.

The Chest Register

This is a speaking voice or a shouting quality that carries the heaviness upward until the younger singer experiences a breaking point above which he or she cannot make a free, unforced vocal sound. If the chest register is used continually in combination with demands for more volume, the child's voice cannot expand in range or improve in tone quality and beauty of sound. Exaggerated and continued use of this kind of production can result in vocal disorders such as hoarseness, breathiness, vocal fatigue, and sometimes vocal nodules. It is often associated with too low, too loud music and is encouraged by too heavy accompaniment.

Head Register

The head register for 8-to-12-year-old trebles is best developed by training the upper medium-high voice *downward,* beginning with the best sound as a standard of tone. These tones can be developed from rather soft forward tones on clear, pure vowels to tones that are full and free and have carrying power because of the pure vowels, not excessive volume. Helping a child discover the head voice quality is of prime importance for long-term vocal development.

The One-Register Concept

After the description of chest and head registers, I would like to suggest that the standard of tone quality be established on these pitches:

As the notes descend, keep the sounds in the singing, head-register channel. Avoid dropping heavily and abruptly into the chest-register speaking or yelling channel. However, I am not advocating weak, whispery tones from G to middle C. These need to be carefully developed by carrying the quality of the *head voice downward,* encouraging a bright, light, clear, forward, resonant tone. I try to develop this tonal concept by exercises like the following:

H. Kemp

O - ver   on   the   top   tones,   light and clear the low - er tones.

*The symbol ⌐ seeks to convey the idea of approaching high notes from the top; ⌐ is a visual reminder to *lift* or support lower notes that often tend to slip downward and out of tune.

Round and free on   A   and   G,   keep the ping on D   and   C !

Although we are dealing in this chapter with the older elementary singers, it would be beneficial for the reader to make a study of the following information concerning the sequence of vocal development for children in kindergarten through sixth grade. The material is meant to stimulate a sense of awareness of these developmental stages and how they affect the singing ranges and the vocal goals. Since there is a wide spectrum of innate musical and vocal capacity at every age level, this information is presented in the form of suggestions and guidelines rather than as a tight set of rules.

Vocal Development: Ranges and Goals

Five- and Six-Year-Olds

Vocal goals: Establish the *feel* of singing in contrast to speaking. I call this the "singing channel." Children should be encouraged to become in-tune singers in this limited range in the head register. Sound-making (vocal games) can go several tones above and below this range.

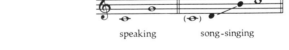

speaking   song-singing

There will be many directional singers who approximate phrase shapes but are not accurate on every pitch of a tune.

Middle C is a pitch on which many children switch into a speaking or chest quality if they are encouraged to sing louder.

Seven- and Eight-Year-Olds

Vocal goals: Same as above plus developing the ability to match pitch. Establish the experience of unison singing. Many children learn to sing in tune at this age. It is wise to train the voices from medium-high downward, rather than from low upward.

Range settles into an octave (plus). Vocalizing can go above and below this range.

song-singing   vocalizing

Keep the concept of *one* register, not allowing the break into chest register on the first line (E) or below. "The lower the lighter" is good vocal advice while head-voice is being developed.

Nine- and Ten-Year-Olds

Tessitura should be median, not lying constantly in either *extreme* of the vocal range. Voice box (larynx) is still flexible cartilage, not hardened. Straining and forcing for loudness is not appropriate. Work for clarity and purity of vowels and for vitality. Many singers, if helped, are able to develop upper tones, fourth line D′ to G′ above. Some children do not develop the high F and G, but most will with a teacher who teaches "how-to."

song-singing   vocalizing

Eleven- and Twelve-Year-Olds

The volume spectrum increases not through loudness but by the development of pure vowel sounds, good posture, and breathing technique. Improving diction greatly enhances clarity and vitality. Treble singers of this age reach the pinnacle of the vocal beauty possibilities for the child's voice. Part-singing should be introduced to allow comfort in singing for those who are good second sopranos and for the *very* few who are altos. Though range often increases, the tessitura should be median, not lying *constantly* in either extreme of vocal range.

song-singing   vocalizing

In each age category I have suggested guidelines for tessitura considerations by a slash spanning certain notes. Tessitura is the term used to indicate where *most* of the notes of a song lie. The total range may be from low B♭ to high F′, but most of the notes might lie in a very comfortable head-voice F and D′.

Scheme for Pitch Indications

a   b   c   d   e   f   g   a′   b′   c′   d′   e′   f′   g′   a″

Developing Singing Skills

There are two basic principles involved in learning to carry a tune and to use the voice in singing experiences with increasing success and satisfaction. (1) The child must learn to hear, judge, and control his own voice, and (2) he must be able to sing *in tune* with another voice, to match pitch, and to experience unison. These principles involve concepts in the mind that spark the development of singing skills, including the ability to sustain a vocal sound, to move from high to low or low to high with the voice, to recognize matching pitches and *match* the pitch of another voice, to move from one tone to another with the voice, and to reproduce a melody with the singing voice.

A child needs to experience what it *feels* like to sing and how that is different from the feel of speaking. I like to use a chart that I had designed for this purpose. It is titled "Your Voice Can Make Different Sounds."[6] It is conceptual in that it helps the young singer *recognize* the difference between whispering, speaking, yelling, and singing. The concepts are then put to the test in action:

a. "I whisper like this." (Whisper.)

b. "I speak like this." (Speak in a normal voice.)

c. "I YELL LIKE THIS!"

d. I sing like this. (Sing in this range to demonstrate "head" voice.)

I call these different "channels." One can switch mentally and transfer that concept into the sound one wants to produce. The child learns to perceive with his mind and to reproduce with his voice at will. It is necessary that each one of these abilities mentioned above be *reinforced* with many opportunities to *listen* and to use the developing skill of singing.

One of the best teaching aids for reinforcing the "singing channel" sound with developing inexperienced choristers is to have them listen to several good head-tone singers in the group. A model sound by someone in the peer group helps to create the mental image of the desirable tone and volume level. This promotes in the slowly developing choristers the *sound,* the *feel,* and even the *look* of singing. Some children progress very quickly, seeming to master all of the concepts and skills at once. Others progress slowly, having to master one ability at a time at a slower learning pace.

The Whole Person Sings: Philosophy and Procedure

This conceptual singing chant embraces many important aspects of training children to use and improve their singing skills. Singing well does indeed require physical, mental, and spiritual involvement. The following material can be used with grades four through seven. It is too disciplined for primary age singers.

Two main physical aspects of singing are *posture* and *breathing.* If you observed a good baseball or swimming coach, you have noticed that basic body positions are thoroughly taught: "Hold the bat this way." "Prepare for the dive with your body in this position." The act of singing is somewhat like learning the skills of an athletic activity. There is a stance, a seated and standing position that helps the young singers hold the singing instrument. Here are a few suggestions:

A Posture-Check Chart

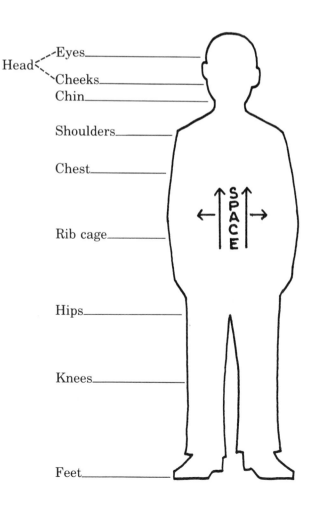

Eyes sparkle — Eyes

Cheeks up — Cheeks
Parallel with the floor—not jutting forward — Chin

Back a bit and down — Shoulders

Comfortably high — Chest

Expand when you breathe, all the way around — Rib cage

Keep rib cage lifted from hip bones

Tucked under slightly to keep back nice and straight — Hips

Very slightly bent, not locked — Knees

On the floor and a little bit apart for balance — Feet

Posture Tips

1. Sit up when you sit down.

2. Stand as if you were a puppet being suspended by the crown of your head from the ceiling.

3. Pretend you are squeezing through a narrow space. Think tall.

4. Think proud.

5. Don't let the chest descend with descending pitches or phrase endings or when singing from *f* to *p*.

I often use this chant to verbalize a singing posture:

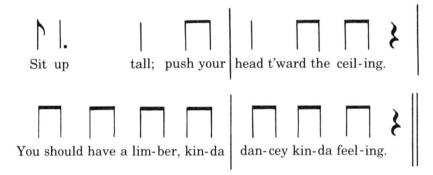

To illustrate how it should feel to use a singer's posture, try these minidramas:

Feel like a ⸮ (bent over—no)

Feel like an ! (stretched tall—yes)

Feel like a robot. (rigidity—no)

Feel like a space person. (buoyancy—yes)

To summarize, good posture for singing is a *way* and a *feeling*.

The other physical activity is *breathing*. Although we have been alive and breathing successfully since birth, there is a difference in breathing for singing. Air must be taken quickly, quietly, and deeply. It has to be exhaled *under control,* slowly, in order to sustain a singing phrase and to sing with different dynamic levels and with good intensity (purity) of tone—all of this while sustaining pitches and producing vowels and consonants.

A few simple exercises can help young trebles to train for singing as they train for swimming:

1. Inhale quickly, quietly and deeply. Chant on a single tone in unison, counting from 1 to 10, then from 1 to 20, perhaps even from 1 to 30. The alphabet may be chanted lightly and clearly, one or two times through. Choose a comfortable head-voice pitch, possibly from G to D'.

2. Breathing exercises (repeat four times in rhythm):

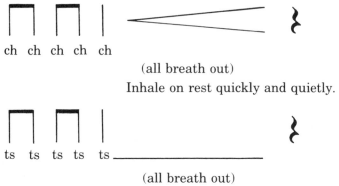

ch ch ch ch ch

(all breath out)
Inhale on rest quickly and quietly.

ts   ts   ts   ts   ts

(all breath out)
Inhale on rest quickly and quietly.

3. Visual images:
Breathe with a *surprise in your eyes!*

Take a Christmas tree breath. The lower boughs are the lower ribs; they expand. The star is the animated face and spirit of the singer.

The slow hiss—breathe quickly, quietly, and deeply. Exhale on a sustained s-s-s-s (controlled exhalation). Sing on one breath as long as I am pulling this ribbon through my fingers.

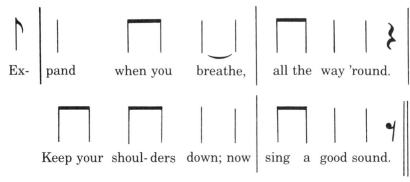

Ex- | pand   when you   breathe, | all the way 'round.

Keep your shoul- ders   down; now | sing   a good sound.

The *mental connection* is essential to the development of singing skills. There are first of all three A's—*awareness, alertness,* and *anticipation.* These are attitudes of an active mind and are prerequisites for the development of *concentration,* which is of prime importance for the developing chorister.

Singing on pitch with other voices requires both concentration and *control,* since the brain sends the message to the voice box (larynx) from a mental image of a certain *pitch.* Those miraculous vocal cords respond to the brain impulse and vibrate the proper number of cycles per second to produce a given pitch. Yes, the brain is at work in fine singing! The brain is also involved in the mental image of vowels, consonants, words, articulation, and diction. *Memoriza-*

tion of tunes and texts also requires the mental connection. The brain is much like a computer with memory. The image of pitch and word can be stored until called on to be produced physically.

Children who have difficulty matching pitches or who sing melodies out of tune need to have lots of practice *listening to* and *thinking* the tone or the melody before the physical act of singing. The sequence has to be aural (listening), mental (retaining a mental image of sound), and physical (breathing and producing vocal sound).

In speaking of *spirit,* I am thinking of the affective, or feeling, level of singing. Even with your youngest choristers, the *expression* of feelings is one of the prime reasons for singing. Expression is often the result of *imagination* and a desire to communicate. Spirit links up with breathing, because singers "breathe in" a mood, a spirit, in order to express. Spirit, or soul, also implies the *individuality* and the *personality* of the singer. The human voice is a truly incredible gift. Even when choristers are trained to sing in the same way or method, the individual child still retains a uniqueness of sound. We owe all children the opportunity to learn to use this gift "to glorify God and enjoy him forever."

Summary: Training the Child's Voice— 15 Vocal Suggestions

Focus on Fourth- Through Seventh-Grade Trebles

1. Have a clear mental concept of the kind of tone you want to hear. Think of the child's singing voice as a long-term musical instrument, one that requires consistent training and constant encouragement.

2. Consider a four-point beginning: stand (or sit) tall, think, breathe, sing. Remember that "tall" means stretching the spinal column upward, while keeping the chin downward. The feeling is buoyant rather than rigid.

3. Relate singers' posture to correct body positions in various sports: Prepare for diving, batting, aiming for a basket. These postures demand coordinated mental and physical alertness and readiness.

4. Phrases must start on pitch and on the first sound in the phrase. There must be no preliminary scoops or slides or glottal attacks. Preparation of body, mind, and breath is required.

5. Sing to the end of the last sound in a phrase, rounding the phrase as you finish within the duration allotted. The last syllable

must go somewhere, must be somewhat elastic, must either decrease or increase. The release at the end should be a little lift, like loosening a soap bubble from a pipe.

6. In children's singing, remember: the lower, the lighter. Do not allow voices to push or drop into speaking production, separating upper voice and lower voice with an obvious break. The two registers should be blended so that the passage from head voice to a mixture (overlap) of head and chest cannot be easily detected. Freedom and vitality (not force) should be maintained throughout the entire range.

7. Consonants take less time but more energy than vowels. They enter the stream of vowel sounds with definiteness but without stopping the flow of the stream. This is one of the secrets of legato singing. Children usually need help in the area of articulation. They need practice with developmental exercises.

8. Pronunciation in singing is the same as in speech. The rise and fall, the accented and unaccented syllables are the same as in speech. (On high pitches—F', G'—certain vowels must be modified *toward* a neutral sound—"uh" or "aw"—to retain the necessary space and height inside the throat.)

9. As is true with pronunciation, speech is the basis for phrasing. Read texts aloud as poetry, not just as metered lines. Too many regular accents create thumps rather than rhythmic flow.

10. Think in musical phrases instead of notes. Think of thoughts instead of words. Think of phrases in swinging pendulum movement instead of thumping beats. (This advice is given for thinking of creating beautiful singing after the initial learning of correct pitches and time values has been done. There is no substitute for careful preparation of basic requirements.)

11. Keep singing rhythmically alive. In conducting a children's choir, the accent is an upward rather than a downward impulse. Internalize rhythmic flow. Conduct phrase shapes to encourage better vocal sound.

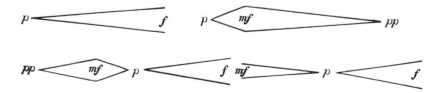

Avoid conducting entire songs like this:

12. Teach children to listen, to distinguish between good and poor tone, to keep their ears alert to pitch accuracy, to be their own critics.

13. Vocal exercises should be simple and have specific purposes that are understandable to the children. A cappella singing should be a part of every rehearsal in order to develop a sensitivity to tone quality and a sense of pitch responsibility.

14. Use a minimum of part singing until the concept of singing is established. After unison singing is secure, canons, rounds and two-melody songs are best to introduce independent singing.

15. Encourage vitality of mind, body, spirit, and voice. Children develop vocal abilities and a love for singing by imitation of a model, by effective instruction, by empathetic reaction, and by gaining a feeling of self-worth. Remember that the *whole person* sings!

Vocalises, Chants, and Breathing Exercises

Activating the Generator (Breath)

A Consonant Caper with F, S, Sh

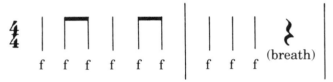

Do the entire exercise in sequence. Use a little diaphragm bounce and a gentle impulse from below the waistline.

Chest and shoulders should remain quiet.

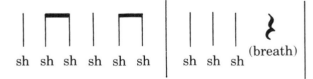

Think of posture as tall and buoyant.

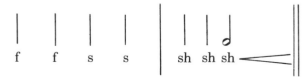

Singers crescendo to release all remaining breath as they bend over from the waist, relaxed and "dangley."

Suggestions:

— Do this exercise in rhythm, not too fast, encouraging choristers to think of the inhaled air as going down into the lungs.
— Make a visible chart of the exercise to create a focus for the "unison eye."
— Create your own rhythmic patterns. Try using the rhythms of a three-part round (e.g., "Row, Row, Row Your Boat") with each entering group using a different breath consonant (f, s, sh, ch).

Breath and Sound

A One-Tone Chant

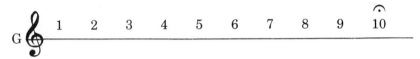

Purposes:

— To sustain one pitch through the consonants and vowels.
— To identify choristers who have difficulty singing a unison pitch in tune with other voices.
— To develop controlled exhalation.

Suggestions:

— Use medium pitches. I suggest G, A', B'. Be aware constantly of the quality of the singing sounds. Be sure children are in the singing channel rather than the talking or shouting channel
— To sustain a longer phrase, try singing to 20 or 25 or chanting the alphabet or the months of the year.

Psalm Fragment Chants

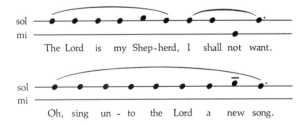

Purposes:

— To sustain pitch accurately.
— To develop a legato line and a consciousness of stressed and unstressed syllables.

— To improve diction by singing long vowels and short consonants (no excess mouthing).

Suggestions:

— Choose a variety of psalm fragments that can gradually be lengthened to prepare children to participate in the sung psalm in worship.
— Make a series of large flash cards to mount on the wall as a visual focus for this vocal activity.

A Gregorian Chant — "Alleluia"

Solo voice, echoed by all. Sing the chant in ascending keys until the highest tone is E′ or F′.

Purpose:

— To provide a vocal model for children to hear, to imagine, and to imitate. The solo voice can be an adult with a clear, unpushed voice or a child from the group.

Variations on "Alleluia"

a. Unison Alleluia (pronounced in singing as indicated below)

Suggestions:

— Sing in unison at a lively tempo, one beat to a measure.
— Sing on one breath.
— Inhale on the rest, and transpose 1/2 tone higher. Repeat until the highest tone is F♯′ or G′.
— Use a relaxed, quiet lower jaw with tip of the tongue agility and no excessive mouthing.
— If children use an undesired glotted stroke on each "Ah-," I suggest the addition of a gentle "H," making the word "Hah- leh- loo."

b. Antiphonal Alleluia

— Antiphonal singing provides variety, creativity, and fun and gives practice in entering with the voice after a rest with a control of pitch, rhythm, and consistent voice quality.

c. Harmonic Alleluia

Suggestions:
    — Listen for tuning of intervals.
    — Sometimes use a variety of texts for the last four measures for different consonant and vowel combinations.

Examples:
    —Sing to the Lord above.
    —Sing to the Lord of love.
    —Go now and serve the Lord.
    —Go now and spread the Word.
    —With the addition of simple ostinati on a classroom tuned instrument, this can be used as a short introit or closing response.

No-No Vocalise

Purposes:

- To encourage choristers to sing forward with the *n*.
- To be able to change from *no* to *nah* without spreading the vowel. Strive for vowel uniformity by keeping the *nah* closer to the sound of *no*.

Suggestions:

- Keep molars apart with the lower jaw quiet and relaxed even when the tongue is making the *n*.
- It is best to *descend* by half tones on this exercise. Children usually need to have a triad in the new key played on the piano to establish the fifth of the chord and the tonic. The singing should be a cappella.

Descending Scales - "Hosanna"

Purposes:

- To develop an awareness of half-tone and whole-tone intervals in the diatonic scale.
- To develop an awareness of free tones on upper notes and of the concept of *lifting* (suggested on these examples with the symbol ⌒) into lower tones rather than *pushing* or pressing them out.

Suggestions:

- Sing descending scales on a variety of consonant-vowel combinations. Try "lah" or "loo," "dah" or "doo," "mah" or "moh."

Descending Arpeggios

* This symbol suggests keeping the note "high" since a descending half step often causes flatting because the second note is not sung on pitch.

Vi - va la mu - si - ca!   Vi - va la mu - si - ca!

Purposes:

— To coordinate breath and space needed for beginning on
upper tones.
— To create a bright attitude for singing.

Suggestions:

— Establish a rhythmic pulse. Rhythmic security affects vocal
confidence.
— Establish the key by playing a triad on the piano in the
established rhythm.
— Remember: "Over on the top tones; light and clear on the
lower tones," as introduced on p. 71. (That is the idea suggested by the symbol ⌐ .)

Three Singing Encounters
(Sol, Fa, Mi, Re, Do)

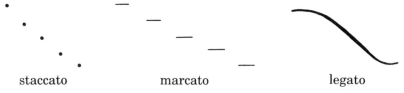

staccato   marcato   legato

Purposes:

— To create an awareness of different vocal articulations.
— To develop the singing skills necessary to produce these
variations.
— To prepare for variety in vocal line and expressions.

Suggestions:

— Use the vowels *oo, oh,* and *ah* on a five-tone descending
scale, articulating short, separated notes for staccato; accented but not separated notes for marcato; and smooth
and flowing notes for legato.
— Use hand "choreography" to picture and feel the different
modes.
— Use a wall chart picturing the three encounters above.

A Closing Chant

Use at the conclusion of the rehearsal.

The Lord bless us and keep us; the Lord make His face to shine up-on us. A- men.

Additional Resources

Finn, William. *Child Voice Training—In Ten Letters.* Chicago: H. T. FitzSimons Co., 1948. Father Finn wrote this material at the request of nuns who were training treble choirs in parochial schools. He addressed the sisters in a series of 10 witty, eloquent, and informative letters. It also is a choir library classic.

Gould, Oren A. *Developing Specialized Programs for Singing in the Elementary Schools.* U. S. Department of Health, Education, and Welfare. Project No. 5-0241. Washington, D.C., 1968. This government grant project was the forerunner of *Teaching Children to Sing.* Much valuable material is documented in the original project, which is more scholarly and pedagogical than the later publication.

Gould, Oren A., and Edith J. Savage. *Teaching Children to Sing.* Dubuque, Iowa: Kendall/Hunt Publishing Co., 1972. The purpose of this manual is to provide practical approaches and answers to children's singing problems. Special techniques and materials are given for helping out-of-tune singers.

Jennings, Kenneth. *Sing Legato.* San Diego: Neil Kjos, 1982. A collection of original studies in vocal production and musicianship. These exercises are imaginative, purposeful, and useful for children and adults. The book is available in a vocal-line edition and an accompaniment edition.

Woodburn, Dawson. *Teaching Singing: A Handbook for Elementary and Secondary Schools.* London, Ontario, Canada: Faculty of Education, University of Western Ontario, 1981. This book was written by a highly successful Canadian music teacher. It consists of a series of pragmatic ideas dealing with such topics as "Teaching a Song: A Five-Step Approach," "Voice Production," and "Improving Breath Control." Equally useful for elementary and secondary school music teachers.

Notes

1. Used by permission of the Choristers Guild, Garland, Texas, which publishes a large, attractive chart listing these purposes. It is useful for the choir room or as a visual reminder for choir parents and congregations.
2. *The Children's Music Leader* (July 1967), Sunday School Board, Southern Baptist Convention.
3. "The Monotone," a poem by Charlotte Harris.
4. Oren A. Gould and Edith J. Savage, *Teaching Children to Sing* (see Additional Resources).
5. "Sing and Rejoice," a 90-minute video cassette demonstrating examples and successful techniques for both classroom and performance (Order numbers: VHS—87MZ0231, Beta II—87MZ0233); "Body, Mind, Spirit, Voice: Developing the Young Singer," a 45-minute video cassette in which Helen Kemp demonstrates techniques choir directors can use in assisting boys with changing voices, youngsters with intonation problems, hesitant singers, etc. (Order number: VHS—87MZ0236, Beta II—87MZ0238).
6. Published by the Choristers Guild. Used by permission.

"The use of instruments throughout the seasons can give children an understanding and feel for the liturgical year."

Chapter Six

Using Instruments with Children's Voices

David S. Walker

Part I
Planning for and Acquisition of Instruments

Throughout the history of worship, instruments have joined with voices to sound praises to God. The simple reed, the crashing cymbal, the strings of the harp, the brassy trumpet—all have added to the richness and excitement of the Word in tone. Man with his God-given inventiveness has searched for and created instruments to express feelings, thoughts, and truths. What better way to fill the temple of God than with sounds of rejoicing and praise!

Rationale

The playing of instruments need not be limited to adults or professionals. Indeed, if they are used correctly and with imagination, instruments can expand the role of the children's choir. They can also effectively teach musical as well as worship concepts. All rehearsals, if planned well, should include the use of instruments. They serve many purposes, and as a handmaid in achieving the long-range objectives of the children's choir, they can add immeasurably to the spirit, excitement, and routine of the rehearsal. Many children who are not turned on to music through the singing experience will become active and eager participants through the use of instruments.

Selection and Care

The kinds of instruments and the various tone colors available for use with children are quite varied—autoharps, guitars, recorders, percussion (both tuned and untuned), resonator bells, handbells, harpsichord, as well as the usual piano and organ. Some are readily available; others require budgetary commitment. The richer the resources, the richer can be the program. The imaginative director will find ways to provide these resources if convinced of their usefulness, appropriateness, serviceability, and direct appeal to children.

When selecting instruments, keep two things in mind: quality of sound (Is the tone color appealing and pleasant?) and durability (Is the instrument well constructed? Are the parts that wear out replaceable?). Even with the best intentions children use instruments with enthusiasm and zeal. Cheap, shoddy instruments do not hold up. When selecting ethnic instruments such as maracas, bongos, claves, fuiro, etc., try to obtain authentic ones. Above all, avoid instruments in the toy category. To enjoy quality sounds children need to be exposed to them directly and consistently.

All instruments should be treated with respect, an attitude children need assistance in learning. Simple, less expensive claves should be handled with as much care as an elaborate, expensive chromatic xylophone. Plan storage space. A church or school that has invested in instruments should protect this investment. Percussion instruments hanging on a pegboard in the choir or music room can both look attractive and make for easy use.

Guiding Their Use

The trained director will, it is hoped, know how to organize and effectively use these instruments with children. The intent of this chapter is not to discuss the techniques of large ensembles—handbell choirs, Orff Instrumentarium, etc.—but rather to investigate and discuss practical and musical ways to use single instruments and small ensembles in both rehearsal and worship. The second half of this chapter provides practical information, simple techniques for immediate involvement, and suggestions for teaching concepts of both music and worship. This will assist both the skilled and the unskilled. Most music examples are taken from the least used but most fertile source of material—the hymnal.

Body Control Precedes Playing

A word of caution before incorporating instruments into the rehearsal or worship: The playing of instruments, whether keyboard, percussion, or mallet type, is an extension of the body. Include much use of body motions in the rehearsal—hand clapping, finger snapping, *patschen* (lap clapping), foot stamping, etc.—before expecting a child to play an instrument successfully. Placing an instrument in a child's hands before much exploration with body motions compounds the problem in many ways: *how* to play, *what* to play, and *when* to play. Imitation using the call and response technique is usually a successful approach. Don't incorporate too many instruments at any one rehearsal. Make each presentation a special event, a discovery, and above all a valid musical experience for children.

Prerehearsal Planning

To avoid confusion and unnecessary noise, plan a definite order for distribution and collection. Don't expect things simply to happen in a rehearsal. Plot and plan. Practice centers can be set up for children who arrive early. Special rhythm patterns, chord progressions on the Autoharp, ostinatos on the mallet instruments, etc., can be written out on tagboard for children to practice. Once children have respect for the instruments and know the basic playing techniques, let them explore the instruments on their own. They may find new ways to play the instrument that will point out a subtle meaning in a hymn text, psalm, canticle, or another item in the repertoire.

Fortunately, the playing of many of the instruments mentioned in this chapter, especially the nonpitched items, is immediate. It involves the child in musical awareness and music making without resort to long hours of practice or the learning of fingerings, notation, correct embouchure, etc. How appealing to children who want things *now*! If directed correctly, children are immediate and inventive music makers. Playing instruments extends their musical imagination and their understanding of how sounds are put together and provides a sense of accomplishment.

The *activity approach* to music learning has been a time-honored tradition in music education. A well-planned lesson usually includes singing, moving, and playing, with some attention given to reading—all focused on the listening experience. Plan rehearsals with these activities in mind, since children respond best to a musical experience that has variety and change of pace. A rehearsal with only singing can turn off even the most eager, enthusiastic child.

With careful planning all the activities can fit together to focus on a musical concept or learning that is necessary for a musical performance in the worship service. Indeed, the activity may remain as a part of the child's understanding of how music works and why it is used in worship much longer than a specific anthem.

Working with Concepts of Music

One of the objectives in working with a children's choir is to build a basic vocabulary that describes both music and worship events. Children can use these words consistently and correctly if they have been exposed to them over a period of time. The objective of a rehearsal should not be to "learn an anthem." The focus, rather, should be on the music and worship elements contained in the piece. That will remain with the children throughout their "stretching cycles of years."

Instruments are ideal means to explore and direct children's attention to the concepts of musical organization. Usually these are divided into the categories of rhythm, melody, dynamics, tone color (timbre), texture (harmony), and form. Although instruments add to the mood and effect, this is *not* the objective. We add instruments for musical reasons and for the illumination they can give to the content of the text. If the director wants to influence children and enrich their lives so they value music in worship, they will need to learn not only the immediate anthem but also its musical worth and its significance in worship. The performance in the worship service should be the culmination of both music and worship elements to which the children have been exposed and that they understand and possess.

An abundance of music arranged for children's choir and instruments has been published in recent years. In either octavo or collection form, these arrangements include not only standard orchestral instruments but also tuned and untuned percussion instruments ranging from the very simple to the very complex. In many cases these arrangements can be adapted to meet the needs and resources of local congregations. They also provide ideas, countermelodies, and possible instrumental combinations for the director. Select wisely and with taste. Not all published materials, even though they are aimed at the child's musical experience, are of equal value and use. Disregard any with inappropriate or questionable text. Build a personal library of these materials based primarily on resources from the hymnal and Biblical texts, so that when they are performed, they will fit into the worship service naturally and not merely as adornment.

Much published folk material features ethnic instruments

such as bongos, cowbell, claves, etc., especially in calypso and Latin American carols. This style often appeals to children, and they love to perform in such ensembles. However, these presentations are often better limited to carol services and church and Sunday school programs rather than at a formal corporate worship service.

Performance

The atmosphere and openness of a children's choir rehearsal, especially when it involves playing and experimenting with instruments, should not spill over into the sanctuary. Attention should be given not only to proper vestments but also to instrument placement, music stands and tables, if needed, as well as the transporting of the instruments. This is most important if the children's choir sings in view of the congregation. The management of both chorister and instrument should be well planned and practiced with proper decorum and with an understanding of why this activity is included in a worship service. Dropping an instrument or playing it during a prayer can be detrimental to the overall worship atmosphere. It may be best to collect or remove the instruments in a quiet manner immediately after their use. Choir parents, adult choir members, or ushers can be trained to assist.

Never perform in church with children without adequate rehearsal in the church. Neglecting this important detail could result in a negative appreciation of what should be a source of enrichment—the complementary use of instruments with children's voices.

Part II
A Dictionary of Instruments and Suggestions for Their Use with Children's Choirs

In order to discuss similar types of instruments in close proximity, a modified dictionary approach has been used with the entries that follow. Families of instruments are treated under more encompassing, usually descriptive, headings. For example, harpsichord, organ, and piano are found under *Keyboard;* drums, triangle/finger cymbals, gong, wood block, etc., are under *Nonpitched Percussion.* Additional categories of this type are *Pitched Mallet* (Orff—Glockenspiel, Metallophone, and Xylophone—and Resonator Bells) and *Orchestral,* which includes woodwinds, strings, and brass. Autoharp, guitar, handbells, and recorder are listed individually as single instruments in alphabetical order.

Autoharp

The Autoharp, invented in the late 1800s, is a useful accompaniment instrument for those directors who are not skilled with the guitar. Although some advanced players, especially in Appalachia, have developed techniques to "pick out" melodies, its primary use is to provide accompaniments using primary and secondary chords. After several trial sessions most directors will become expert in providing these chordal accompaniments for children's voices. More use should be made of this tone color in rehearsals than of the piano. With experimentation, different strums, plucked tones, and rhythmic accompaniments will aid the director in supporting the child's voice. In addition to rehearsals, it is especially effective when accompanying various hymns, usually those from the folk tradition—for example, *Jefferson, New Britain, Consolation, Go Tell It,* etc. Some models are equipped with contact microphones, which offer more possibilities for volume and special effects.

Many models are available through church supply stores and instrument suppliers. At least a 15-bar instrument should be purchased from the start, since a smaller model soon becomes inadequate. The Autoharp is limited in its selection of keys; the more bars there are, the more possible chords.

The director who spends time exploring the possibilities of the Autoharp sometimes thinks of the instrument as a personal tool. But its simplicity, chordal organization, and ease of performance also appeal to children. Let them experiment with the instrument, exploring chordal patterns, rhythmic strums, and other techniques mentioned below. They can learn and perform accompaniments for fellow choir members. In grades one and two, children can learn to press the chord bars while the director or older children strum. It is best to begin with one-chord melodies and later advance to those that use two or more chords. In their initial experiences, the children can strum while someone presses the correct chord bars.

All respond quickly to the different quality of sound created by different chords. The response is to the total sound of the chord and not to separate tones that compose the chord.

It is important that the Autoharp be handled with care and that children learn to respect the instrument.

An Autoharp must be kept in good tune. This is a major problem and discouragement for those who have not had experience with stringed instruments. A tuning fork is provided, and after a determined effort, most directors can tune with reasonable efficiency.

Since it is a chordal instrument, tune it through the use of chordal structure: do—mi—sol (1—3—5). Start with the C chord, reproducing the C from a known pitch on the piano, bells, or a pitch pipe. Then tune the C chord (C—E—G). Pressure to the right *raises* the pitch; pressure to the left *lowers* the pitch.

Then proceed by the circle of fifths. Since the G is in tune, next tune the G chord (G—B—D), then the D chord (D—F♯—A). Go on to the A chord (A—C♯—E). Continue until all strings are tuned. Always check by strumming the complete chord. Above all, don't be discouraged. After several tunings you will become an expert. Some directors can tune an Autoharp in 10 minutes. Courage and determination will pay dividends.

As children learn melodic organization by singing and playing melody instruments, their understanding of harmonic function and development of aural discrimination can be increased by experimenting with the Autoharp.

Suggestions

• Always place the correct finger on the chord bar. Notice that the chords are arranged in a family—the I—IV—V⁷ in each key. If the tonic or home-base key is C major, the index finger should be placed on that chord bar. The middle finger will fall on the V⁷ chord (G⁷) and the fourth finger on the IV chord (F). This placement of fingers—index, middle, and fourth—will usually be straight across. The one exception is the G chord family. This will be a triangle with the middle finger above covering the V⁷ chord (D⁷).

• Always strum with a definite chord pattern in both mind and ear. Folk music, "pop" music, and some hymnals, when appropriate, have chordal indications above the top staff. Study these and their pattern before strumming.

• If children are to play the Autoharp, prepare an Autoharp strumming chart. Tagboard or index cards may be used. As notated below, include the *key* and *time signature*. Change the chord as indicated. After some practice, the children can deviate from the basic strum and improvise patterns of their own.

Autoharp Strumming Chart

Angels We Have Heard on High
(Melody: *LW* 55; *LBW* 71)

F Major

4/♩	F	F	C⁷	F
	Angels	we have	heard on high,	

	F	F	F C⁷	F
	Sweetly	singing	o'er the plains	

F F	C⁷ F	F F	F C⁷ F
And the mountains	in reply,	Echoing their	joyous strains.

• The Autoharp comes with several different picks—plastic, soft felt, hard felt, etc. Experiment with others—rubber doorstops, wooden spoons, charge cards, etc. Children are especially resourceful in finding unusual sounds on the Autoharp. Try hitting the strings with a wooden mallet, placing the instrument on top of a metal wastepaper basket, or playing it with a comb. Some of these effects highlight the meaning of the text, especially of certain psalms or canticles. When using special effects, evaluate their usefulness and contribution to the music and to its meaning within the worship service.

• The Autoharp is particularly effective with certain psalm tones. In some remote keys the chords may have to be transposed to fit the limits of the instrument. Adding a recorder or flute on the chant melody adds further interest. Children, whenever possible, should be involved with the liturgical portions of the service, not merely in anthems.

• Children can sing selected stanzas of hymns with Autoharp accompaniment if the alternation practice is used in congregational singing. When this is done, it is very important that the service folder clearly indicates the stanzas to be sung by the children's choir.

Of all the pitched instruments, the Autoharp is the most immediate and the most fun. Its exploitation in rehearsals will add interest and help retain membership, not to mention its value in recruitment.

Additional Resource
Peterson, Meg. *The Complete Method for Autoharp.* Northbrook, Ill.: Music Education Group.

Guitar

Without doubt the guitar has never been more popular or more widely used than it is today. With the many kinds available—from electric rhythm to acoustic nylon-string or steel-string—the guitar has become the instrument of youth. Its folk character and tone color provide superb accompaniments for the child voice, especially with folk hymns, carols, spirituals, and some contemporary music. Its portability is an asset when a piano, organ, or harpsichord is not available or would be inconvenient or overpowering.

There are two styles of guitar play—folk and classic—that serve well with children. Older children who have studied the folk style and have a knowledge of chords and picking-strumming techniques can assist. However, the more useful is the classic style with attention to beautiful tone, fundamentals of reading, and musicianship. This lute style of playing is usually more suitable and tasteful in a worship service.

The recommended guitar for beginners, and the one most suited for accompanying children's singing, is the classic guitar, which has a round sound hole, a flat top, and nylon strings. It provides a pleasant, warm tone that complements young voices. While amplification is occasionally needed when accompanying adult choirs, it is usually unnecessary with children's voices. Experimentation is the best guide. If a contact microphone is not available, simply have the guitarist play into a standard microphone, and use very light amplification.

A good guitar player always plays on a well-tuned instrument. Tuning the guitar with its six strings is far easier than tuning the Autoharp. In time older children can tune with accuracy and ease. The strings on the guitar, from lowest to highest, are E, A, D, G, B, E. (The high E is a third above middle C; the low E is two octaves below.) Tune these to a piano, bells, or a pitch pipe.

Another way to tune the guitar is called *relative tuning:*

● After tuning the low E string, place your finger just behind the fifth fret on that string. This will give you the correct pitch for the next highest string, the A string. As you pluck the fingered string, tune the A string until the pitches match.

● Next, finger the A string in the fifth fret, and tune the D string until the pitches match. Continue in this way until all the strings are in tune. Check the low E with the high E; they should sound in tune with each other.

● *Note:* The G string is fingered in the fourth fret rather than the fifth.

Suggestions

● Be selective when choosing anthems that indicate guitar accompaniment. Few have the accompaniment written out; most only indicate chords. Always read the text first. If it is inappropriate, trite, or questionable, do not use it. Give the guitarist the music well in advance of the rehearsal so an appropriate accompaniment can be worked out.

● Prepare your own folk hymn arrangement. Such tunes as *Maria ist geboren, Land of Rest, The Ash Grove,* and *Bunessan,* all derived from the folk tradition, can be sung with guitar accompaniment. Prepare a tagboard chart with melody, text, and appropriate chords for the guitar player. This can assist less advanced players, who often have difficulty extracting the melody line from the closed scores found in hymnals.

For an introduction, interludes, and a coda, add a melodic instrument such as a recorder, bells, or a flute. Or teach a child who plays keyboard how to play the melody on a distinctive solo stop on the organ.

Not all stanzas need to be sung. Select those that are most effective, and if congregational singing in alternation is used, be sure instructions and the sequence of the stanzas are clearly listed in the bulletin.

• The repetitive chord structure of rounds encourages simple guitar accompaniment. (This is also true for the Autoharp.) For each chordal repetition, have the guitarist vary the strum and rhythm pattern. Because of children's general developmental growth and awareness of harmony, do not attempt round singing until the middle or end of the third grade.

• Some rounds and folk melodies lend themselves to one-chord accompaniments, with the tonic chord (I) usually on the strong beats in each measure. Return the strings of the guitar to this chord, and with the guitar on a table top, gently hit all the strings at once with a pencil, ruler, or wooden mallet. Experiment with different rhythm patterns.

Selected portions of the liturgy can also be accompanied successfully on the guitar. Some settings of the Kyrie lend themselves to this treatment, as well as settings of the Magnificat and chant versions of the Lord's Prayer. Advanced guitar players are usually needed to provide the proper style for these accompaniments. Never impose bad musicianship, poor performance, or trite music on a congregation involved in corporate worship.

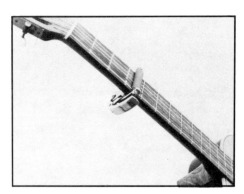

• Explore the use of the capo, a device that can be clamped over the fingerboard of the guitar, making it easy to change key quickly. The choice of key influences the range and register. Often a hymn, folk song, or spiritual sounds better in a key other than the one in which it was written. Do not be limited by the printed page. Learn to transpose, and have children explore their complete range. The glory of the child voice is not its low register but rather its medium and high tones. Hearing children soar to their high register in climaxes creates an unforgettable sound.

• The classic guitar has a wealth of fine literature. Many Baroque pieces sound well in transcription. When using the guitar with children, ask the guitarist to provide other appropriate music during the service, for example, Prelude, Voluntary, or music during the distribution of Communion. Most performers like to play, and the more involvement they have, the more willing is their participation.

The guitar has a definite place in both rehearsal and performance of today's children's choir. Even minimum technique is of great advantage to the director. Take time to learn and study; it will pay rich dividends.

Additional Resources
Seeger, Peter. *Folksinger's Guitar Guide.* New York: Oak Publications.

Synder, Jerry. *Basic Sing Book for Guitar.* 2 vols. New York: Hansen Music and Books.

Handbells

Bells have long been associated with Christian worship. Legends and superstitions about bells—"Sanctus" bells, tower bells, *cymbala,* handbells—abound. There is no doubt that bells played a part in medieval religious life and were used to a great extent in liturgical worship.

Of all the bells, the handbell has become part of the music program in many churches today. Bells are rung by both young and old alike. Much music is published for special choirs of handbell ringers. Although the technique of playing bells is easily learned, playing in an ensemble and playing musically require long hours of practice, determination, and discipline. However, a few handbells to highlight hymns, chants, and processionals can add richness and variety to the children's choir program. The more complicated pieces are best left to the handbell choir. Simple, immediate handbell parts are enjoyed by children and open ears to this ancient and fascinating sound that can further enrich contemporary worship.

Suggestions

- Handbells should be handled carefully. They should not touch while vibrating.
- Bells do tarnish over a period of time and should occasionally be cleaned with special solutions prepared for that purpose. Using white gloves helps prevent fingerprints.
- It is helpful to realize that, for convenience in notation, handbell parts sound one octave higher than written.
- Many rings are possible with the handbell but the simple *straight* ring is the easiest for children: Grasp the leather handle and bring the bell back to shoulder height with a slight backward tilt so the clapper rests toward the player's body. The bell is then rung by a quick forward motion of the forearm with a supple snap of the wrist. The bell is then returned to the starting position in an upward arc. The strike occurs at the point furthest away from the ringer.

Only for rare special effects dampen the bell. The characteristic style allows the bell to continue to vibrate after striking.

- Any simple ostinato parts scored for resonator bells or metallophones can be played on handbells (see Pitched Mallet instruments). Repetitive parts that require few bells are most successful with the children's choir.
- If appropriate to the text and spirit of the hymn, children

can ring the tonic (do) or the complete tonic triad (do—mi—sol) between verses of a hymn. Do this sparingly.

• In medieval times the use of bells was quite simple, even improvisatorial. Often in processionals and longer chants an ostinato was played on several bells, creating interesting rhythmic clashes and chance harmonies. If the Entrance Hymn is used and its style lends to this treatment (melodies derived from the Gregorian tradition), create a simple ostinato of three or four bells that children can ring throughout. Select tones within the key of the hymn. Children love to play bells in procession.

• When chanting liturgical portions of the service (for example, the Venite in Matins), have the children sound the reciting tone(s) throughout.

• Giving pitches for chant by playing the incipit on bells provides variety. Practice this beforehand. Some people have difficulty finding correct pitches from handbells.

• Bells have often been associated with certain sections of the Ordinary, for example, the Gloria and the Sanctus. Simple bell parts can be arranged for these portions, depending on the setting used. Because of its form, text repetition, and liturgical significance, the number three has been associated with the Sanctus. Have children toll the tonic (do) bell three times before beginning congregational singing.

• When responsorial singing is used (between cantor and congregation or cantor and choir), ring the tonic, an open fifth, or a cluster of bells between responses. This serves to signal the congregational or antiphonal refrains. This is especially effective when singing the psalm tones or when using the Litany in procession. When playing in procession, it is best to place performers in the middle of the choir. Let older children experiment with ringing bells high above their heads in procession so the tone floats above the congregation.

• When singing hymns either as complete anthems or in alternation with the congregation and the harmony uses mostly the primary chords (I, IV, V⁷) on the strong beats, children can learn to play the root tones of these chords throughout on handbells.

Some examples:

Hymn Tune	Key (in *LW, LBW*)	Bell Tones
Rathbun	B♭ Major	B♭—F
Tempus Adest Floridum	G Major	G throughout
Azmon	G Major	G—C—D
Llanfair	F Major	F—B♭—C
St. Thomas	F Major	F—B♭—C
Olivet	D Major	D—G—A

• Pentatonic melodies, those that use only the do—re—mi—sol—la of the scale, invite improvisation on the bells. The Irish folk tune *Gartan,* using the text "Love Came Down at Christmas" (*LW* 46), is such a melody. The tune *New Britain* with the text "Amazing Grace, How Sweet the Sound" (*LW* 509) is another. Both melodies use only the tones F—G—A—C—D. Have five children, each playing one bell, prepare an ostinato or improvise softly throughout. Experienced handbell players aim for rhythmic precision and good dynamic control. For soft playing, the wrist movement alone may be sufficient.

When working with pentatonic melodies make sure the text and spirit of the hymn is appropriate for the tone color of the handbell.

In short, the imaginative director will think of many ways to use the handbell, not the handbell choir, to enrich the child's understanding and involvement in all aspects of the worship service.

Additional Resource
Allured, Donald E. *Joyfully Ring! A Guide for Handbell Ringers and Directors*. Nashville: Broadman Press, 1974.

Keyboard

Harpsichord

With the increasing interest and availability of fine harpsichords, this instrument deserves to be considered for accompanying children's voices. Not all piano and organ accompaniments lend themselves to effective use on the harpsichord. Keyboard parts of thinner texture—two or three voices—frequently work well, especially if they are of a linear style. Chordal music, unless of a moderate tempo, tends to decay too fast, leaving a feeling of unconnected sounds. Highly reverberant rooms can sometimes redeem this problem, however.

Suggestions
• Use a piano for keyboard accompanying until the last one or two rehearsals.
• Do not rely on the harpsichord for support while children are learning a selection. Begin to use it after the choir is confident with the music.
• Rehearse with the harpsichord in the church or room where the performance will take place. Remember, unlike the piano and organ, this instrument has a very limited volume range.

• Harpsichord sound is most satisfying in a reverberant environment. Dry or acoustically dead rooms suppress the delicate clarity characteristic of this instrument.

• Experiment to find the best location for both singers and congregation to hear the harpsichord. An open lid may not be necessary in a smaller "live" room.

• Music from the Renaissance and Baroque eras, or music in that style, usually lends itself to harpsichord accompaniment. Some contemporary music with the qualities mentioned above is equally effective with harpsichord.

• Even-temperament tuning is preferred for accompanying children because their musical development seldom encompasses historic unequal temperaments.

• In the basso continuo style of the Baroque period, add a cello, bass clarinet, or bassoon to the bass part. A treble instrument playing the vocal part or descant can be a fine complement to the harpsichord sound, as well as offer reinforcement to the bass and upper parts.

• When introducing the harpsichord to children for the first time, acquaint them with the way in which the sound is produced. They also need to know that the sound is not made louder by depressing the keys with more force and to be aware of the somewhat more fragile nature of its moving parts in comparison to the piano.

• During rehearsal, spend a brief time with each of the children, allowing them to play a few notes or a short melody or piece. Once they are familiar with the uniqueness of the instrument, they will sing better with its accompaniment and delight in its engaging sound.

Organ

Because of the diversity of organs available in local congregations, it is difficult to be definite about its use as an accompaniment to the child's voice. Placement, tonal resources, acoustics, and voicing all play crucial roles. In addition, the organist's technique—articulation, touch, intelligent use of agogic accents—contributes to a quality performance. Unlike the piano, many organs do not have a percussive attack, the immediate response to rhythm, or the control over a singing tone. These must be provided by the skill and knowledge of the organist. However, the organ does provide a myriad of tone colors, a sustained tone, and a variety of contrasts that should be used to advantage when accompanying children's voices.

Suggestions

• Never cover children's voices with organ sound. Too little rather than too much should be the rule. Loud organ playing often encourages children to shout rather than sing. Rehearsal techniques that encourage independent singing will pay dividends when adding organ accompaniment.

• A definite 8' pitch should be provided. Usually this is from the flute family, but a small-scaled principal or even a string may prove adequate. If louder volume is needed, add a 4' flute or small, modestly voiced principal. The addition of a 2' often adds too much brilliance unless this stop is under expression where it can be delicately controlled, as in the Swell division. However, skipping pitches—an 8' and 2' only—sometimes provides a good, clear accompanying tone, especially in faster tempos. Usually avoid quints (2-2/3' and 1-1/3') and other compound stops (for example, Sesquialtera—2-2/3' plus 1-3/5'). Sometimes a small mixture in appropriate pieces can be useful. Above all, experiment and listen. Plan registrations before the children rehearse with the organ. Endless changes of registration and experimentation can lead to disinterest and discipline problems. Keep a record of effective registrations.

Avoid a booming bass or growling pedal part using the 16' register. If the organ has a gentle 16' that blends with the manual registration, use it. If not, couple down manuals at 8'. Not all anthems must use 16'. In fact, this pitch often interferes with the register of the child's voice. Use the 16' sparingly. Some organs have a soft 16' on one manual. Use this in the left hand as if playing a basso continuo part, or couple to the pedal.

• Do not use overly loud combinations for introductions, interludes, or codas. Think of the overall dynamic scheme. Introductions should provide three things: pitch, tempo, and style.

• Except for very, very special effects, avoid the tremolo.

• In general, do not duplicate the children's vocal line. If taught and prepared in rehearsal, the children will sing with assurance and security provided the harmonic and rhythmic intent is felt.

• If the accompaniment includes a distinct countermelody, do not hesitate to use a solo stop such as a small-scaled reed, a cornet, or even a louder flute stop. Sometimes individual children can play these countermelodies on an orchestral instrument, bells, or recorder. If the countermelody can be registered on a separate manual, prepare a child to play it on the organ. Children can be taught to play melody parts on the organ. Less advanced students can play simple harmonic parts such as drones, ostinatos, and pedal points. Using children in many ways adds to the excitement of being in the choir. Let your imagination soar.

• Always plan at least one rehearsal with the organ before performing in the worship service. The sound and security of the rehearsal room is changed when the children are in the surroundings of the church. If children get restless, practice the processional or entrance hymn in the middle of the rehearsal. Do not always start with the process of getting in and getting seated.

• If the director of the children's choir is not the organist, prepare thoroughly together beforehand. Do not accept a cursory, offhanded accompaniment for the children's choir. The accuracy, taste, and style of the accompaniment for this choir is as important to a worship service as the performance of the most elaborate anthem or cantata and takes as much skill and sensitivity.

• End the first rehearsal of the season in the choir loft so children can hear the instrument, have it explained, and play it themselves. Above all, sing with it. Children respond to familiar surroundings and do their best when they are secure and comfortable in special situations.

• Become familiar with the acoustics of the parish auditorium, the school stage, the church, or wherever the children's choir will perform. This will determine tempo, one of the most important considerations when preparing music. If the children have rehearsed in the music room and then have to adjust at the performance site, the sense of security and confidence also readjusts.

• When the children's choir is involved with a multiple choir performance that includes organ and/or instruments, do not expect them to respond or act like adults. Plan the rehearsal very carefully, considering their attention span, seating, special cues, etc. Always make sure the children understand their special role in the performance and their contribution to the worship service. Rehearse the complete ensemble first with particular attention to the children's part. After dismissing the children, continue the rehearsal with the other choirs and instrumentalists if needed. Do not expect children to sit through a lengthy rehearsal. Ask choir parents to assist at these special rehearsals so the burden of assembly and dismissal is not part of the director's responsibility.

• Vary accompaniments for the children's choir. Do not always use the organ. The harpsichord, if available, could be a welcome alternate for some selections, as may be the Autoharp, guitar, or mallet instruments combined with nonpitched percussion. If available, use a recorder consort or string trio or quartet. Explore the possibilities that are available in your congregation and community. Children as well as adults respond to variety.

Piano

Although most children's choir directors have keyboard skills for solo performance, many have not developed techniques for using the keyboard as a tool in rehearsal. Often *too much* piano sound is used. The piano is an excellent instrument to lead group singing, but its tone color, percussive attack, and volume conflict with producing an acceptable singing tone with children's voices. Playing through a piece or "banging out" a melody or countermelody generally defeats the objectives of musicality and excellence. Children, over a period of time, must become independent singers, secure and musically aware of their part in the total ensemble. This will never be achieved if the piano constantly assumes the role of providing accurate pitches (if it is in tune), precise rhythms, and accurate tempo. Elaborate, loud, obtrusive keyboard playing will never redeem poor singing or choral preparation. The piano, at best, should provide a definite but subtle harmonic support, a secure tempo, and a sense of musical drive.

Suggestions

- Get away from the piano during some or all of the rehearsal.
- Play musically. Children respond to musical sounds such as clean, crisp rhythms, feeling for the phrase, and melodic movement.
- For pitches, rely on your own voice, the children's voices, bells, or a recorder instead of the piano. (If the director is a man, he should sing in his own register. The children will compensate for the octave difference. Do not use falsetto.)
- When playing the piano, use simple but accurate chordal accompaniments. Avoid thick textures, lush harmonies, and complicated polyphony. (Research has found that harmonic function is the last element developed in a child's awareness of musical events. The concept of dynamics develops early, followed by rhythm and melody. Simple form can be taught at all ages.)
- Experiment with the placement of the piano. Do not always have the piano in front of children. If it is a large upright, place it sideways so eye contact can be maintained; if it is a spinet or console, place children and piano in a circle. This arrangement also helps children hear the effect of ensemble. If children are seated in traditional straight, parallel rows or shallow semicircles, only the director hears the results.
- Do not duplicate the vocal line on the piano. Provide a guitar-like chordal accompaniment so children will "think" their part(s) and not rely on the piano.
- Insist that the piano be maintained and tuned regularly. An out-of-tune piano will never help children become sensitive to pitch.
- Although most directors are responsible for all aspects—playing, teaching, and conducting—enlist, if possible, an advanced piano student or adult to assist on occasion. Prepare the accompanist carefully before the rehearsal, establishing tempo, key (if it is transposed), dynamics, etc. An accompanist can make or break a rehearsal; a good one is a treasure.
- While some of the repertoire for the children's choir will be taught by rote from the hymnal or other sources, children should be exposed to music notation so they see and discover how sound is put on paper. When selecting octavos or collections with keyboard accompaniment, base your selection on the principles listed above.

Nonpitched Percussion Instruments

Pitched mallet instruments can provide children with melodic and harmonic concepts; nonpitched percussion instruments, if used correctly, can add to their understanding of concepts about rhythm. Indeed, sometimes these instruments are simply called *rhythm instruments*. Every director of a children's choir should have a variety of these instruments and use them extensively in a planned rehearsal. More often their use in a rehearsal is a means rather than an end. In a worship service they are not always appropriate. Their use during rehearsal to highlight beat, meter and rhythm pattern, and other concepts of music is of inestimable value to the final musical performance. Of course, some anthems, especially those derived from ethnic sources, demand their use.

Cheap, shoddy, toy-like instruments should not be used. Select and purchase the best and most authentic. It is better to use only a few with the finest tone quality and construction than to use a battery of poorly sounding, inferior instruments.

Some useful instruments to collect are the following:

Latin American		**Other Percussion**	
maracas	cowbell	triangle/finger cymbals	wood block
claves	bongo drum	tambourine	cymbal
guiro		gong	temple blocks

Suggestions

● Movement activities precede the playing of instruments. Before transferring the feeling to an instrument, be certain children are accurate in their body motions.

● Children should be taught how to play the instruments correctly. Insist on a good tone quality with accurate, musical responses.

● When using these instruments, avoid the so-called "rhythm band" approach in which every part is preorchestrated and imposed on the children. Instead, let the children discover and extract the beat, meter, and rhythm patterns contained in the piece, and suggest various ways of highlighting these components with the rhythm instruments.

● Every use of percussion instruments should contribute to a child's understanding of how a piece is put together musically. Not only the components of rhythm need to be extracted. Experiment with the following:

Beat   Let a child discover the tempo (speed of the beat) by playing a drum softly. (Pull the sound out; don't push it in.)

Meter	Play a claves to respond to the metric accent in sets of twos, threes, or fours.
Rhythm Pattern	Play the pattern of long and short sounds of the melody on a triangle. Add this to the above, and most children will hear that rhythm is a combination of several ingredients working together.
Melodic Phrase	Play a triangle or finger cymbals at the beginning and/or end of a phrase. This will call attention to the way long and short phrases are used to create contrast in music and also help the children breathe on the phrase.
Dynamics Accents	Experiment with loud and soft sounds and accents. Evaluate which are most appropriate to a particular piece of music. Consider also whether percussion instruments are appropriate to the text and musical setting.
Register	Explore the high, middle, and low registers of these instruments. Some will only sound at one register; others, if played in different ways, can produce either low, middle, or high tones. Which is appropriate?
Form	Orchestrate the first section (called A) of a piece with children's suggestions using certain tone colors played on percussion instruments. During the first contrasting section (called B), change the orchestration. Children will hear the same/different quality. This is a musical way to expose children to the contrasts and repetitions in music that work together to create form.

• When using ethnic material (calypso, black spirituals, Japanese folk melodies, American Indian chants, etc.), be authentic and true to the style. Proper nonpitched percussion is a distinctive element of ethnic style.

• Enriching the worship service with the glory of the vocal tone of the children's choir is a main objective. Avoid cute and pretentious instrumental arrangements that might overpower and detract from this objective.

Orchestral Instruments

In recent years some materials for the children's choir have included orchestral instruments such as flute, oboe, strings, and brass, either as a solo or in ensemble. Most children, of course, are not capable of playing these parts. However, with some investigation, older children and adults in the community, either professional or amateur, can be discovered. What a musical experience for children to see and perform with these instruments! And what a climate in the rehearsal room when performers finally appear!

This valuable and enriching experience takes time, effort, and planning, but the final results can be musically and educationally rewarding.

Suggestions

• Search for and locate instrumentalists in the community who would be willing to participate in a worship service. Keep an up-to-date file card for the various categories of brass, strings, woodwinds, and percussion (also include recorder and classical guitar).

• If possible, audition instrumentalists before agreeing to a performance. Not all musicians work well in a church situation, and not all can submit to the rehearsal situation of a children's choir. Also, agree on a fee, if requested, the number of rehearsals, and the time, dates, and length of the service(s) in which they will participate. Some directors insist on a written, signed contract, but this is seldom necessary. In addition, make sure music stands are available, and if a fee is involved, make sure it is given, perhaps with a thank-you note, immediately after the service is completed.

• Do not waste instrumentalists' time. Plan your rehearsal so that they appear at the middle or end of a rehearsal after the preliminaries, warm-ups, and other items have been covered. Some instruments, such as brass, are very loud to children; others, like the bassoon, are "gunny" sounding. Let the children know what to expect, and encourage them to behave professionally.

• If possible, prepare the instrumentalists in a separate rehearsal before combining parts with children. Agree on tempo, phrasing, repeats, dynamics, and other musical matters.

• Always rehearse where the performance will take place. Acoustics, seating arrangements, the visibility of the conductor, etc., are important aspects to consider for a successful performance.

• If the instrumentalists are willing—and they usually are—use them throughout the service—Prelude, voluntaries, hymn introductions, descants, etc. Be prepared for the B♭ instruments such as the trumpet and clarinet. These are called transposing instruments, and the parts must be indicated as such. Most professional musicians can transpose on sight, but if this is not the case, write out the parts legibly. B♭ instruments play one whole step *above* the notated pitch; thus, if a piece is in B♭ major, these instruments will play in C major; if it is in C major, they will play in D major, etc.

Pitched Mallet Instruments

An excellent way to develop elementary concepts about melody and harmony, as well as to enhance the final performance in the worship service, is to include pitched (tuned) mallet instruments such as resonator bells and/or the Orff instruments in the children's choir experience. The purchase of good, in-tune, well-constructed instruments is essential. These instruments, although expensive, are versatile, and when they are used imaginatively, they can enrich the singing activity, develop aural skills, and promote interest and skill in reading simple melodies and tonal patterns observed in music notation.

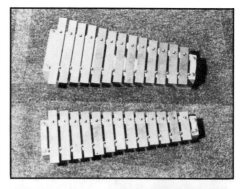

Orff Instruments

Since the introduction of the Orff *Schulwerk* approach to music education in the United States, many directors have included not only the speech and movement techniques of this method but also the mallet instruments especially designed for Orff ensembles. (This ensemble may also include many nonpitched percussion instruments as well as recorder, string, and timpani.)

The mallet instruments include glockenspiels, metallophones, and xylophones; each category has its own special tone color. The glockenspiels (a distinctive, delicate bell-like sound) come in two sizes, soprano and alto. The metallophones (also a bell-like sound but more mellow and longer lasting than the glockenspiels) come in three sizes: soprano, alto, and bass.

The xylophones (a crisp, wooden sound) also come in three sizes: soprano, alto, and bass. In their respective ranges most will include an octave and a sixth—C to A.

These instruments, of excellent quality, are more closely related to those of non-Western cultures (such as the Indonesian gamelan) than to their modern orchestral counterparts. The bars are not fixed permanently over the wooden resonator chambers but are arranged in a single, straight row. Supplementary bars are provided for playing in different keys. Most instruments come with a B♭ and an F♯ bar; all other pitches can be purchased separately. (Chromatic instruments of the same type also are available.) Bars can be removed easily, leaving only those that are needed. This can be an advantage, especially for the inexperienced child, and can provide an immediate, successful instrumental experience. It is strongly suggested, however, that when bars are removed, those that remain

should stay in their relative positions. This will aid children to *see* as well as *hear* intervallic relationships.

It is not necessary to purchase all the instruments at once. When money is available, new instruments can be added to the ensemble. Delightful musical ensembles with contrasts of different tone colors can be planned even with a few instruments.

Special mallets made of different materials are used to play these instruments. For the best possible tone, experiment with the hard felt, rubber-tipped, wood-tipped, and felt-covered mallets provided.

Free and unhindered body movement, including clapping, *patschen* (slapping of the knees or thighs with the palms of the hands), stamping, and finger snapping, should precede the playing of these instruments. Children must internalize a feeling for beat, meter, rhythm pattern, and phrase before transferring these concepts to a pitched or nonpitched instrument.

Mallet Techniques for Orff Instruments

As with the playing of all instruments, good tone quality demands certain techniques. Here are some suggestions for producing the best possible tone from these instruments that all *children* can learn quickly:

• Sit or stand with good posture. Hold the arms slightly away from the body. Bend the elbows so the forearms are several inches above the instrument keyboard.

• Holding the mallets is like holding bicycle handlebars. Hold them between the thumbs and curved index fingers, lightly wrapping the other fingers around each handle. The ends of the handles should be visible. Thumbnails face each other; palms are toward the floor. *Note:* Don't let the index fingers straighten to point down the mallet.

• To avoid hitting the mallet sticks against each other, hold one mallet slightly further away from the body than the other. The mallet sticks should also slant toward each other at a 45-degree angle. This helps keep the arms and hands in position for good wrist action.

• Whenever possible, alternate left and right hands. This helps with coordination, playing fast passages, and playing both hands simultaneously.

• Play in the center of the bar.

• Play with a flexible wrist. Begin from a ready position above the bar, and return to this position after each stroke. Think of pulling the tone out of the bar, not beating it in.

• Special techniques such as the fork hold, the crossover, the tremolo, and the glissando can be easily mastered after the basics have been learned.

(This list was adapted from *Silver Burdett MUSIC* [Morristown, New Jersey: Silver Burdett Company, 1981].)

Although improvisation is an integral part of the Orff concept of elemental music—the idea that music, movement, and speech are inseparable and that they form a unity—many prearranged settings for speech, movement, and instrumental ensembles have been published for use in the worship service. These perhaps sound best when performed with the mellow, delicate tone color of the Orff ensemble, but they can, of course, be adapted for use with any available pitched and nonpitched instruments. It is suggested that directors who have not had training in the Orff approach (many local colleges and universities offer several levels of certification) should study these arrangements, noting particularly how the instruments are scored and the use of certain techniques: pentatonic melodies, *bordun* (a drone based on the open fifth), minors, Dorian and Phrygian modes, canons, rhythmic and melodic ostinati, etc.

The tone color of these mallet instruments is musically appealing and intimate. They can be used with great effect in any worship service. They provide children with an outlet and sense of accomplishment, and if they are used with taste, they can not only teach concepts about music but also bring richness and variety to corporate worship.

The following suggestions are aimed at the inexperienced *director* who wants to make immediate use of these instruments.

Suggestions for the Director

• Although percussion instruments, strings, guitar, lute, and recorder may be included in the Orff ensemble, the keyboard instruments such as piano and organ are not used as an accompaniment for singing. Single piano tones, soft flute stops, and perhaps a small-scale reed, if used sparingly, can be effective in the ensemble sound. The intended sound with its clear, transparent texture is meant to support the child voice. The Orff ensemble as such does not have the strength to support congregational singing. It is best reserved for those portions of the liturgy in which the children's choir sings alone—anthems, alternation stanzas of hymns, psalm tones sung antiphonally, etc. An example of a psalm tone in the Dorian mode scored for the Orff ensemble is on page 111.

The universal "sol—mi" (5—3) chant of childhood is exploited in the earliest singing experiences in the Orff approach. Other tones are added in the order "la, re, do" (6, 2, 1) to complete the pentatonic scale. "Fa" and "ti" (4, 7) are added later. Since the combined tones of the pentatonic have less dissonance and less pull to a tonal center than major or minor scales, experiment with vocal and instrumental improvisation using just these tones in C pentatonic: first the descending minor third (G—E), then adding A. Create your own psalm tone or Gloria Patri. Capitalize on the rhythm of the words; add a *bordun* (a drone using the open fifth C—G) and at least one simple ostinato based on the tones G—E—A played on mallet instruments.

A finger cymbal played lightly at the end of the musical phrase will complete an effective ensemble. Children are natural improvisers if the avenues are open for them to explore what they know in new and unusual ways.

• Use the mallet instruments to play the melody of hymn introductions, interludes, alternation settings, etc. Use them alone or with soft guitar or Autoharp accompaniment. Play in octaves or in several ranges, depending on what instruments are available. Add a vocal countermelody played on a recorder and/or a soprano or alto glockenspiel. The instruments are designed to require only large-muscle movements, but they do require some playing technique, especially when playing melodies. Those children who are responsible for such performance should be allowed adequate rehearsal time. *All* playing should be done from memory.

• Mallet instruments can also provide the incipit for parts of the liturgy to be chanted or sung.

• When singing rounds, any phrase can be extracted and treated like an ostinato. Play this part throughout the singing of the round on any appropriate mallet instrument. Even the melody sung in unison with just one ostinato sounds effective. If children are ready, add two or more phrase ostinati while the round is sung. As with all melodies, it is especially important with rounds that the children know and possess a song before adding instrumental accompaniment.

• Many ensembles have been composed for instruments alone. These usually include recorder and strings such as gamba or bass. Experienced performers, either children or adults, can practice and perform these as voluntaries, during distribution, or at other appropriate times during a worship service.

• These instruments are a distinctive feature of the Orff *Schulwerk* approach. Indeed, they distinguish it from all other methods. They are not toys, and all performers must treat them with respect and care. Whether the performance is in the choir loft, the sanctuary, or any other location, definite plans must be made for their transport, setup, arrangement, etc. Large ensembles may be used for festival services, carol services, and the like, but smaller ensembles can perform just as effectively.

• When used with taste, musicianship, and discretion, these instruments add immeasurably to a child's growth and understanding of music concepts and performance and of the ingredients of corporate worship.

Additional Resource

Keetman, Gunild. *Elementaria*. Trans. Margaret Murray. St. Louis: Magnamusic-Baton.

PITCHED MALLET INSTRUMENTS

Psalm Tone

Legend

All mallet instrument parts are notated in the treble clef. This permits the ease of reading only one clef and also allows for greater flexibility in substituting one instrument for another if necessary.

Notes with a down stem are played with the mallet in the left hand; notes with an up stem are played with the mallet in the right hand.

Rec.	Recorder	
	Sop. Soprano recorder	(sounds one octave higher)
	Ten. Tenor recorder	(sounds as written)
SG	Soprano Glockenspiel	(sounds one octave higher)
AG	Alto Glockenspiel	(sounds as written)
AM	Alto Metallophone	(sounds as written)
BM	Bass Metallophone	(sounds one octave lower)
FC	Finger Cymbals	
☰	Tremolo	Play by alternating between the two hands slowly and then more quickly. Keep a loose wrist.
〰	Glissando	Play by loosening the wrist, holding the mallet loosely so as to avoid giving any resistance to the glide effect.

Resonator Bells

While sets of diatonic bells with fixed tone bars in the key of C are available, they are limited in their use and application. It is suggested that a set of resonator bells—tuned metal bars mounted separately on either wood or hard plastic—be purchased. When properly arranged, they form a chromatic scale, or they can be rearranged to form any single scale, chord, or selected group of tones. Some larger sets have a range of G^3—G^5. Smaller sets include C^4 (middle C) to G^5. The distinctive bell-like sound of resonator bells attracts children and can be used for musical devices suggested below.

Suggestions

• Many of the suggestions listed under Handbells (pp. 97—99) can be performed using resonator bells.

• Resonator bells are not usually included in the Orff Instrumentarium but can be used to perform many of the musical devices suggested on pp. 109—10.

• Any repeated tonal pattern (ostinato) can be played on resonator bells.

• Solo parts scored in the keyboard accompaniment can be extracted and played on resonator bells.

• Children can perform simple melodies, either alone or accompanied by Autoharp, guitar, organ, or harpsichord, as an introduction, interlude, or coda. Make sure performers have adequate rehearsal time. (Do not punch the sound into the bells; pull it out with a quick flip of the wrist.)

• A simple device to maintain pitch is to play the appropriate bell just before the first note of each phrase. This is especially useful when performing without accompaniment. If this is difficult for the children, enlist the help of an adult choir member.

• Accompany a simple melody with chords played on resonator bells. Divide all the tones of the scale among the choir. Using finger signals—one finger for the I chord; four fingers for the IV Chord; five fingers for the V^7 chord—the conductor can indicate when the bells should be played.

C Major	I chord (Tonic)	All C—E—G bells play
	IV chord (Subdominant)	All F—A—C bells play
	V^7 chord (Dominant Seventh)	All G—B—D—F bells play

Experiment with one strike or with a *tremolo*—a rapid, repeated hitting of the bells with a loose wrist. (This technique is equally effective using handbells.)

Recorder

The recorder has a rich historical tradition and a worthy literature that church musicians should explore. Its tone color, more than that of the transverse flute or other woodwinds, blends beautifully with the child's voice.

Many children learn to play the soprano and/or alto recorder in school music programs. Encourage those who play to bring their instruments to rehearsal. Several techniques listed below can involve them in both rehearsal and performance.

Some directors include the study of the soprano recorder in the curriculum of the children's choir. Indeed, the ground rules for singing—good posture, deep breathing, careful articulation, and constant pitch awareness—apply equally well for recorder playing as for singing. Playing an instrument is also one of the best approaches to accurate music reading.

Do not confuse the recorder with other flutelike plastic toys intended for children's use. These imitations have no place in a child's musical education. The recorder is a legitimate woodwind instrument with a dignified history. Children can continue to enjoy and play the recorder throughout their lives.

Excellent recorders, usually made from wood, are expensive. However, with recent technology many manufacturers have produced excellent inexpensive models made of plastic. These are the best buy for children.

Two fingerings exist for the soprano recorder: the so-called "German" and the "English/Baroque." Some educators think that the German fingering is best for children. However, most professionally trained recorder teachers insist on the English/Baroque from the start. (Most manufacturers, whether German or not, provide both kinds of fingering.)

Recorders come in all sizes, ranging from the one-foot C soprano to the three-foot F bass. Playing in ensemble with other instruments (called a consort) is a real joy. Adult groups exist in abundance throughout the country. The director should approach such music makers and enlist their help in providing music and accompaniments for the worship service. A quartet of soprano, alto, tenor, and bass recorders in a resonant church is an exciting musical experience. For the most part adult recorder players are amateur musicians who enjoy playing. Use such groups extensively when they prepare for a service.

The recorder, whether played by children or by an adult consort, is a worthy addition to the sounds of praise in the house of the Lord.

Suggestions

- Use those children who already play soprano and alto re-

corder. Most children can play simple melodies in the key of G. With practice, some can play the melodies of hymn tunes. Have them introduce the hymn, either as a solo or with accompaniment. A melody alone provides variety and change from the usual texture heard during a worship service.

● Many mallet parts, if within the recorder range, can be played on the recorder. Some scores include a separate recorder part.

● The soprano recorder sounds one octave higher than notated. The addition of one or more alto recorders helps to tame down the sound. Adding percussion instruments such as triangle, finger cymbals, tambourine, or drum also helps to solidify the sound of ensembles. In medieval and Renaissance times, percussion parts were freely improvised. Let children create and improvise their own percussion parts on appropriate instruments, using what they know about rhythm—beat, meter, pattern, etc.

● If a performer is reliable, the recorder can provide the pitch for the cantor by playing the incipit.

● If an anthem suggests the flute, try substituting the soprano, alto, or tenor recorder.

● Use the recorder to strengthen part singing. Since they blend well with children's voices, have recorders duplicate parts in rounds or countermelodies. (This is also useful in adult groups. The practice of doubling vocal parts with instruments has had a long tradition in much Renaissance and Baroque music.) In some instances a group of recorders can play the round while the children sing the melody in unison—a very pleasing musical experience.

● Three or more recorders, either all sopranos or in combination with an alto, can provide a chordal accompaniment for children's singing. Most of the time these parts have to be arranged by the director or someone knowledgeable about scoring for the recorder. The addition of an Autoharp or guitar makes for a pleasant accompaniment.

● When using a consort of amateurs or professionals, the possibilities are limitless. Most can play all the instruments and enjoy performing the four-part harmony provided for many hymns. Use this combination when varying hymn singing with the congregation. One verse played alone by the recorder consort is an effective sound. A recorder consort can also announce the hymns to the congregation or play short interludes between hymn verses. In quieter, more contemplative hymns it can support the congregational singing.

● Above all, explore the recorder sound and seek out those who have played the recorder in their adult life. Once they are involved, the director will find many opportunities to enrich the musical life of both children and congregation.

Additional Resource

Wollitz, Kenneth. *The Recorder Book*. New York: Alfred A. Knopf, 1982.

The use of instruments throughout the seasons can give children an understanding of and feel for the general character of the liturgical year. Subdued playing or sparse use during penitential seasons contrasted with a joyous outburst of song and instruments on festival days and periods of prominent rejoicing will provide a personal involvement with the church's spiritual calendar of events. Children who are fortunate to experience such a sensitive use of instruments in worship will have a richer experience from which to respond as worshipers throughout their lives.

The broad palette of sounds that instruments can offer in the context of worship is a reward for which to plan. Engaging these "voices" to enrich worship and express proclamation, prayer, and praise is to allow them to "speak" in an important way. What greater service can an instrument or instrumentalist perform than to participate in the worship and praise of the Almighty? Just as those who sing, speak, or preach in worship are in ministry, so are the instruments and players who offer their gifts to the glory of God and the spiritual enrichment of the saints on earth.

Let ev'ry instrument be tuned for praise;
Let all rejoice who have a voice to raise;
And may God give us faith to sing always: Alleluia!

Chapter Seven

"Successful children's choir directors are resourceful, and it is through their resourcefulness that they build confidence and increase their effectiveness."

Nonmusic Resources

Donald Rotermund

Developing a Resource Library

What an unreal expectation it is to ask an artist to create a work of art without any materials. It would be equally unreasonable to request a craftsman to produce a quality product without adequate tools. Both would be seriously handicapped, if not virtually paralyzed, in accomplishing their task.

The children's choir director, who, like both artist and craftsman, creates, molds, and shapes young lives and voices into beautiful musical ensembles, is similarly handicapped without a reservoir of resources. Observe effective children's choir directors, and it soon becomes apparent that they are resourceful individuals, capable of responding to most needs as, or even before, they arise. And as directors expand their resourcefulness, they naturally become more confident, effective leaders.

A *basic reference library,* whether personal or church-owned, is an indispensable resource for the successful director. This library should include not only music but also quality books, recordings, tapes, teaching aids, games, and pertinent catalogs and helpful addresses. With these materials at hand, most of the needs that arise can be met. With perseverance and selectivity such materials can be acquired at a reasonable cost.

In the ever-expanding arena of life, where creative people continue to develop and often share their ideas and discoveries in print or on recording, the potential always exists for finding new resources to meet current or future needs more effectively and to help expand one's present knowledge, reference materials, and skills. Like true professionals, who seek to remain current with information in their field of expertise, resourceful children's choir directors do not cease the effort to become ever better equipped for their ministry to children.

A primary goal of this chapter is to provide a compendium of quality nonmusic materials that will directly assist the children's choir director who serves in a liturgically oriented church in which the three-year lectionary series and the historical liturgy provide the framework for the corporate worship expression of the congregation. Coordinated with these ingredients is an extensive group of psalms, verses, offertories, and hymns, all of which offer opportunities for a rich and meaningful choral participation in worship. Many of the resources and information will help choral directors in nonliturgical churches also.

Selecting quality music is important for spiritual, musical, and economic reasons. From the spiritual perspective, both the director and the choir need to challenge themselves continually to offer their best efforts in worship. The attitude of faithful Christian service in which one seeks to give the "first fruits," as evidenced in such eminent church musicians as J. S. Bach and others, needs to permeate every aspect of the music ministry. This positive attitude will further manifest itself in guiding the selection of texts that have both strong content and an excellent literary quality. Musically this will be reflected in compositions possessing a high degree of craftsmanship and sensitivity to the servant role in worship. For the choir this dedication will be translated practically in careful preparation of the music being sung. To offer God less is to replace Him with a lesser god. For children especially, a good working guideline is to feed them on music and texts they can grow into rather than out of. To do so is to avoid spending time on fleeting, transitory material that has no substance; it lacks the qualities to endure occasional reuse.

It may be well to recall that the great composers—Bach, Handel, Purcell, and many others before and after them—wrote church music in which the treble parts were sung by children. They did not compromise quality just because children would sing it. Rather, they provided the finest music they were capable of writing. Experience repeatedly has demonstrated that great spiritual and musical benefits are the positive returns for the time invested.

Practically speaking, the result of using quality materials, whether that is good music or other supportive resources, is a better stewardship of both the people's time and the church's treasury.

The church is constantly teaching by its actions, through its leaders—not the least of which are those who shape the worship and music experiences—and by the materials it uses to carry out its spiritual ministry. Recognizing both their position of influence and the power music has to teach and edify, those in leadership roles must continue to remind themselves of the responsibility entrusted to them. They are in a unique position to supply some of the most valuable experiences and "food" for those whose lives are in the most receptive stages of development.

Children's choir directors, whether given the title or not, truly function as ministers of music by faithfully pursuing their calling in a style and with a dedication consistent with the important content they seek to share with the children.

Quality resources are important, supportive tools, but only in the hands of committed, dynamic leaders are they imbued with life. The director who pursues these objectives and who uses such tools to develop young lives and voices is both a craftsman and an artist. Fortunate is the church that is endowed with such leadership for its young saints. Leaders with such qualities and dedication will communicate that the Lord is served best when His disciples give their best to glorify Him in the service of His flock that so importantly includes the "little lambs." As the verse that Heinrich Schütz has inscribed on his music cabinet states:

> When you praise the Lord, exalt Him as much as you can; for He will surpass even that. When you exalt Him, put forth all your strength, and do not grow weary, for you cannot praise Him enough. (Ecclus. 43:30)

Three-Year Lectionary Materials

Devotional

Patt, Richard. *Psallite*. St. Louis: Concordia Publishing House, 1976—78. One-page devotions with prayers for church choir singers. Separate books for series A, B, and C. Can be adapted for use with children.

Syverud, Genevieve. *This Is My Song of Songs*. Minneapolis: Augsburg Publishing House, 1966. Devotions and prayers related to the church year.

Planning Resources

Worship Blueprints Series. Minneapolis: Augsburg Publishing House. Includes the following:

Ferguson, J. *Guide to Planning for Worship Music* (12-1554). Offers many suggestions, including ways to incorporate children's voices into the fabric of the liturgy.

Huffman, W. *Guide to Planning Congregational Worship* (11-1550).

Walhof, K., ed. *Series A/Planning Ideas for the Seasons of the Church Year* (12-1551).

———. *Series B/Planning Ideas for the Seasons of the Church Year* (12-1552).

———. *Series C/Planning Ideas for the Seasons of the Church Year* (12-1553).

Each volume in the series devotes specific attention to pertinent liturgical participation by the choir, much of which is applicable to children's choirs.

Liturgy

Alleluia Series. Minneapolis: Augsburg Publishing House, 1980. Eleven individual booklets for preschool through grade eight based on the Gospels used in the three-year lectionary. Christian worship, music, and the arts are integrated in innovative ways. A rich resource for guiding musical growth in singing and sight-reading skills, Biblical knowledge and faith, and more meaningful participation in the music ministry in liturgically oriented worship. Each student course has an accompanying teachers manual. A scope and sequence chart is available. Based on the content and lectionary in the *Lutheran Book of Worship*.

Aune, Michael. *Holy Communion—Narrative for Children*. Minneapolis: Augsburg Publishing House, 1978 (62-0206). The sharing of this colorful booklet with the children should increase their understanding of both the order of worship and the music that they prepare and sing in the services.

Herder, M., and S. Peebles. *Celebrate a Season*. Dallas: Choristers Guild, 1977. An animated, colorful booklet for elementary children to become more aware of the structure of a liturgically oriented order of service. 39 pages.

Ihli, Jan, Sr. *Liturgies of the Word for Children*. Ramsey, NJ: Paulist Press (545 Island Rd., 07446), 1979. While based on the lectionary and accents of the Roman Catholic Church, which occasionally vary from the Lutheran pericopes, many creative ideas are included to enrich the understanding and presentation of the appointed Scripture texts, including some pertinent music suggestions that will assist even the younger children to function in a more active way.

Pfatteicher, Philip. *Festivals and Commemorations*. Minneapolis: Augsburg Publishing House, 1980 (10-2259). Handbook to the calendar in *Lutheran Book of Worship*. Includes many hymn writers and composers.

Sladen, Kathleen. *Let Them Worship*. Toronto: S. K. H. S. Publ. (619 Ave. Rd., Toronto, Ontario, Canada M4K 2K6). A cross-denominational book on integrating children into the corporate worship of the congregation. Resources for ages 4—18. Contains valuable suggestions for hymn study, psalmody, and singing.

Gospel and Epistle (Second Lesson) Texts

These thematic presentations correlated with visual aids can be helpful in preparing devotions for the choir or in enriching the children's understanding of one of the appointed readings for the day.

Year A

Weisheit, Eldon. *The Gospel for Kids*. St. Louis: Concordia Publishing House, 1977 (15-2711). Devotional presentations on the Gospel for the day with visual aid suggestions.

———. *To the Kid in the Pew*. St. Louis: Concordia Publishing House, 1974 (15-2132). Devotional presentations on the Epistle (Second Lesson) for the day with visual aid suggestions.

Year B

Weisheit, Eldon. *The Gospel for Kids*. St. Louis: Concordia Publishing House, 1978 (15-2713). Same approach as in companion volumes.

———. *To the Kid in the Pew*. St. Louis: Concordia Publishing House, 1975 (15-2160). Same approach as in companion volumes.

Year C

Franzen, Lavern. *Good News from Luke*. Minneapolis: Augsburg Publishing House, 1976 (10-2183). Devotional material based on the Gospel for the day.

Weisheit, Eldon. *The Gospel for Kids*. St. Louis: Concordia Publishing House, 1979 (15-2723). Same approach as in companion volumes.

————. *To the Kid in the Pew*. St. Louis: Concordia Publishing House, 1976 (15-2169). Same approach as in companion volumes.

Vocal Training

Books on Training Children's Voices

Alleluia Series. Minneapolis: Augsburg Publishing House. Each of the 11 volumes contains practical information on the preschooler through grade eight.

Finn, William J. *The Art of the Choral Conductor*. 2 vols. Evanston, Ill.: Summy-Birchard Co., 1960. A solid resource for the children's choir director who is committed to understanding physiology, psychology, and musical principles in guiding the voices of young singers. Available in paperback.

Hardy, T. Maskell. *How to Train Children's Voices*. New York: G. Schirmer. Gives specific helps for guiding the child's singing voice to obtain the "head tone."

Ingram, Madeline, and William Rice. *Vocal Technique for Children and Youth*. Nashville: Abingdon Press, 1962. Treats vocal matters from preschool through high school.

Noble, T. Tertius. *The Training of the Boy Chorister*. New York: G. Schirmer, 1943. A miniature 24-page booklet giving brief sections on correct vocal production, sight-reading, and the rudiments of music.

Swanson, Frederick J. *The Male Singing Voice Ages Eight to Eighteen*. Iowa City: D. M. Phillips (P. O. Box 446, Iowa City, IA 52240—Sole distributor), 1977. Especially helpful in understanding and guiding boys' voices. Challenges the director to improved competence with respect to the singing voice.

Wright, Edred. *Basic Choir Training*. Litchfield, Conn.: R. S. C. M. in America. Valuable reading for all trainers of children's voices.

Yarrington, John. *Sound Recipes for Teenage Voices*. Dallas: Choristers Guild, 1980 (BK-14). Contains helpful tips for use with upper elementary voices.

See also Cassettes and Recordings under Teaching Aids.

Sight-Singing Exercises

Kodály, Zoltán. *Let Us Sing Correctly*. Choral Method. Oceanside, N.Y.: Boosey & Hawkes (17233). For unison and two-part exercises for reading and intonation.

————. *333 Elementary Exercises in Sight Singing*. Choral Method. Ed. Percy M. Young. Oceanside, N.Y.: Boosey & Hawkes (19157). For unison singing.

See also *Sight-Singing Flash Cards* under Teaching Aids.

Philosophy and Practice

Books

The following have been selected for their direct assistance in guiding a children's choir ministry focused on worship.

Halter, Carl, and Carl Schalk, eds. *A Handbook of Church Music.* St. Louis: Concordia Publishing House, 1978. A valuable resource related to the practice of worship and music in the Lutheran Church. The introduction and chapter 4 will be of significant value to the choir director.

Ingram, Madeline. *A Guide for Youth Choirs.* Nashville: Abingdon Press, 1967. Focuses on how to organize and direct more effectively.

Jacobs, Ruth Krehbiel. *The Children's Choir.* Vol. 1. Philadelphia: Fortress Press, 1957.

Lawrence, Joy E., and John A. Ferguson. *A Musician's Guide to Church Music.* New York: The Pilgrim Press, 1981. Chapter 6 on youth and children's choirs is especially recommended, but the whole book is a valuable resource.

Schalk, Carl, ed. *Key Words in Church Music.* St. Louis: Concordia Publishing House, 1978. A reference resource to expand the choir director's knowledge of terms used in church music.

Tufts, Nancy Poore. *The Children's Choir.* Vol. 2. Philadelphia: Fortress Press, 1965. An extension of volume one (see Jacobs above) with specific chapters on the various youth-oriented choirs in the church. A resource with many practical helps.

Booklets, Monographs, Articles

Anderson, Norma. *How to Have a Good Children's Choir.* Minneapolis: Augsburg Publishing House, 1976. A concise, 15-page treatment of all important phases of children's choir work. A starter.

Butler, JoAnn. *22 Ways to Teach a Song.* Dallas: Choristers Guild (CGD-25). Varied methods using rote and note teaching, many with visual aid suggestions.

Fisher, Martha. *Music in Church History.* Dallas: Choristers Guild, 1979. Student Book (BK-1); Teacher Guide (MM-24). 28 sessions tracing music and worship from the Old Testament to the present century.

Hadler, Rosemary. *Tricks of My Trade.* Dayton, Ohio: Lorenz Publishing Co., 1966. Tested ideas for junior choir directors.

Hunnicut, Judy. *Teaching Hymns to Children.* Springfield, Ohio: The Hymn Society of America. Written for directors of children's choirs primarily serving grades 3—6. Practical ideas for learning and using hymns in creative, fulfilling ways.

Jacobs, Ruth Krehbiel. *The Successful Children's Choir.* Chicago: H. T. Fitzsimmons Co., 1948. Offers the director practical assistance for virtually all phases of children's choir work. A standard resource.

Kemp, Helen. *Helen Kemp on Junior Choirs.* Dayton, Ohio: Lorenz Publishing Co., 1962. Covers many phases of children's choir work from disciplining to achieving tone.

———. *Music in Christian Education with Children.* Dallas: Choristers Guild, 1970. Provides basic assistance for both the beginning and the experienced director of children's choirs.

Lowe, Helenclair. *Sing for Joy.* Dallas: Choristers Guild, 1980 (BK-13). Chorister's handbook prepared especially for children's use.

Nelson, Ronald. *Children's Choir Is a Ministry.* Minneapolis: Augsburg Publishing House, 1981 (23-9495). A small, threefold leaflet especially useful for sharing with parents and congregation, accenting the service aspect of children's choirs. Pricing encourages quantity distribution.

———. "The Ministry of Children's Choirs." *Liturgy: Celebrating with Children* (810 Rhode Island Avenue NE, Washington, DC), vol. 1, no. 3 (1981).

Schalk, Carl. *The Hymn of the Day and Its Use in Lutheran Worship.* Church Music Pamphlet Series. St. Louis: Concordia Publishing House, 1983. A vital resource for pastors, choir directors, and organists who serve in a Lutheran church.

———. *The Pastor and the Church Musician: Thoughts on Aspects of a Common Ministry.* Church Music Pamphlet Series. St. Louis: Concordia Publishing House, 1984. Offers positive, substantive points for mutual benefit of co-workers.

Teaching Aids

Books and Tapes

Abramson, Robert M. *Music for Rhythm Games.* Pittsburgh: Volkwein Bros. Inc. Two cassette tapes with teacher guide book. Uses games and physical movement to increase cognition and perception of tempo, dynamics, beats, etc.

Athey, Margaret, and Gwen Hotchkiss. *A Galaxy of Games for the Music Class.* West Nyack, N. Y.: Parker Publishing Co. Over 200 tested games to illustrate important concepts in music.

Butler, JoAnn. "22 Games for Teaching Music Facts." *Choristers Guild LETTERS.* Part I—September 1983; part II—October 1983; part III—November 1983. Each requires some advance preparation of materials. Rhythm, notation, chords and intervals, famous composers, and movement are treated in interesting and enjoyable ways.

Hotchkiss, Gwen, and Margaret Athey. *A Treasury of Individualized Activities for the Music Class.* West Nyack, N. Y.: Parker Publishing Co. Nearly 500 tested activities to enrich, enliven, and give variety to the teaching of music skills of all kinds.

Moore, Karen. *Note.* Stevensville, Mich.: Educational Service Inc. (P. O. Box 219, Stevensville, MI 49127). Gamelike activities for all ages to motivate, teach, and review elements of music.

Flash Cards

Interval Cards. Dallas: Choristers Guild (D-43). Teach melodic intervals via familiar hymns and carols. Specific interval is red to aid recognition.

Miniature Flash Cards. Dallas: Choristers Guild (CGD-23). 24 cards, 2-3/4" x 3-1/2". Clef sign, simple note values, and meter signatures (#1—11); seven pitches on treble clef staff (#12—19); sol—la—mi patterns (#20—22); one-octave keyboard (#23—24).

Music Symbol Flash Cards. Buffalo, N. Y.: Kenworthy Education Services, Inc. 3-1/2" x 8". 138 music symbols and 22 practice staves.

Lundstrom, L., and R. Nelson. *Sight-Singing Flash Cards.* Dallas: Choristers Guild (D-48). 4-1/2" x 10-1/4". Cards are printed on medium-heavy stock for group or individual use. Teaches intervals and rhythmic patterns. A Teachers Guide (D-48a) is available. A proven tool.

Cassettes and Recordings

Choristers Guild Workshop—At Home Series:
> Butler, J. "Planning a Rehearsal" (ECT-101).
> Campbell, D. "Heading Toward Perfection" (ECT-103).
> Lovelace, A. "Hymns and Children" (ECT-102).
> Ramseth, B. "Celebrate with Voices and Instruments" (ECT-104).

Crocker, Charles F. "Children Can Learn to Sing!" Nashville: Convention Press, 1978. A cassette tape and accompanying manual that is helpful as a model of the child's singing head voice.

Nelson, Ronald. "The Children's Choir." Part I (C-7); part II (C-8); part III (C-9). American Guild of Organists Educational Cassettes available from AGO national headquarters. Cost: $5.00 per tape.

Recordings Featuring Children's Voices

Discriminating record dealers and music catalogs are good sources for quality recordings of children's voices, especially for choirs using boys for the treble parts, such as many of the cathedral choirs in England and the United States. While the repertoire on these recordings is often technically demanding, they illustrate the glorious potential of children's voices and are splendid models of the beauty and range of the head voice. The following recordings, however, present simpler music and a blend of girls' and boys' voices. These are readily available and should not intimidate either the children or their director.

"Children Sing of Christmas." Edith Norberg and the Carillon Singers. Minneapolis: Augsburg Publishing House (23-1455).

"Great Hymns for Children." The Westwood Choristers, Ronald Nelson, director. Order from Westwood Lutheran Church, 9001 Cedar Lake Road, St. Louis, MN 55426. $7.50 plus postage.

"O Come, Little Children." The Westwood Choristers, Ronald Nelson, director. Price as above; order from the church.

"Sing for Joy." The Winnipeg Mennonite Children's Choir. Dallas: Choristers Guild (CT-3).

"Singing the Seasons of the Lord." The Winnipeg Mennonite Children's Choir, Helen Litz, director. Dallas: Choristers Guild (CSC-1).

"With Joyful Hearts and Voices." The Westwood Choristers, Ronald Nelson, director. Price as above; order from the church. At Westwood Lutheran Church this recording is given as a gift to the family of a newly baptized infant with an accompanying letter (see Appendix A, page 179).

Visuals

Art Masters Studios, Inc. (AMSI), 2614 Nicollet Ave., Minneapolis, MN 55408, offers attractive postcards, announcements, note cards, etc., designed for use with children's choirs. Catalog available on request.

Bovet, Guy. "Peep the Piper." Introduction to the pipe organ. Filmstrip and cassette tape. Dallas: Choristers Guild, 1982 (D-59).

Choristers Guild Catalog. Pictures many visuals to support a choral program with children. New catalog published annually.

Horn, George F. Bulletin Boards. New York: Van Nostrand Reinhold Co. (450 W. 33d, New York, NY 10001). Many ingenious and valuable suggestions for charts, posters, three-dimensional designs, and attractive bulletin boards.

Periodicals

The Choral Journal. Published by the American Choral Directors Association, P.O. Box 17736, Tampa, FL 33682. A professional journal with specific articles and material concerned with children's voices. Inquire for current subscription and membership fees.

Choristers Guild LETTERS. Published monthly by the Choristers Guild. Editor: Donald Jensen. Subscription also provides national membership in the guild. Contains creative teaching helps and shares ideas related to all facets of children's choir work. Includes hymn studies and sample copies of new guild choral releases. Nondenominational. Individual and church memberships are available. Inquire for current subscription rate.

Church Music Memo. Published several times each year. Lutheran Church in America provides free copies to organists, choir directors, and pastors in its synods through its office at 2900 Queen Lane, Philadelphia, PA 19129. The American Lutheran Church provides the same service to the same groups in its churches from its Division for Life and Ministry, 442 S. Fifth St., Minneapolis, MN 55415. Practical and church-year-oriented with both educational and informational material correlated with the pericopes and Hymn of the Day.

The Church Music Quarterly. Published by the Royal School of Church Music of England in January, April, July, and October. Issued free to members of RSCM. *Church Music Today* is an additional pamphlet U. S. members receive through RSCM in America. Membership in the latter provides, in addition to the *Quarterly*, discounts on the purchase of music and choir training materials.

Journal of Church Music (2900 Queen Lane, Philadelphia, PA 19129). Published monthly September through June. Offers assistance with music related to the church year for choirs, organ, handbells, hymnody, and liturgy. Inquire for current subscription rate.

Lutheran Worship Notes. Published summer, fall, and spring by the Commission on Worship, Lutheran Church—Missouri Synod, and Concordia Publishing House. Free. Available to pastors and church musicians. Write to Concordia Publishing House, 3558 S. Jefferson Ave., St. Louis, MO 63118-3968.

Music Educators Journal. Published by the Music Educators National Conference, 1201 Sixteenth St. N.W., Washington, DC. Write the office for membership and subscription information.

Catalogs

These catalogs are oriented toward liturgical worship, the church year, and children's choirs and feature supportive materials for a coordinated program. The last two offer nonmusic items, both educational and incidental (charms, pins, etc.).

Augsburg Music Catalog. Minneapolis: Augsburg Publishing House. Published annually and features an octavo listing of Augsburg publications according to the three-year lectionary. Free on request.

Choristers Guild Catalog. Dallas: Choristers Guild. Published annually and sent to all guild members. Includes anthems, hymn studies, posters, awards, games, music postcards, birthday cards, and note cards. Primarily oriented to serve children's needs.

Concordia Music Catalog. St. Louis: Concordia Publishing House. Features liturgical music, including a considerable number of settings related to the pericopes. Issued annually to those on their mailing list. Free copy on request.

G. I. A. Publications, Chicago. Roman Catholic oriented, but offers some liturgical music useful in Lutheran worship. Free copy on request. Issued annually.

Laster, James. *Catalogue of Choral Music Arranged in Biblical Order.* Metuchen, N.J.: Scarecrow Press, 1983. Contains over 5,000 titles of music based on Scripture texts from Genesis through Revelation. Helpful in locating music related to specific pericopes for the day. All voicings are included; some are appropriate for children's voices.

Music in Motion (122 Spanish Village, Suite 645, Dallas, TX 75248). A catalog with many choir-related materials, including games, teaching aids, etc. Selected materials. Cost: $2.00.

The Music Stand (Norwich, VT 05055). A catalog issued several times annually. Contains many gifts and ideas for the areas of music and dance. Helpful for securing unique gifts for choir parents and awards for choir participants.

Publishers and Suppliers

This is an abridged list of publishers of materials included in chapters 7 and 8.

Abingdon Press, 201 Eighth Ave., South, Nashville, TN 37202.

Agape (see Hope Publishing Co.).

C. M. Almy and Son, Inc., 37 Purchase Street, Rye, NY 10580. Choir vestments.

American Choral Directors Association, P. O. Box 17736, Tampa, FL 33682.

The American Guild of English Handbell Ringers, Inc. (AGEHR), 601 West Riverview Ave., Dayton, OH 45460.

American Guild of Organists, Suite 318, 815 Second Avenue, New York, NY 10017. National headquarters.

Art Masters Studios, Inc. (AMSI), 2614 Nicollet Ave., Minneapolis, MN 55408.

Artneedle Cap and Gown Co., 400 First Avenue North, Minneapolis, MN 55401. Choir vestments.

Augsburg Publishing House, 426 South Fifth Street, Minneapolis, MN 55440.

Belwin-Mills Publishing Corp., (order from Columbia Pictures).

Boosey and Hawkes, Inc., P. O. Box 130, Oceanside, NY 11572.

Alexander Broude, Inc., 225 West 47th St., New York, NY 10019.

Chantry Music Press, Inc., Wittenberg University, Springfield, OH 45501.

Choristers Guild. Home office: 2834 W. Kingsley Rd., Garland, TX 75041. Order Choristers Guild music publications from their distributor/publisher: Choristers Guild Distributor, P. O. Box 802, Dayton, OH 45401.

Collegiate Cap and Gown Co., 1000 N. Market St., Champaign, IL 61820. (Choir vestments)

Columbia Pictures, 15800 North West 48th Ave., Hialeah, FL 33014.
Concordia Publishing House, 3558 S. Jefferson Ave., St. Louis, MO 63118.
Convention Press, 127 Ninth Avenue, North, Nashville, TN 37234.

J. Fischer (order from Columbia Pictures).
H. T. Fitzsimmons Co., 615 N. LaSalle St., Chicago, IL 60610.
Harold Flammer, Inc., Delaware Water Gap, PA 18327.
Fortress Press, 2900 Queen Lane, Philadelphia, PA 19129.

G. I. A. Publications, Inc., 7404 South Mason Ave., Chicago, IL 60638.
Galaxy Music Corp. (order from E. C. Schirmer Music Co.).
H. W. Gray (order from Columbia Pictures).

Hinshaw Music Inc., P. O. Box 470, Chapel Hill, NC 27514.
Hope Publishing Co., 380 S. Main Pl., Carol Stream, IL 60187. (Agape)
Hymn Society of America, Wittenberg University, Springfield, OH 45501.

Ireland Needlecraft, Inc., 4126 San Fernando Rd., Glendale, CA 91204.
    (Choir vestments)

Neil A. Kjos Music Co., 4382 Jutland Dr., San Diego, CA 92117.

Lorenz Publishing Co. (see Sacred Music Press).

Magnamusic-Baton, 10370 Page Industrial Blvd., St. Louis, MO 63132.
Malmark, Inc., 21 Bell Lane, New Britain, PA 18901. (Handbells)
E. R. Moore Co., 7700 Gross Point Road, Skokie, IL 60077. (Choir vestments)

C. F. Peters Corp., 373 Park Ave. S., New York, NY 10016.
Petit Fritsen Bell Foundry, Bellfounderstreet, Aarle-Rixel, Holland. U.S.A.
    agent: G.I.A. (address above). (Handbells)

Rhythm Band, Inc., P. O. Box 126, Fort Worth, TX 76101. (New Era Orff
    instruments)
Royal School of Church Music *or* RSCM in America, Box 369, Litchfield, CT
    06759. Source for music published by the Royal School of Church
    Music, Croydon, England.

Sacred Music Press, 501 E. Third Street, Dayton, OH 45401.
Scarecrow Press, Inc., 52 Liberty St., P. O. Box 656, Metuchen, NJ 08840.
E. C. Schirmer Music Co., 112 South St., Boston, MA 02111.
G. Schirmer, Inc., 866 Third Ave., New York, NY 10022.
Schulmerich Carillons, Inc., 177 Carillon Hill, Sellersville, PA 18960. (Hand-
    bells)
Suzuki Musical Instruments Corp., P. O. Box 261030, San Diego, CA 92126.
    (Suzuki Orff instruments)
Swartwout Enterprises, P. O. Box 476, Scottsdale, AZ 85252.

Volkwein Bros., Inc., 117 Sandusky, Pittsburgh, PA 15212.

Walton Music Corp. (order from Sacred Music Press).
Whitechapel Bell Foundry, 32 & 34 Whitechapel Road, London E1 1DY,
    England. (Handbells)

Liturgical Choral Vestments

Addresses may be found under Publishers and Suppliers.

C. M. Almy and Son, Inc. In addition to ready-made choir robes, surplices, and cassocks, kits providing precut material, thread, and instructions are available. Sewing saves approximately 50 percent of the finished cost. Quantity discounts are offered on orders of 12 or more.

Artneedle Cap and Gown Co. Offers ready-made children's choir robes in several basic sizes.

Collegiate Cap and Gown. Offers robes made to specific measurements.

Ireland Needlecraft, Inc. Offers robes made to specific measurements.

E. R. Moore Co. Offers robes made to specific measurements.

Organizational Aid for Recording Service Music

Pictured is a portion of a liturgical calendar, including 12 non-Sunday services (September through August) with space for recording choral music for the day. It becomes a ready reference of music used in past years as well as that projected for the current year. This and other Thorson organizational aids for recording budget, robe, and attendance information are available through Augsburg Publishing House and Malecki Music, Inc., 3404 South Eleventh St., P. O. Box 411, Council Bluffs, IA 51502.

Quotable Quotes . . .

These succinct statements gleaned from Scripture and from the writings, sermons, lectures, and informal exchanges of respected people can be useful for the following purposes:

- personal thought and reflection;
- stimulating the thinking of others in bulletins, letters, announcements, articles, programs, etc.

Quoting the words of others can often:
      —challenge—
        —enrich—
          —encourage—
            —heighten sensitivities—
          —persuade—
          —reinforce—

. . . from Scripture

I will sing to the Lord, because He has dealt bountifully with me. (Psalm 13:6 RSV)

Sing a new song to the Lord, for He has done marvelous deeds. (Psalm 98:1 NEB)

Come, let us praise the Lord! Let us sing for joy to God, who protects us! Let us come before Him with thanksgiving and sing joyful songs of praise. (Psalm 95:1-2 TEV)

Sing to the Lord, all the world! Worship the Lord with joy; come before Him with happy songs. (Psalm 100:1-2 TEV)

Let the word of Christ dwell in you richly as you teach and admonish one another with all wisdom, and as you sing psalms, hymns and spiritual songs with gratitude in your hearts to God. (Colossians 3:16 KJV)

Be filled with the Spirit. Speak to one another with the words of psalms, hymns, and sacred songs; sing hymns and psalms to the Lord with praise in your hearts. (Ephesians 5:18-19 TEV)

Open my lips, O Lord, that my mouth may proclaim Thy praise. (Psalm 51:15 NEB)

He taught me to sing a new song, a song of praise to our God. (Psalm 40:3 TEV)

For lo, the winter is past, the rain is over and gone. The flowers appear on the earth, the time of singing has come. (Song of Solomon 2:11-12 RSV)

I will praise Him as long as I live; I will sing to my God all my life. (Psalm 146:2 TEV)

Let everything that breathes praise the Lord! Praise the Lord! (Psalm 150:6 RSV)

. . . of Thoughtful, Respected Men

Clergy and Theologians

I would that all the arts, and music in particular, be used in the service of Him who hath given and created them. (Martin Luther)

Music: The only art of heaven given to earth; the only art of earth we take to heaven. (Martin Luther)

Music is the noblest gift of God, next to theology. I would not change my little knowledge of music for a great deal. (Martin Luther)

Worship is faith's first response. (George Hoyer, homiletician/ pastor)

To be a Christian artist is extremely difficult; to be an artist is difficult, to be a Christian is difficult; but to be both in a society which is indifferent to both makes it extremely difficult. (Martin J. Naumann, theological professor/pastor)

Music belongs to the history, the tradition, the very life of the church; music has played a role in public worship for a long time and that role has been magnificent; music is a means of trans-verbal praise, both a way of evoking expressive responses *from* the congregation and a particularly felicitous way of proclamation *to* the congregation; music is a stimulant to devotion, a lubricant to piety, and a powerful evocation of an appropriate mood. (Joseph Sittler, theologian)

Doubt builds no cathedrals, sings no Te Deums, frames no liturgies. Faith builds and prays and sings. (Luther D. Reed, liturgiologist/professor)

Liturgy is an orderly way of doing things. (Hugh Beck, clergyman)

There are not many genuine geniuses in any fields of endeavor. There are talented men and women. Some of these hide their talents (not through modesty or humility, but generally through laziness or self-deception) in the dark. Others develop them, bringing them out into the full light, and, glorifying God who gave them their gifts, influence for better the lives—spiritual, cultural, and physical—of all whom they serve. (Father Finn, clergyman/musician)

What a church sings is the very core of its faith and life; and what kind of music a congregation hears determines the musical taste and level of its membership. (Ludwig Fuerbringer, clergyman/ professor)

A pastoral musician has to become a "theologian of sound." (Nathan Mitchell, clergyman)

We need to write, to play, and to sing music that is theology, not theology that is "put into musical form." (Nathan Mitchell)

Pastoral musicians are not "sound technicians"; they are "sound theologians," sound poets, ministers of sound. (Nathan Mitchell)

We have no "fillers" in a well-planned liturgical action. No part or element is introduced simply because we have to pass the time. We do not "throw in" a song because someone likes it, or interpose a gesture because it is familiar, or include a dance because we have a dancer. . . . Anything that is to be part of a liturgy must pass the tests of quality and appropriateness. (Robert W. Hovda, clergyman)

Quality is no less important for children's celebrations than it is for adult or general ones. Perhaps it is even more important when dealing with children, because children are open and in the process of formation. (Robert W. Hovda)

Musicians, Composers, Educators

It has been my constant aim that church music should be so performed as to exalt God's glory. (J. S. Bach, organist/composer)

I have always kept one end in view, namely, with all good will to conduct well-ordered church music to the honor of God. (J. S. Bach)

The better the voice is, the meeter it is to honor and serve God therewith; and the voice of man is chiefly to be employed to that end. (Wm. Byrd, composer)

Only the best is good enough for a child. (Zoltán Kodály, composer/educator)

The first month of a nightingale's life determines its fate. . . . A "master bird" is borrowed that daily sings its lovely song, and the infant bird listens for a period of about a month. In this way the little wild bird is trained by the master bird. . . . Whether the wild bird will develop good or bad singing quality is indeed decided in the first month by the voice and tone of its teacher. It is not a matter of being born a good or a bad singer. (Shinichi Suzuki, musician/educator)

Good taste is a moral concern. (Ralph Vaughan Williams, composer)

Unless music has something to contribute to worship it is useless and may be actually harmful. It is better to have no music at all than the wrong music badly performed. (Joseph Clokey, composer)

Discipline cannot be maintained in any church choir where the major decisions are made by someone other than the director. (Clarence Dickinson, musician/teacher)

As I prepare the special music to be offered at worship, I must be convinced of its worth and relevancy. If it is not great, and if it does not relate, it will not be used. I would rather there be silence than something grossly inappropriate. In America we have been led to believe that silence is frightening, so we cushion the crevices with sounds—"Let there be Muzak!" (Paul Manz, organist/composer)

Our musical diet needs attention. As a rule we are all interested in securing wholesome and nutritious foods for the body, especially for the body-building of the growing youth. We are also interested in clean and uplifting literature for the development of the mind. In view of these and other similar concerns one is often overwhelmed with the lack of interest, knowledge and taste on the part of the same people when it comes to selecting food for the spirit. The most sentimental, crude and destructive music is the regular diet of so many choirs and directors. If music which has not power of growth or inspiration in it is permitted to poison the taste and interest of the church people, there can be only one result, that of decreasing life and general decadence. The church holds to an ideal which embodies the spirit of love and truth, and relies on it for a more abundant life. That same adherence to purpose and love of purity and inspiration must, in its peculiar sense, be felt in our music if it shall be in harmony with the church and be worthwhile. (F. Melius Christiansen, choral conductor/composer)

It is the great artist that can achieve results with simple means. (Heinrich Fleischer, concert organist/professor)

The squirrel has a trait the choirmaster can emulate. What he cannot use immediately, he stores away for future use. What a hollow tree is to the squirrel, a filing cabinet is to the director. (Ruth Krehbiel Jacobs, children's choir director/author)

We must awaken in our people the faculties to honor Him, by ordinary and extraordinary gifts. (Heinz Werner Zimmermann, composer)

The music used to offer thanks and praise ought to be of a different type than that used to entertain and excite us. (Heinz Werner Zimmermann)

Writers and Philosophers

In art all things are possible, providing you like them, providing you really like them—which takes years and years to know. (Goethe, German philosopher)

Nothing should be done or sung in the church which does not aim directly or indirectly either at glorifying God or edifying the people or both. (C. S. Lewis, British writer)

Other

The Holy Spirit is our divine energy. (Anonymous)

Procrastination is the thief of time. (Anonymous)

Triumph is merely the *umph* added to try. (Anonymous)

If you hear the music, join in the singing. (Anonymous)

Additional Resource

Shapiro, Nat, comp. *An Encyclopedia of Quotations About Music*. New York: DaCapo Press, Inc. (227 W. 17th Street, New York, NY 10011), 1977. 350 pages of quotations plus over 50 pages of index to key words and phrases.

"The church is constantly teaching by its actions, its leaders (not the least of which are those who shape the worship and music experiences), and the materials it uses to facilitate its spiritual ministry."

Chapter Eight

Music Repertoire Resources

Donald Rotermund

Organizing a Choral Reference File

Of all the resources to which the choir director has access, one of the most practical and most frequently used is the choral reference file. Once an octavo is filed to coordinate with the pericopes of a Sunday, festival, or season, planning the choral music for the day becomes much more efficient and gratifying to do.

For a variety of reasons, it is unlikely any two choir directors organize their files in precisely the same way. The method outlined here has served a number of them well and is offered to assist those who have not yet established an organized system based on the pericopes of the church year. It may be modified, expanded, and adapted quite easily. If a plan such as this is followed and continually supplemented, the time required to establish it will be repaid many times.

Until the resource file becomes quite voluminous, begin with broad categories according to the festival and nonfestival halves of the church year. For the festival half, individual file folders can be designated as follows: ADVENT; CHRISTMAS, which may be subdivided into at least two groupings: (1) anthems, motets, and texts *not* using carol or hymn tunes and (2) carol and hymn settings; EPIPHANY; LENT; SUNDAY OF THE PASSION/PALM SUNDAY; EASTER DAY; EASTER SEASON; ASCENSION; and PENTECOST DAY. The nonfestival half should include: PENTECOST SEASON (the Sundays of *after* Pentecost Day); FULFILLMENT/ CHRIST THE KING; REFORMATION/ALL SAINTS; THANKSGIVING; PRAISE; BAPTISM/ CONFIRMATION; TRUST; COMMUNION; STEWARDSHIP/LOYALTY/ DISCIPLESHIP;

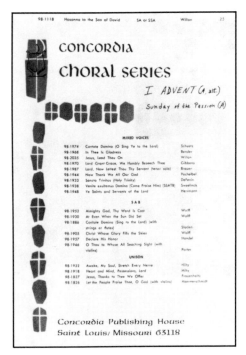

ANNIVERSARIES (church, pastor, teacher, etc.); DESCANTS; CANONS; and any other headings, as desired. Hymn settings, psalms, and other liturgical music may be filed in separate folders.

The second step in arranging the choral library is to place all single octavos in categories, writing on the cover of each the day it is most likely to be used. (See example at left.) This labeling is determined on the basis of the text. (A reference index with all Scripture texts used in the three-year lectionary and the days on which they are used is included in Appendixes B and C, pp. 183—208.)

When texts are used more than once in the three-year cycle, such as Matthew 21:1-11, which is the alternate for the First Sunday in Advent of Series A, and is in some sources offered as an additional reading to be used early in the service on Palm Sunday/Sunday of the Passion, two alternatives are possible: (1) purchase multiple copies of the octavo and put one in *each* of the folders, or (2) secure one reference copy and file it in the folder of the season in which it will more likely be considered for use with the children. In place of the second copy of the octavo, put the title of the piece on a three-by-five-inch card with the composer's name and file the reference card in the other seasonal folder as if there were a second reference copy of the same selection. It would be helpful to add a note on the card indicating which file retains the copy of the octavo.

Collections of pieces with a variety of texts that are not organized according to the church year or limited to a single season pose a challenge for referencing in the choral library. Those that are limited to a specific theme or season can be filed with the octavos of that group. However, collections containing texts for specific pericopes of the church year should be noted on cards, and these reference cards should be placed in specific folders with other music for the day or season. Some directors prefer simply to file all collections together alphabetically by title.

Liturgical music, which includes psalms, introits, graduals, verses, offertory sentences, and canticles (see the various lists of this material later in this chapter), can be filed together in a drawer or on a designated shelf area. Cross-filing or indexing with cards is helpful since some verse and offertory texts are also found in the Scripture readings throughout the year, but this requires diligence if it is to be done in detail.

Extended works, such as cantatas, are usually best filed under the theme they treat, since the number of these for children is relatively limited.

Hymn-based materials, such as concertatos, hymn anthems, and choral settings of hymns, with or without instrumental accompaniment, can be grouped either by title or by hymn tune. Some may prefer to organize them by hymn texts, either in alphabetical or seasonal order. (It is suggested that canons and descants be filed under their own headings.) A brief notation in the margin of a hymnal reserved for music planning helps to jog the memory whenever the particular hymn is projected for use.

Notes that directors take at clinics, workshops, and seminars and articles they read in various publications often contain useful information. Unless these are retained in some easily accessible arrangement, they often become lost or forgotten. Even a modest system of file folders with headings on choral techniques, choir publicity, games, etc., can often prevent this problem. Too often "out of sight out of mind" is the situation unless one spends a brief time after gaining the information filing it rather than tossing it on some pile or in a box. Some cross-filing with cards can be done, if so desired. For example, a choral collection for children may include a helpful discussion of choral techniques, and unless this is noted in a file on that subject, the information will be forgotten by most busy directors.

The expansion and organization of the choral reference library should be an ongoing endeavor of the director. Establishing such a resource and keeping it as current as possible for the person it most directly serves, the director, is an activity that will provide ever more valuable support for a vital ministry of music.

Augmenting Choral Resources

Among the positive characteristics of effective choral leadership is the continuing effort by the director to find new music—both recently published material and unfamiliar music that has been in print for some time. Discovering these resources can be a fulfilling experience for the director while also offering continuing enrichment for the choir's ministry.

With the large number of publications presently available and with more and more appearing from the many smaller publishers in the area of church music, the efficient director is well advised to channel this pursuit in the most efficient ways available. The following avenues are suggested with the above objectives and concerns in mind:

1. Establish contacts with colleagues active in children's choir work, and offer to reciprocate in any manner possible to make the exchange of mutual benefit.
   a. Ask to look at their choral library.
   b. Exchange choral schedules at least once a year with colleagues and friends in other churches. Doing this each semester would be better because of the potential short-range elements to be gleaned and possibly used in one's own ministry in that current year.
   c. Exchange Sunday service bulletins with those you feel

have similar objectives in their choir's ministry, especially with those who correlate the music of the choir with the pericopes of the church year.

2. Attend seminars, clinics, and workshops at least once a year that emphasize children's choir repertoire, techniques, and worship. Ask for congregational support for this.
   a. If you are unfamiliar with the time and place of these educational opportunities, become acquainted with energetic directors both within and outside of the denomination in which you presently serve.
   b. Be especially alert during repertoire sessions for music that complements the themes and texts of the three-year lectionary series.
   c. Become a member of the Choristers Guild and/or the American Choral Directors Association—Children's Choirs (addresses in previous chapter).

3. Ask to be placed on the mailing list of the following:
   a. Publishers of church music (see addresses of music publishers and suppliers in chap. 7, pp. 125—26).
   b. Any department of your own denomination that is oriented toward publishing regular or occasional articles on worship and/or church music, especially those that could relate to children's choir work.
   c. Nondenominational organizations, such as Choristers Guild, and other denominations that offer helpful articles on children's choirs (for example, *The Music Ministry* published by The United Methodist Publishing House, 201 Eighth Avenue South, Nashville, TN 37202).

Hymn of the Day and the Children's Choir

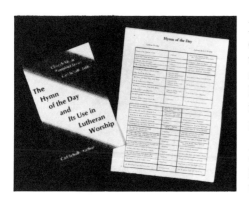

Enlisting the children's choir as an integral participant in the Hymn of the Day (see lists in Appendix D) is a ministry to be encouraged. Such involvement necessarily requires advance consultation and planning with the pastor(s) to ensure mutual support. As a general guideline, children need four to six weeks for adequate learning and maturing with the music. Satisfying results are the fruits of the combined efforts of all who are directly involved in the plan.

The alternate singing of stanzas is one of the hallmarks of the Hymn-of-the-Day plan. At the initial level, the children may become participants by singing one or more of the inner stanzas in good unison with or without the hymnal accompaniment. Occasionally, especially on festivals, more embellished variations that are still within the choir's capabilities deserve preparation and use.

In the absence of specially prepared hymn embellishments for children's choirs that offer immediate application to the Hymn of the Day, the director will need to arrange these settings from extant publications where the tunes are treated, sometimes with alternate texts, or from some that are separate from any Hymn-of-the-Day emphasis.

Under Hymn Accompaniments (see p. 139) it is suggested that the director consider accompanying unison choir singing with varied harmonizations or varied accompaniments (settings in which the hymn tune is not directly or clearly stated but is supported by the harmonies).

Another suggestion is to extract individual stanzas that can be effectively used with children from available chorale or hymn concertatos and Hymn-of-the-Day arrangements for adult choirs (for example, descants and simpler two-part arrangements with keyboard). As the director discovers appealing accompaniments and settings in collections and hymn anthems, they should be noted for prospective use when the schedule calls for that hymn to be sung as the Hymn of the Day. Both the key and the arrangement should be compatible and supportive of the stanza they will serve in the complete hymn. It is important to note the name of the tune clearly (for example, *Nun komm der Heiden Heiland,* Advent 1). The following examples include a variety of sources and types of material children can sing well:

Advent 1

Hymn-of-the-Day tune: *Nun komm der Heiden Heiland.*

1. T. Beck, "Savior of the Nations, Come," *12 Seasonal and Festival Hymns for Handbells and Organ* (Concordia, 97-5312), p. 10. Introduction for handbells can serve well as an accompaniment for unison voices; so also can the organ and handbell descant setting.

2. The same tune but with an alternate text, unison and two-part canonic settings, is in C. Schalk, *Crown Choir Book I* (Concordia, 97-7618), pp. 5ff.

Lent 1

Hymn-of-the-Day tune: (a) *Gott der Vater wohn uns bei,* (b) *Ein feste Burg* (alternate hymn).

1. "God the Father, Be Our Shield" (Concordia, 98-2627) offers several options: unison choir and organ; unison choir, flute, and guitar; unison choir, flute, and organ. The alternate translation (F. Samuel Janzow) for stanza two could replace the hymnal version.

2. P. Thomas, ed., *SSA Chorale Book* (Concordia, 97-7592), includes a canon in unison for four voices by S. Scheidt. Several of

these canonic voices could be played by treble instruments. If three stanzas of the hymn are planned, this setting might best be used as stanza two with the beginning words "Jesus Christ," the alternate text indicated in *LW* 170. For use in Lent the *LBW* 308 text could be concluded with "So sing we all Hosanna," as the Alleluia is traditionally silenced during this season.

Easter 4

Hymn-of-the-Day tune: *St. Columba.*

1. Canonic setting for voices in D. Busarow, *All Praise to You, Eternal God* (Augsburg, 11-9076). This organ setting would permit several possibilities, including unison choir voices in canon, a canonic singing of a stanza with congregation and choir, or choir versus an instrument in canon.

2. Orff accompaniment with unison choir. N. Thoren, *Children's Carols for Improvisation* (Augsburg, 11-9115), pp. 17ff. Consider this for several inner stanzas in alternation with the congregation. Bass metallophone may replace organ pedal point. *Note:* This setting is in C; hymnal versions are in D.

The search for potential hymn alternation settings should be ongoing, if for no other reason than to prevent deadening repetitions. As creative composers and publishers of church music continue to make new arrangements available, some of these will serve better than some used in the past. To discover or even create new settings is rewarding and sometimes can be accomplished by using the creative juices of the children and/or the director.

For a fuller discussion of the Hymn-of-the-Day concept and its development, the reader is encouraged to obtain Carl Schalk, *The Hymn of the Day and Its Use in Lutheran Worship* (Concordia, 99-1252).

Hymn Study Resources

References to *LUTHERAN WORSHIP*

Luther, Martin. *Liturgy and Hymns.* Ed. Ulrich S. Leupold. *Luther's Works,* American Edition. Vol. 53. Philadelphia: Fortress Press, 1965. A one-volume compendium of Luther's thoughts and contributions to liturgy and hymnody.

Lutheran Worship: Altar Book (Concordia, 1982). Particularly helpful for meaningful planning of children's choir participation will be the information on pages 549—51 (Hymn-of-the-Day list) and pages 558—80 (Scripture references coordinated with specific hymns and correlated with the one- and three-year lectionaries). Appendix B includes some of the above material.

References to the
LUTHERAN BOOK OF WORSHIP

Luther, Martin. *Liturgy and Hymns.* Ed. Ulrich S. Leupold. *Luther's Works, American Edition.* Vol. 53. Philadelphia: Fortress Press, 1965. A one-volume compendium of Luther's thoughts and contributions to liturgy and hymnody.

Lutheran Book of Worship: Minister's Desk Edition. Minneapolis and Philadelphia: Augsburg Publishing House and Board of Publication, Lutheran Church in America, 1978. Pages 38—39 and 467—78 are especially helpful for planning meaningful choral participation.

Pfatteicher, Philip H., and Carlos R. Messerli. *Manual on the Liturgy: Lutheran Book of Worship.* Minneapolis: Augsburg Publishing House, 1979. Chapter 3, "Music and Worship," is recommended for serious study and reference.

Stulken, Marilyn Kay. *Hymnal Companion to the Lutheran Book of Worship.* Philadelphia: Fortress Press, 1981. Historical, biographical, and musical information on all hymns and canticles in the *Lutheran Book of Worship.*

Hymn Canons

Buszin, W. *32 Canons on Sacred Texts.* Peters (66166). On the church year, ordinary canticles, Baptism/mission. For two to seven voices.

Krapf, G. *Rounds for the Church Year.* Concordia (97-4922). Two-, three-, and four-part rounds for the church year, two per season or day, with optional instruments. For two and three voices.

Parker, Alice. *Sunday Rounds.* Hinshaw (HMC-106). Some are useful as psalm antiphons or refrains. For two to four voices.

Schalk, Carl. *Two-Part Canons on Classic Hymns and Chorales.* Concordia. Set I (98-1762), 8 hymns. Set II (98-1763), 9 hymns. Set III (98-1764), 8 hymns.

Stein, H. *Hymns in Canon.* Augsburg. Two- and three-part with accompaniment: keyboard, treble, instrument.

Hymn Accompaniments

Perceptive directors of children's choirs recognize the importance of teaching Christian hymnody to young, developing choristers. They do not consider the learning of quality hymns to be of secondary value, but rather of high priority. Thus they conscientiously teach both tunes and texts. Equipping children with a rich repertoire of hymnody enriches both their present and future worship.

Among the hymns deserving particular focus in a hymn curriculum is the Hymn of the Day—the central hymn of the service (see Appendix D for the lists). Almost all children, except perhaps those in the lowest grades, are capable of learning these classic, quality hymns if they are encouraged and guided by an enthusiastic, committed director who provides regular rehearsal time for this endeavor. What this inclusion tacitly conveys to children about the importance and quality of strong hymnody must not be underestimated.

While emphasis is given to the Hymn of the Day, many other noble hymns also deserve special attention. Almost all of these hymns lend themselves to embellished accompaniments that sustain and add interest for both singer and listener when used judiciously. Their occasional use with unison children's singing, especially on one or more interior stanzas and/or on the final stanza when the hymn text seems compatible with this type of variation, can be very effective.

It is possible for the resourceful director to develop complete hymn anthems for the children's choir by selecting such accompaniments to complement those of the basic hymnal and provide the components for a simple but effective hymn-based choral composition with the addition of a prepared intonation/introduction. These embellishments, however, are only effective when the choir can sing the hymn with confidence, clarity, and tonal beauty.

One word of caution: Since not all of the following resources were composed specifically to coordinate with the hymn settings in *Lutheran Worship* and the *Lutheran Book of Worship*, it will be necessary for the director to check the key and the melodic and rhythmic structure of the settings contemplated for use and to make adjustments as necessary. When different keys are used, it is usually preferable to select the one in the higher key to facilitate the head voice of the children.

Varied Harmonizations and Varied Accompaniments

Bairstow, Edward. *Organ Accompaniments*. Oxford University Press (no number given). For unison singing of 24 hymn tunes.

Bender, Jan. *The Hymn of the Week*. Concordia (97-1444).

———. *New Organ Settings for Hymns and Carols*. Concordia (Set I, 97-1454; Set II, 97-1461).

Bunjes, Paul. *New Organ Accompaniments for Hymns*. Concordia (97-5348). Some with instrumental descants.

Busarow, Donald. *All Praise to You, Eternal God*. Augsburg (11-9076). Selected hymns for canonic singing.

Cassler, G. Winston. *Organ Descants for Selected Hymns*. Augsburg (11-9304).

Goode, Jack. *Thirty-four Changes on Hymn Tunes*. Belwin-Mills (GB-644).

Hancock, Gerre. *Organ Improvisations for Hymn Singing*. Hinshaw (HMO-100).

Johnson, David. *Free Accompaniments for Manuals*. Augsburg (Book II, 11-9186; Book III, 11-9189).

Knight, Gerald H., ed. *Accompaniments for Unison Hymn-Singing*. The Royal School of Church Music, Croydon, England. Available through RSCM in America. Uses 50 different tunes.

Noble, T. Tertius. *55 Organ Accompaniments to Well-Known Hymn Tunes*. J. Fischer and Bro. (8430).
——. *Free Organ Accompaniments to One Hundred Well-Known Hymn Tunes*. J. Fischer and Bro. (8175).
Powell, Robert. *Organ Descants (48)*. G.I.A. (G-2504). On well-known hymn tunes.
Rohlig, Harold. *Thirty New Settings of Familiar Hymn Tunes*. Abingdon Press (APM 286).
Routley, E. *25 Festival Hymns for Organ and Choir*. Augsburg (no number given).
Shaw, Geoffrey. *The Descant Hymn-Tune Book*. Novello. Book I has 30 settings; Book II has 34 settings.
Thiman, Eric. *Varied Accompaniments*. Oxford University Press.
Wasson, D. DeWitt, ed. *Free Harmonizations of Hymn Tunes*. Hinshaw Music, Inc. Treats over 120 different tunes, some with two and three settings.

Collections by groups of composers:

Hymn Preludes and Free Accompaniments. Augsburg. 15 separate volumes, each by a different contemporary composer; approximately 12 hymn tunes per group.
New Organ Accompaniments for Selected Hymns of Paul Gerhardt. Concordia (97-5369). Composed by 12 contemporary composers.

Intonations and Introductions

Beck, Theodore. *Forty-seven Hymn Intonations*. Concordia (97-5018).
——. *Intonations for the Hymn of the Week*. Concordia (97-4899).
——. *Intonations on Selected Hymns*. Concordia (97-5392).
Greenlee, Anita. *Hymn Intonations*. Fortress Press (no number given).
Herman, David. *11 Hymn Intonations*. G.I.A. (G-2378). Includes free accompaniments and instrumental descants.
——. *12 Hymn Intonations*. G.I.A. (G-2519). Includes free accompaniments with instrumental descants.
Videro, Finn. *Twenty-one Hymn Intonations*. Concordia (97-5004).
Young, Michael. *Creative Intonations*. G.I.A. (G-2340).

See also *Hymn Preludes and Free Accompaniments* (Augsburg), listed above. Each prelude is brief and can be used effectively for an introduction to a choral singing, perhaps as a hymn anthem.

Psalm Texts for Children's Voices

See the list of abbreviations on p. 148 for sources. The number in the left column is the number of the psalm. Numbers in parentheses after each item refer to difficulty: 1 = easy; 2 = easy/medium; 3 = medium; 4 = medium difficult; 5 = difficult.

1   Metrical paraphrase: *LW* 388.
    Marshall, J. *Psalm 1* (selected verses). CG (A-248). Unison/keyboard (3).
    Proulx, R. *Happy the Man Who Fears the Lord* (paraphrase). APH (11-0312). S(S), organ, flute, oboe (4).

4 Ramseth, B. "An Evening Prayer of Trust" (select verses based on Ps. 4). *Making Happy Noises,* p. 14. APH (11-9280). Unison/autoharp or guitar (2).
Schütz, H. *O Hear Me, O Lord* (v. 1). APH (ACL-1512). S(A), organ (3).
Schwartz, C. *Hear Me When I Call to Thee* (vv. 1, 8). AMSI (347). S(S), keyboard (2).

5 Haan, R. *A Song of Joy* (v. 11). AMSI (277). Unison/keyboard, (2).

8 McAfee, D. *Three Psalm-Hymns for Juniors* (Psalm 8). CPI (6703). Unison/keyboard (2).
Ramseth, B. "O Lord, Our God" (based on Ps. 8). *Making Happy Noises,* p. 13. APH (11-9280). S(S/or/A), dulcimer, opt. timpani (2).
Telemann, G. "O Lord, Our Master" (v. 1). *MSCB*II. CPH (97-4702). Unaccomp. canon (3).
Wagner, D. *How Excellent Is Your Name* (vv. 1, 4—10). SMP (S-HB5-2). Speech choir or narrator, handbells, opt. C-inst. (3).

9 Rohlig, H. "I Will Praise You" (v. 1). *Explode with Joy.* CPH (97-5165). Unison/keyboard, opt. C-inst. (3).

13 Willan, H. "I Have Trusted in Thy Mercy" (vv. 1, 2, 5, 9). *We Praise Thee.* CPH (97-1032). Unison/keyboard (2).

17 Marcello, B. "Give Ear unto Me." CPH (97-4702). SA, keyboard (4).
———. "Oh, Hold Thou Me Up" (vv. 5, 6). *MSCB.* CPH (98-1046). SA, keyboard (4).

19 Selby/Owen. *The Heavens Declare Thy Glory.* CG (CGA-261). Unison, keyboard, opt. 2 B♭ trumpets (3).

23 Metrical paraphrases: *LW* 412, 416, 417; *LBW* 451, 456.
Jacob, G. *Brother James' Air.* OUP (44P047). Unison (descant) (2).
McCabe, M. *The Shepherd Song* (Ps. 23 adapted). SMP (S-8632). Unison (descant), organ (3).
Sister Theophane. *Psalm 22* (Vulgate numbering). GIA (G-1608). Unison, flute, organ (3).
Thoren, N. "The King of Love My Shepherd Is" (select verses). *Children's Carols for Improvisation.* APH (11-9115). Unison, Orff (2).

24 Metrical paraphrases: *LW* 23, 24; *LBW* 452.
Hopson, H. *Enter His Sanctuary Singing* (paraphrased). CG (A-1070). Unison, antiphonal choirs, keyboard, brass (3).
Willan, H. "Lift Up Your Heads, O Ye Gates" (vv. 7—10). *WPT*II. CPH (97-7610). S(SA), keyboard (3).

Williamson, M. *Who Is the King of Glory*. B&H (W.004). SS, keyboard (4).

Wills, A. *Popular Psalm Settings* (Psalm 24). GS (11771). Unison, antiphonal choirs, keyboard, opt. brass (3).

25 Rohlig, H. "Teach Me Your Ways, Lord" (vv. 4—5). *Explode with Joy*. CPH (97-5165). Also available separately (98-2358). S(A), keyboard (3).

27 Schütz, H. *The Lord Is My Light and My Strength* (v. 1). McAfee Mus. (DMC-1208). Distributed by Belwin-Mills. S(S), keyboard, opt. trumpets (3).

29 Schütz, H. "Give to Jehovah" (vv. 1—2). *MSCB*II. CPH (97-4720). Unison/keyboard (3).

30 Parker, A. "Hear, O Lord" (v. 10). *Sunday Rounds*. HMI (HMC-106). Two- or three-voice canon (2).

Schütz, H. *Sing, O Ye Saints* (vv. 4—5). CPH (98-1414). S/A, organ (5).

31 Metrical paraphrase: *LW* 406.

32 Weber, P. *Psalm 32*. APH (11-0682). SS(T), organ (3).

33 Proulx, R. *Of the Kindness of the Lord* (vv. 1, 5, 6a). APH (11-1539). S(A), keyboard (4).

Rohlig, H. "God Is Here—Let's Celebrate" (contemp. paraphrase). *Explode with Joy*. CPH (97-5165). S(A), keyboard, percussion (3).

34 Handel/Hopson. *I Will at All Times Praise the Lord* (selected verses). CG (GGA-243). Unison, keyboard (2).

Ramseth, B. "Never Cease Praising God" (select verses). *Making Happy Noises,* pp. 8, 9. APH. Unison, autoharp (or guitar), tambourine (3).

38 Metrical paraphrase: *LW* 372.

40 Hopson, H. *Blest Are They Whose Spirits Long* (v. 4). CG (GGA-183). Unison (SATB or) keyboard (2).

Young, P. "Psalm 40" (vv. 1, 16, 26). *MCCB*I. APH (11-9288). S(A), organ (3).

42 Bach, J. S. *Psalm 42*. Arr. J. Green. CMP (CLA 7817). SA, organ (4).

43 Willan, H. "Oh, Send Out Thy Light" (vv. 3, 4). *WPT*II. CPH (97-7610). S(A), keyboard (3).

46 Metrical paraphrases: *LW* 297/298; *LBW* 228/229.

47 Hopson, H. *Antiphonal Praise*. SMP (S-255). Unison, organ (3).

Hunnicutt, J. *Clap Your Hands, All Children*. APH (11-1632).

Unison, keyboard (2).

Nelson, R. "Clap Your Hands, Stamp Your Feet" (paraphrase). *MCC*II. APH (11-9285). Unison, keyboard (4).

Rohlig, H. "Clap Your Hands" (paraphrased). *Explode with Joy*. CPH (97-5165). Unison, keyboard (3).

Webb, C. *Psalm 47* (adapted). CG (CGA-207). Two-part, keyboard (2).

51 Metrical paraphrase: *LW* 373.

Bouman, P. *Create in Me a Clean Heart, O God* (vv. 10—12). CPH (98-1143). S(S), organ (4).

Willan, H. "Create in Me a Clean Heart, O God" (vv. 10—12). *MSCB*II. CPH (97-4702). Unison, keyboard (2).

See also Offertory for Ash Wednesday in Verse and Offertory collections.

55 Frederici, D. "Cast Your Burden on the Lord" (v. 22). *32 Sacred Canons*. CFP (66166). Two voices (3).

57 Webb, C. *Psalm 57* (adapted). CG (CGA-219). Unison, keyboard (2).

62 Ramseth, B. "As for Me" (select verses). *Making Happy Noises*. APH (11-9280). S(SA), autoharp or guitar (2).

Willan, H. "Truly My Soul Waiteth upon God" (vv. 1, 2, 7a). *WPT*. CPH (97-1032). S(A), keyboard (3).

65 Greene, M. "Thou Visitest the Earth." *MSCB*. CPH (97-6287). S(A), keyboard (3).

66 Ramseth, B. "Making Happy Noises" (select verses). *Making Happy Noises*. APH (11-9280). S(S), autoharp or guitar (2).

67 Metrical paraphrases: *LW* 288; *LBW* 335.

Bouman, P. *God Be Merciful*. APH (11-0696). S(A), keyboard (4).

———. *God Be Merciful unto Us*. CPH (98-2471). S(A), keyboard (3).

Willan, H. "God Be Merciful unto Us and Bless Us." *WPT*II. CPH (97-7610). S, SA, keyboard (3).

———. "Let the People Praise Thee, O God" (vv. 3—5). *WPT*. CPH (97-1032). S(A), keyboard (3).

Wills, A. *Popular Psalm Settings* (Psalm 67). GS (11771). Unison, organ, and guitar (2).

72 Metrical paraphrases: *LW* 83, 312; *LBW* 530.

75 Parker, A. "Give Thanks" (v. 1). *Sunday Rounds*. HMI (HMC-106). (2).

78 Metrical paraphrase: *LW* 472.

81 Clawson, D. *Sing We Merrily unto God* (vv. 1, 23). H. W. Gray (2938). SA, organ (3).
Webb, C. *Psalm 81*. CG (CGR-38).

84 Roff, J. *How Lovely Is Thy Dwelling* (vv. 1—3). CPH (98-2622). S(A), keyboard (3).
Willan, H. "Oh, How Amiable Are Thy Dwellings." *WPT*. CPH (97-1032). S(A), keyboard (3).

Also see Offertory settings in Verse and Offertory collections for the Tenth Sunday After Pentecost (vv. 3, 4).

86 Willan, H. "Give Ear, O Lord, unto My Prayer" (vv. 5, 6). *WPT*. CPH (97-1032). SSA, acc. (4).

89 Mendelssohn, F./C. Young. *I Will Sing of Thy Mercies* (v. 1). Agape (AG7228). S(A), keyboard (4).

90 Metrical paraphrases: *LW* 180; *LBW* 320.

92 Parker, A. "O Lord, How Great Are Thy Works" (v. 5). *Sunday Rounds*. HMI (HMC-106). (3).

95 Kirby, C. *A Psalm for Singing* (vv. 1, 3). LP (AN-4039). SS, keyboard (2).
Leaf, R. "Rejoice, Be Glad in the Lord" (vv. 1, 7). *MCCII*. APH (11-9285). A(A), keyboard (3).
Mawby, C. *O Come, Let Us Sing unto the Lord* (vv. 1—5). GIA (G-1098). SS, organ (5).
Sprunger, R. "O Come, Let Us Sing" (vv. 1—7). *Orff in the Church*. CMP (see Orff Collections). SS, Orff (3).

96 Beck, J. *Sing unto Him* (select verses). CG (A-52). S(A), keyboard (3).
Rohlig, H. "Sing a New Song to the Lord" (vv. 1, 3). *Explode with Joy*. CPH (97-5165). S(A), keyboard (3).
Smith, D. *Sing unto the Lord*. CG (CGA-70). Unison, finger cymbals, tambourine, keyboard (2).

97 Metrical paraphrases: *LW* 53; *LBW* 39.
Beck, J. *Sing unto Him*. (See entry under Psalm 96).
Smith, S. *Sing unto the Lord*. CG (CGA-70). Unison, finger cymbals, tambourine, keyboard (2).
Willan, H. "Oh, Sing unto the Lord a New Song" (vv. 1, 2). *WPT*II. CPH (97-7610). S(A), keyboard (3).

100 Metrical paraphrases: *LW* 205, 435, 454; *LBW* 245, 531.
Owens, S. *Jubilate Deo Psalm 100*. CG (CGA-288). Unison, keyboard (3).
Pavone, M. *Psalms to Ring and Sing*. CG (CGA-263). 10 handbells, unison (canon 2-4 parts) (2).
Ramseth, B. *Make a Joyful Noise* (complete). APH (11-9132).

Unison, Orff (2).

Rohlig, H. "Sing for Joy to the Lord." *Explode with Joy.* CPH (97-5165). S(A), keyboard (3).

Willan, H. "Make a Joyful Noise unto the Lord." *WPT* II. CPH (97-7610). S(A), keyboard (3).

101 Mawby, C. *My Song Shall be of Mercy and Judgment* (vv. 1—4). GIA (G-1098). SS, organ (5).

103 Metrical paraphrases: *LW* 444, 453, 457; *LBW* 519, 549.
Handel, G./L. Kirby. *O My Soul, Bless God the Father.* HFC (EA-5015). SA, keyboard (3).
Lovelace, A. *Bless the Lord, O My Soul.* CG (CGA-225). Unison, keyboard (2).
Ramseth, B. "The Eyes of All" (v. 1 plus Ps. 145:15, 16). *Prepare Ye the Way.* APH (11-9365). Unison (canon), autoharp (2).

104 Metrical paraphrases: *LW* 458; *LBW* 548.
McAfee, D. *Three Psalm Hymns for Juniors.* CPI (6703). Unison, keyboard (2).

105 Beck, J. *Sing unto God* (selected verses of Ps. 105 and 107). CG (CGA-52). Unison, keyboard (2).

107 Beck, J. *Sing unto God* (selected verses of Ps. 105 and 107). CG (CGA-52). Unison, keyboard (2).
Pavone, M. *Psalms to Ring and Sing.* CG (CGA-263). 10 handbells, unison (2).

108 Metrical paraphrase: *LBW* 538.
Johnson, M. *My Heart Is Ready* (v. 1). AMSI (258). S(A), keyboard (2).

113 Proulx, R. *Praise Ye the Lord, Ye Children* (paraphrased). APH (11-0322). Unison/handbells (resonator bells) f.c. (2).

115 Telemann, G./Nelson, R. *O Not to Us, Good Lord* (based on Ps. 115). APH (11-311). Unison, organ, flute (4).

117 Metrical paraphrases: *LW* 440; *LBW* 550.
Watson, W. *Praise the Lord, Alleluia* (paraphrase). CG (A-133). Unison, keyboard (3).
Willan, H. "O Praise the Lord, All Ye Nations." *WPT.* CPH (97-1032). SSA, a/cap. (4).

118 Metrical paraphrase: *LW* 200.
Lenel, L. *Let Us Be Glad in This Day.* APH (11-1311). S(A), keyboard. Uses the Hymn of the Day, "Christ Jesus Lay in Death's Strong Bands" (4).
Parker, A. "This Is the Day" (v. 24). *Sunday Rounds.* HMI (HMC-106). Canon 2—3 parts (1).
Sleeth, N. *This Is the Day* (select verses). HMI (HMC-229).

S(A), keyboard (2).

119   Metrical paraphrase: *LW* 392 (vv. 5, 33—35), 474 (v. 9).
      Willan, H. "Blessed Are the Undefiled" (vv. 1, 2, 33). *WPT*.
      CPH (97-1032). S(A), keyboard (3).

121   Metrical paraphrase: *LBW* 445.
      McAfee, D. *Three Psalm Hymns for Juniors* (Ps. 121). CPI
      (6703). Unison, keyboard (2).
      Pavone, M. *Psalms to Ring and Sing*. CG (CGA-263). 9 hand-
      bells, unison, SA (SATB or keyboard) (3).
      Sleeth, N. *Psalm* (adapted). AMSI (441). Unison (2-part), key-
      board, opt. flute (3).
      Wills, A. *Popular Psalm Settings* (Ps. 121). GS (11771). Unison,
      organ, or guitar (3).

122   Hallock, P. *I Was Glad*. GIA (G-2079). SS, 7 handbells (2).
      Willan, H. "I Was Glad" (vv. 1, 2, 7). *WPT* II. CPH (97-7610).
      SSA, a/cap. (4).
      Kreutz, R. *Psalm of Rejoicing* (adapted). CG (CGR-46). Unison
      (divided), keyboard (2).

126   Sherman, R. *Psalm 126*. GIA (G-2196). S(AB), handbells (2).

130   Metrical paraphrases: *LW* 230; *LBW* 295.
      Horman, J. *A Psalm of Blessing*. CG (CGA-266). Unison, key-
      board (2- or 3-part, opt.) (3).

134   Proulx, R. "Psalm 134" (paraphrased). *Tintinnabulum*, pp.
      24—28. GIA (G-2358). SA, handbells (3).

136   Metrical paraphrases: *LBW* 520, 521.

137   Metrical paraphrases: *LW* 296; *LBW* 368.
      Mawby, C. *By the Waters of Babylon* (vv. 1—4). GIA (G-1098).
      SS, organ (5).

138   Butler, E. *A Joyous Psalm* (adapted). CG (CGA-74). Unison,
      keyboard (3).

139   Sprunger, R. "Search Me, O God" (vv. 23, 24). *Orff in the
      Church*. CMP (see Orff Collections.) Unison, Orff (3).

145   Ramseth, B. "The Eyes of All" (vv. 15, 16, plus 103:1a). *Prepare
      Ye the Way*. APH (11-9365). Autoharp (guitar), unison (canon)
      (2).

146   Metrical paraphrases: *LW* 445; *LBW* 539.
      Ramseth, B. "I Will Sing to the Lord" (v. 2). *Making Happy
      Noises*. APH. Unison (canon to four voices), Orff dulcimer, f.c.
      (2).
      Rohlig, H. "Alleluia, Praise the Lord, My Soul" (vv. 1, 2). *Ex-
      plode with Joy*. CPH (97-5165). Unison, keyboard (3).

147 Young, P. *A Little Psalm for Singing* (adapted). CG (CGA-279). Unison, keyboard (2).

148 Metrical paraphrases: *LBW* 540, 541.
Mawby, C. *O Praise the Lord of Heaven* (vv. 1—5). GIA (G-1098). SS, organ (4).

150 Metrical paraphrase: *LW* 444.
McNair, M. "150th Psalm" in Junior Choir with Orff instruments (see Collections). Speech choir with choral introduction, Orff (2).
Rohlig, H. "Praise God in His Temple." *Explode with Joy*. CPH (97-5165). Unison, keyboard (3).
Hopson, H. *Antiphonal Psalm* (150). Agape (HH-3901). S(S), keyboard (3).

Abbreviations

Publishers/Distributors (addresses on page 125)

AMSI	— Art Masters Studios, Inc.
APH	— Augsburg Publishing House
B and H	— Boosey and Hawkes
B-M	— Belwin-Mills
CFP	— C. F. Peters Company
CG	— Choristers Guild
CMP	— Chantry Music Press
CPH	— Concordia Publishing House
CPI	— Canyon Press, Inc.
GIA	— Gregorian Institute of America
GS	— G. Schirmer
HFC	— Harold Flammer Company
HMI	— Hinshaw Music, Inc.
HWG	— H. W. Gray
LP	— Lillenas Publishing Company (div. of Belwin-Mills)
OUP	— Oxford University Press
SMP	— Sacred Music Press

Hymnals/Collections

LBW	— *Lutheran Book of Worship* (available through APH)
LW	— *Lutheran Worship* (available through CPH)
MCC	— *Music for the Contemporary Choir*
*MCC*II	— *Music for the Contemporary Choir*—A Second Book
MSCB	— *Morning Star Choir Book*, ed. P. Thomas
*MSCB*II	— *A Second Morning Star Choir Book*, ed. P. Thomas
WPT	— *We Praise Thee*, H. Willan
*WPT*II	— *We Praise Thee*, II, H. Willan

Psalm Collections

Frischmann, C. *The Psalmody for the Day*. Fortress Press. Series A (3-47), Series B (3-48), Series C (3-49). Psalms for the Day, plus entrance and Communion psalms (3).

Gelineau, J. *The Grail Gelineau Psalter*. Ed. J. Carroll. Complete edition. GIA (G-1703). 150 psalms and 18 canticles. Some of these are more easily learned by children than others. The director's skill and technique for interesting teaching and the choir's capabilities are variables that will guide the selection (3/4).

Petrich, R. *Psalm Antiphons for the Church Year*. Fortress Press (3-64). Musical settings for antiphons for the *Lutheran Book of Worship*. Unison, keyboard (2).

Ramseth, B. *MAKING HAPPY NOISES*. Augsburg (11-9280). Psalms in melody and motion for children's voices and bodies. Psalms used are 4, 8, 34, 62, 66, 146. Includes a 20-minute musical of praise and joy using the contents of the collection.

Formulae for Singing Pointed Psalms

Specific assistance for singing pointed psalms can be found in *Lutheran Worship,* pp. 366—67, and *Lutheran Book of Worship*, pp. 290—91. Note also the psalm tone setting arranged for Orff instruments with voices on page 111 in chapter 6 of this book. (This tone is from *Lutheran Worship*.) John Ferguson offers valuable assistance for stimulating psalm singing in chapter 8 and appendix A of *Worship Blueprints* (Augsburg, 12-1554).

Choral Music for the Day

Advent 1 to Pentecost 1 (Holy Trinity)

Recognizing the extended list of general choral music available for the particular season of the church year, the following titles have been selected for their close relationship to the suggested three-year lectionary, i.e. the Psalms, the Readings, and the Hymns for the Day found in *Lutheran Worship* and *Lutheran Book of Worship*. Those who use other worship books with similar readings and hymns will find many of the entries applicable also.

The following abbreviations are used in the list: capital letters for the particular year of the three-year cycle (A, B, C), roman numerals I and II for the First and Second (Epistle) Readings, and G for the Gospel. Since Psalm selections are listed separately on pages 141—48 of this chapter, they are not repeated here. Be sure to refer to them for additional choices for the day. H/D refers to choral settings of the appointed Hymn(s) for the Day.

As with other entries of music titles, numbers are used to indicate the level of difficulty of the choral part, not the accompaniment (1 = very easy; 2 = easy; 3 = medium; 4 = medium difficult; 5 = difficult).

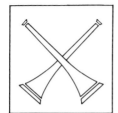

Advent 1

H/D   "Savior of the Nations, Come"

    a. Arr. J. Melby (Augsburg, 11-1660); unison/keyboard (1).

    b. Arr. C. Schalk in *Chorales for Advent* (Augsburg, 11-9134); unison, two treble instruments with keyboard (1).

  "Wake, Awake for Night Is Flying"

    a. F. Tunder/Thomas in *The Morning Star Choir Book* (Concordia, 97-6287); unison/keyboard (2).

    b. Arr. M. Drischner in *Make a Joyful Noise* (Concordia, 97-4684); unison, keyboard, opt. trumpet (2).

I (AB)   "Come, Rejoice Believers," Buxtehude/Hopson (H. Flammer, E-5199); 2-part, keyboard (3).

G (B)   "First Sunday in Advent (B)," N. Maeker (Augsburg, 11-3510); speech choir, percussion, handbell or metal-lophone; uses Mark 13:33-37 (2).

G (C)   "And There Will Be Signs," J. Bender (Concordia, 98-2082); unison/keyboard (3).

I (alt. Gospel ABC)   "Hosanna to the Son of David" (see settings under Palm Sunday/Sunday of the Passion).

I (alt. Gospel ABC)   "Hosanna Now Through Advent," H. Willan in *We Praise Thee* (Concordia, 97-1032); soprano, opt. alto, keyboard (2/3).

Advent 2

H/D   "On Jordan's Bank[s] the Baptist's Cry." Consider using one of the following settings with the same tune (*Puer nobis nascitur*) but substitute the text suggested for the Hymn of the Day:

    a. "Come, Jesus, Holy Child," arr. H. Willan in *We Praise Thee* (Concordia, 97-1032); unison, opt. descant, keyboard (1/2).

    b. "Come, Thou Redeemer of the Earth," arr. R. Haan (Concordia, 98-2429); unison, keyboard, opt. hand-bells (1).

    c. D. Busarow in *All Praise to You, Eternal God* (Augsburg, 11-9076); canonic organ setting for organ and voices (2).

    d. "Lo, He Comes with Clouds Descending," arr. T. Beck (Concordia, 98-2487); keyboard, opt. flute (2/3).

II (ABC)   "Advent Message," M. How (Boosey & Hawkes, M.161); unison, opt. second part, keyboard (3).

II (AC)   "Prepare Thyself, Zion," J. S. Bach (E. C. Schirmer, #1521); unison, keyboard (4).

I (B) and   "Comfort, Comfort Ye My People," J. S. Bach (Concor-

H/D   dia, 98-2045); unison (2), strings/keyboard (3).

Advent 3

H/D   "O People, Rise and Labor" (tune: *Aus meines Herzens Grunde*). Consider using the following setting but substituting the text from the hymnal: "Arise, Sons of the Kingdom," Buxtehude/Bunjes in *The Morning Star Choir Book* (Concordia, 97-6287); unison, keyboard (2). "The Only Son from Heaven," K. Othmayr in *The SSA Chorale Book*, ed. Thomas (Concordia, 97-7592); 2-part a cappella (3).
"Hark a Thrilling Voice," J. Goodman (Augsburg, 11-2074); 2-part, keyboard (2/3).

G (A)   "Behold, I Send My Messenger," H. Willan in *We Praise Thee II* (Concordia, 97-7610); soprano, opt. alto, keyboard (2).

II (C)   "Rejoice in the Lord," H. Willan (Concordia, 98-1815); 2-part, keyboard (3).

Advent 4

H/D   "Oh, Come, Oh, Come, Emmanuel," arr. T. Beck (Concordia, 98-2631); 2-part, keyboard (2/3).
"Come, Thou Long-Expected Jesus," arr. C. Schalk in *Chorales for Advent* (Augsburg, 11-9134); unison, keyboard, two treble instruments (1).
"Come, Thou Long-Expected Jesus," Rameau/Nelson. This setting does not use the tune *Jefferson*, but an original tune by the composer.

G (C)   See Magnificat settings under settings of major canticles.

Christmas (Christmas Eve, Christmas Day, Christmas 1 and 2)

H/D   "From Heaven Above to Earth I Come"
    a. Arr. C. Schalk in *Chorales for Christmas and Epiphany* (Augsburg, 11-9143); unison, keyboard, one or two descanting instruments (1).
    b. Arr. P. Bunjes in *The Hymns of Martin Luther* (Concordia, 97-5453), pp. 15—16; unison, keyboard, treble instruments (2).
"Of the Father's Love Begotten"
    a. Arr. C. Schalk, also in the collection *Chorales for Christmas and Epiphany;* same requirements for voices and instruments.
    b. Same tune, arr. by J. Erickson (Choristers Guild, A-150); unison voices, handbells (2).
"Let All Together Praise our God," arr. J. Goodman

(Augsburg, 11-2076); two-part, keyboard (2).

"All Praise to You, Eternal God," arr. R. Hillert in *The Hymns of Martin Luther,* p. 20 (Concordia, 97-5453); S/A a cappella (3).

Christmas Day

G (ABC)   "Christmas," N. Maeker (Augsburg, 11-3504); unison, Orff, narration; uses the complete Gospel text, Luke 2:1-20 (2/3).

"The Christmas Gospel," M. Mayer in *A Third Morning Star Choir Book,* ed. Thomas (Concordia, 97-4972); unison, keyboard, two treble instruments (3/4).

Christmas 2

G (ABC)   "The Word Became Flesh"
a.   G. Brandon (E. C. Kerby, Ltd., 81571); unison, keyboard (3).
b.   H. Willan in *We Praise Thee II* (Concordia, 97-7610); S(A), keyboard (2).
c.   E. Mauersberger in *A Second Morning Star Choir Book,* ed. Thomas (Concordia 97-4702); S(A), keyboard (2). Uses John 1:14b.

Epiphany

H/D   "O Morning Star, So Pure, So Bright"
a.   Arr. L. Lenel (Concordia, 98-1452); unison, keyboard (4).
b.   Arr. M. Drischner in *Make a Joyful Noise* (Concordia, 97-4684); unison, keyboard, opt. descant instrument (2).

G (ABC)   "And Lo, the Star," J. Petzold (Augsburg, TI-305); 2-part, organ, treble instrument (4).

G (ABC)   "Lo, the Star Which They Saw" (Matt. 2:9-10) in *We Praise Thee II* (Concordia, 97-7610); soprano, opt. alto, keyboard (3).

"To Jesus Who Is King," R. Hillert (Augsburg, 11-2078); unison, keyboard, opt. strings, oboe (3).

"The Lord Our God Is King of Kings," R. Leaf (Augsburg, 11-1582); unison, opt. descant, keyboard (3).

Epiphany 1—The Baptism of Our Lord

G (C)   See Nunc Dimittis settings under Ordinary: Canticles. See selections under Baptism/Affirmation of Baptism for potential use.

Epiphany 2

H/D   "The Only Son from Heaven," K. Othmayr in *The SSA Chorale Book,* ed. Thomas (Concordia, 97-7592); 2-part a cappella (3).

G (A)   "Behold the Lamb of God," P. Bouman (Concordia, 97-1088); unison, opt. 2-part, keyboard; "A" section uses John 1:29 text (3).

Epiphany 3

H/D   "Salvation unto Us Has Come," arr. M. Rotermund (Concordia, 98-2199); unison, flute, string bass, cello, organ, opt. glockenspiel (2).
See another entry under Reformation.

Epiphany 4

G (A)   "The Beatitudes," A. Lovelace (Augsburg, 11-1867); unison, keyboard (3).

II (C)   "The Gift of Love," H. Hopson (Hope, CF-148); unison, opt. descant, keyboard or guitar (3).

II (C)   "More Love," I. Carley (Augsburg, 11-0331); two-part, Orff instruments (3).

Epiphany 5

I (C)   "Holy Is the Lord of Hosts," B. Ramseth in *Open Thou My Lips* (Augsburg, 11-9324); 2-part canon (2).
See also settings of the Sanctus under Settings of Major Canticles.

G (C)   Related to the Gospel accent of discipleship: "Let Us Ever Walk with Jesus," arr. P. Manz (Concordia, 98-2423); unison, organ, (1).

Epiphany 6

H/D   "O Christ, Our Hope, Our Heart's Desire"
a. Arr. M. Schlenker in *Settings of Chorales for Treble Voices* (Augsburg, 11-9382); unison, Orff, opt. timpani (2).
b. Arr. G. Kretzschmar in the same source; two-part, a cappella (2).

I (A)   Consider settings of Psalm 25, which reinforce the focus of this reading.

II (C)   "Thanks Be to God," P. Bouman (Concordia, 98-2342); 2-part, organ (2).

G (C)   "The Beatitudes," A. Lovelace (Augsburg, 11-1867); unison, keyboard (3).
"Beatitudes," M. McNair in *Junior Choir with Orff Instruments* (Swartwout Enterprises); unison with Orff (2).

Epiphany 7

H/D   "O Love, How Deep, How Broad, How High," W. Pelz (Concordia, 97-5675); this is a group of varied harmonizations and accompaniments for organ and unison voices that reflect the content of particular stanzas; effective for alternation of stanzas with the choir and congregation.

G (AC)   "The Gift of Love," H. Hopson (Hope, CF-148); unison, opt. descant, keyboard or guitar (3).

Epiphany 8

H/D   "Sing Praise to God, the Highest Good," arr. L. Lenel (Concordia, 97-1142); consider using the setting with the same tune, *Lobt Gott Den Herren, Ihr,* and another translation in *The Morning Star Choir Book* ("All Praise to God, Who Reigns Above") (2).

"Salvation unto Us Has Come," arr. M. Rotermund (Concordia, 98-2199); unison, flute, string bass or cello, opt. glockenspiel, or organ (2).

G (A)   "Seek Ye First the Kingdom of God," T. Kirk (C. Fischer CM 8043); 2-part, keyboard (3).

Transfiguration

H/D   Consider unison singing of one of the Hymns for the Day with an alternate keyboard accompaniment.

Ash Wednesday

H/D   "From Depths of Woe I Cry to You" ("Out of the Depths I Cry to You"), arr. P. Bunjes in *The Hymns of Martin Luther* (Concordia 97-5455), pp.3-5; unison, keyboard, opt. clarinet, violin or viola descant (2).

See also settings of Psalms 51 and 130 under Psalm Texts for Children's Voices, pp. 144, 147.

Lent 1

H/D   "God the Father, Be Our Stay [Shield]"

a. Arr. R. Hillert (Concordia, 98-2627); unison with either flute and guitar or keyboard, opt. flute (2).

b. Canonic setting: S. Scheidt in *SSA Chorale Book,* ed. P. Thomas, p. 62 (Concordia, 97-7592).

See settings of "A Mighty Fortress" under Reformation.

G (A)   "Begone Satan," J. Bender (Concordia, 98-1848); unison, keyboard (3).

II (B)   "Who Shall Separate Us from the Love of Christ?" H. Hopson (Choristers Guild, CGA-286); unison, keyboard (2).

Lent 2

H/D   "Jesus Refuge of the Weary," J. S. Bach/Bunjes in *The Morning Star Choir Book,* ed. Thomas (Concordia, 97-6287); uses different melody than the hymnals; unison, opt. second part, keyboard (3).

G (C) See "Hosanna" titles under Palm Sunday/Sunday of the Passion.

Lent 3

H/D "Let Us Ever Walk with Jesus," arr. P. Manz (Concordia, 98-2423) unison, organ (2).

II (A) "Now Are Ye Light in the Lord," H. Willan in *We Praise Thee II* (Concordia, 97-7610); unison, keyboard (3).

G (B) "The Kingdom of the Lord," N. Sleeth (AMSI, #301); two-part, keyboard or guitar, opt. flute (3)

Lent 4

H/D "Jesus, Priceless Treasure," G. Kretzschmar in *Settings of Chorales for Treble Voices* (Augsburg, 11-9382); 2-part a cappella (2).

"On My Heart Imprint Thine Image," arr. M. Rotermund (Concordia, 98-2180); unison, keyboard, or double bass or cello, flute, or keyboard (2).

G (B) "Good News" (includes John 3:16), R. Leaf (Augsburg, 11-1762); unison, keyboard, opt. three handbells (3).

G (C) "God Calling Yet," E. Nickel (Augsburg, 11-313); unison, two treble instruments, keyboard (3).

Lent 5

H/D "My Song Is Love Unknown," arr. D. Busarow (Concordia, 98-2336); unison, opt. second part, keyboard (2/3).

G (A) "I Am the Resurrection and the Life," H. Willan in *We Praise Thee II* (Concordia, 97-7610); soprano, opt. alto, keyboard.

G (B) "Children of the Heavenly Father," arr. D. Rotermund (Concordia, 98-2572); unison, opt. second part, organ, opt. treble instrument (2/3).

Palm Sunday/Sunday of the Passion

H/D "A Lamb Goes Uncomplaining Forth," arr. H. Micheelsen in *A Third Morning Star Choir Book* (Concordia, 97-4972); unison, keyboard (2).

"O Sacred Head Now Wounded," G. Handel/Thomas (Concordia, 98-2237); unison, keyboard (3).

I (B) "Rejoice Greatly"
  a. J. Petzold in *Music for the Contemporary Choir,* Book 1 (Augsburg, 11-9288); unison, keyboard (3).
  b. H. Willan (Concordia, 98-1113); two-part, keyboard (4).

II (ABC) "Christ Hath Humbled Himself," H. Willan in *We Praise Thee* (Concordia, 97-1032); soprano, opt. alto, keyboard (3).

II (ABC)   "At the Name of Jesus," H. Willan in *We Praise Thee II* (Concordia, 97-7610); soprano, opt. alto, keyboard (3).

G (ABC)   "Hosanna to the Son of David," H. Willan (Concordia, 98-1118); soprano, opt. second soprano and alto, keyboard (3).

"Sing Hosanna in the Highest," E. Butler (Choristers Guild, A-16); soprano, opt. second part, keyboard, trumpet (3).

"Sing Hosanna Today," R. Schaefer (Fortress, 3-76001); unison, keyboard, opt. finger cymbal and flute (2).

"Ride On, Eternal King," R. Leaf (Augsburg, 11-1581); soprano and alto, keyboard (3).

"Hosanna, Loud Hosanna," P. Brink (Concordia, 98-2284); unison, opt. second part, keyboard; uses the hymn tune *Ellacombe* (2).

See also Collections with Church Year Focus.

Good Friday

H/D   "A Lamb Goes Uncomplaining Forth" [A Lamb Alone Bears Willingly]. See H/D for Palm Sunday/Sunday of the Passion.

"O Sacred Head, Now Wounded." See H/D for Palm Sunday/Sunday of the Passion.

"Sing, My Tongue, How Glorious Battle," C. Schalk (Concordia, 98-2240); unison, keyboard (2).

I (ABC)   "Surely He Hath Borne Our Griefs," H. Willan (Concordia, 98-1769); soprano, opt. alto, keyboard (3).

Consider also settings of Psalm 51 (see separate list of psalms, p. 144).

Easter Day

H/D   "Christ Jesus Lay in Death's Strong Bands"

    a. Arr. R. Hillert in *The Hymns of Martin Luther* (Concordia, 97-5455); unison, keyboard, opt. three trumpets (2).

    b. Arr. R. Schultz (Concordia, 98-2298); unison/two-part, keyboard, opt. trumpet (3).

"Good Christian Friends [Men], Rejoice and Sing," M. Drischner in *Make a Joyful Noise* (Concordia, 97-4684); unison, keyboard, opt. descant instrument (2).

Both of the above are in the key of D; hymnals use C.

"At the Lamb's High Feast We Sing"

    a. Arr. M. Drischner in *Make a Joyful Noise* (Concordia, 97-4684); unison, keyboard, opt. descant instrument (2).

    b. Arr. W. Mudde in *A Second Morning Star Choir Book* (Concordia, 97-4702); three different settings; unison, two-part, keyboard (2/3).

Both of the above are in the key of E-flat; hymnals use D.

I (C) "The Lord Is My Strength and My Song," H. Hopson (Choristers Guild, A-101); opt. drums, bells, tambourine, finger cymbals (2).

II (ABC) "Thanks Be to God," P. Bouman (Concordia, 98-2342); S(A), keyboard (3).

G (A) "Easter," N. Maeker (Augsburg, 11-3503); speech choir with Orff instruments (2/3).

G (alt. A) "The Angel Said to the Women" (Matt. 28:5-6), H. Rohlig in *Explode with Joy* (Concordia, 97-5165); soprano, opt. alto, keyboard (4).

G (B) "Do Not Be Amazed," J. Bender (Concordia, 98-1966); two-part, keyboard (3/4).

"This Is the Day," N. Sleeth (Hinshaw, HMC-229); unison, opt. second part, keyboard; refrain is from the Psalm of the Day (Ps. 118) (2).

"Festival Canticle: Worthy Is Christ," R. Hillert (Concordia, 98-2305); unison with descant, keyboard, opt. brass; useful to embellish the canticle (3).

Easter 2

H/D "O [Ye] Sons and Daughters of the King," C. Schalk in *The Star Carol Book* (Concordia, 98-4858); uses the text but not the same tune as in most hymnals; unison, keyboard, opt. second part, triangle, tambourine (2/3).

"Come, You [Ye] Faithful, Raise the Strain," arr. J. Bender in *The Morning Star Choir Book* (Concordia, 97-6287); this setting is in G; hymnals use F; unison, opt. second part, keyboard (2/3).

"That Easter Day with Joy Was Bright," arr. D. Wood in *Music for the Contemporary Choir,* Book I (Augsburg, 11-9288); uses a different tune than the two new Lutheran hymnals; unison, opt. descant, keyboard (2).

II (C) "Unto Him That Loved Us," R. Vaughan Williams in *The Morning Star Choir Book* (Concordia, 97-6287); unison, keyboard (2).

G (ABC) "Peace Be with You," J. Bender (Concordia, 98-2086); two-part, keyboard (3).

Easter 3

H/D "With High Delight"

a. Arr. T. Beck in *7 Anthems for Treble Voices* (Concordia, 97-5218); soprano, alto, with two treble instruments, no keyboard (3).

b. Arr. H. Micheelsen (Concordia, 98-1942); setting is

in C; hymnals use D; unison, opt. second part, keyboard (2/3).

"The King of Love My Shepherd Is"

a. Arr. N. Thoren in *Children's Carols for Improvisation* (Augsburg, 11-9115); unison, opt. second part, Orff instrument, organ (1).

b. Arr. D. Walker in the anthem "Good Shepherd, May I Sing Thy Praise" (Concordia, 98-2374); each stanza is arranged differently; unison, Orff instruments, flute or recorder (2/3).

II (C) "Festival Canticle: Worthy Is Christ," R. Hillert (Concordia, 98-2305); unison with descant, keyboard (3).

"To the Lamb Be Glory," P. Weber (Concordia, 98-2299); unison (congregation or choir), keyboard (2/3).

Easter 4

H/D "At the Lamb's High Feast We Sing"—see entries under Easter Day.

"The King of Love My Shepherd Is"—see entries under Easter 3.

G (B) "I Am the Good Shepherd," J. Bender (Concordia, 98-1992); two-part, keyboard (3/4).

II (B) "Festival Canticle: Worthy Is Christ"—see entry under Easter Day.

Easter 5

H/D "Dear Christians, One and All Rejoice"

a. Arr. M. Rotermund (Concordia, 98-2198); unison, keyboard, opt. glockenspiel, flute, and string bass or cello (2).

b. Arr. M. Drischner in *Make a Joyful Noise* (Concordia, 97-4684); unison, keyboard, opt. treble instrument (2).

"At the Lamb's High Feast We Sing"—see entries under Easter Day.

G (A) "I Am Jesus' Little Lamb," arr. R. Haan (C. Fischer, CM-8158); unison or two-part, keyboard (2).

II (B) and
G (C) "The Gift of Love," H. Hopson (Hope, CF-148); unison, opt. descant, keyboard or guitar, opt. descant instrument (3).

Easter 6

H/D "Dear Christians, One and All Rejoice"—see entries under Easter 5.

"Our Father, Who from Heaven Above," arr. P. Bunjes in *The Hymns of Martin Luther* (Concordia, 97-5457); unison, keyboard, descant instrument (1).

G (AB) "If Ye Love Me," H. Willan in *We Praise Thee* (Concordia,

97-1032); SSA a cappella (4).

G (AC) "I Will Not Leave You Comfortless," H. Willan in *We Praise Thee II* (Concordia, 97-7610); soprano, opt. alto, keyboard (3).

G (C) "If a Man Loves Me," J. Bender (Concordia, 98-1697); unison, keyboard (2).

Ascension

Choral anthems for Ascension:

"Ascended Is Our God and Lord," arr. M. Drischner in *Make a Joyful Noise* (Concordia, 97-4684); unison, keyboard, opt. descanting instrument (1).

"Ascended Is Our God and Lord," arr. T. Klammer in *The Morning Star Choir Book,* ed. P. Thomas (Concordia, 97-6287); SSA a cappella (2).

"Hail the Day That Sees Him Rise," C. Schalk in *The Star Carol Book* (Concordia, 97-4858); unison, keyboard, tambourine (2).

Consider also settings of "At the Lamb's High Feast We Sing" (see listings under Easter Day) and "Dear Christians, One and All, Rejoice" (see listing under Easter 5).

Easter 7

H/D "Oh, Love, How Deep," W. Pelz (Concordia, 97-5675); accompaniment for each stanza is different; unison, keyboard for organ (3).

"Have No Fear, Little Flock," W. Pelz (Concordia, 97-5692); accompaniment for each stanza is different; unison, keyboard for organ (3).

"Have No Fear, Little Flock," arr. B. A. and M. Ramseth in *Take a Hymn . . .* (Augsburg, 11-2172); coordinated movements for children; unison, keyboard, opt. flute and cello, finger cymbals and wood block (1).

II (B) "The Gift of Love," H. Hopson (Hope, CF-148); unison, opt. descant, organ or guitar, opt. flute (3).

II (C) "E'en So, Lord Jesus, Quickly Come," P. Manz (Concordia, 98-2037); two-part, keyboard (4).

Pentecost Day

H/D "Come, Holy Ghost, God and Lord"

a. Arr. R. Hillert in *The Hymns of Martin Luther* (Concordia, 97-5455); unison and two-part, keyboard, opt. instruments (2).

b. Arr. A. Strube in the *SSA Chorale Book,* ed. P. Thomas (Concordia, 97-7592); SSA a cappella (3).

c. Also a two-part a cappella setting by K. Othmayr in the same collection.

"Come, Holy Ghost, Our Souls Inspire"
a. Arr. R. Hillert in *The Hymns of Martin Luther* (Concordia, 97-5455); unison and two-part settings, keyboard, descant instrument (2).
b. Arr. C. Schalk in *Two-Part Canon on Classic Hymns and Chorales,* Set I (Concordia, 98-1762); equal voices (2).
"To God the Holy Ghost Let Us Pray"
a. Arr. H. Distler in *A Second Morning Star Choir Book* (Concordia, 97-4702); unison and SSA a cappella (2/3).
b. Arr. L. Abraham in *The SSA Chorale Book,* ed. P. Thomas (Concordia, 97-7592); SSA a cappella (3).

II (ABC) "Pentecost," N. Maeker (Augsburg, 11-3506); speech with Orff instruments (2).
"Carol for Pentecost," J. Hunnicutt (Augsburg, 11-1676); based on Acts 2:1-5 with narrator and speech choir; unison, keyboard, opt. descant instrument (2).

G (C) "When the Counselor Comes," J. Bender (Concordia, 98-2055); two-part, keyboard (3).

See the Collections with Church Year Focus for additional selections appropriate for the day.

Holy Trinity (Pentecost 1)

H/D "Creator Spirit, Heavenly Dove"—see entries under "Come, Holy Ghost, Our Souls Inspire" for Pentecost Day above.
"All Glory Be to God on High"—see entries under Gloria in Excelsis (choir settings of the tune *Allein Gott in der Höh* under Settings of Major Canticles, p. 165).

II (A) "Children of the Heavenly Father," arr. D. Rotermund (Concordia, 98-2572); unison, opt. descant, alto, and treble descant instrument (2).

G (A) "Go Ye into All the World," A. Gumpeltzhaimer in *The Morning Star Choir Book,* ed. P. Thomas (Concordia, 97-6287); canon for two equal voices, a cappella (3).
"Go Into the World," N. Sleeth (Choristers Guild, A-209); two-part, keyboard (2/3).

G (B) "Unless One Is Born Anew," J. Bender (Concordia, 98-2056); unison, keyboard (2/3).

G (ABC) "The Trinity," R. Powell (Concordia, 98-2285); unison, keyboard (2).

G (B) "Good News," R. Leaf (Augsburg, 11-1762); unison, keyboard, opt. three handbells (3).

Consider also settings of the Sanctus under Settings of Major Canticles, p. 165.

Last Sunday After Pentecost
Sunday of the Fulfillment/Christ the King

H/D   "Wake, Awake, for Night Is Flying" (Sunday of the Fulfillment)

     a. Arr. C. Schalk in *Two-part Canons on Classic Hymns and Chorales,* Set III (Concordia, 98-1764); for equal voices, a cappella (2).

     b. Arr. M. Drischner in *Make a Joyful Noise* (Concordia, 97-4684); unison, keyboard, opt. descant instrument (2).

     c. Arr. F. Tunder/Thomas in *The Morning Star Choir Book* (Concordia, 97-6287); unison, keyboard (3).

     "O Jesus, King Most Wonderful" (Christ the King, Year C), arr. R. Gieseke (Concordia, 98-2601); this setting uses a different tune from that in the hymnals; stanza 4 only is for SAB but may be sung either as a unison stanza or two-part (without a baritone part) (2).

II (B)   "E'en So Lord Jesus, Quickly Come," P. Manz (Concordia, 98-2037); two-part, keyboard (4).

G (A)   "Come, O Blessed of My Father," J. Bender (Concordia, 98-1834); two-part, keyboard (3).

G (ABC)   "The Lord Our God Is King of Kings," R. Leaf (Augsburg, 11-1582); unison, opt. descant, keyboard (2).

     "Christ Is the King," arr. M. Rotermund (Augsburg, 11-2130); unison, two-part (or SAB setting) with keyboard of *LBW* 386 (3).

Minor Festivals and Sacraments

St. Michael and All Angels

H/D   "Lord God, to You We All Give Praise," arr. Becker-Foss in *Settings of Chorales for Treble Voices,* ed. M. Egge (Augsburg, 11-9382); "Come, Let Us Join" (p. 19) uses the Hymn of the Day tune; substituting the H/D text enables one to use this setting for unison choir and Orff instruments for the Festival of St. Michael and All Angels (choir: 1; Orff: 2/3).

II (ABC)   "With Flame of Might," C. Schalk in *The Star Carol Book* (Concordia, 98-4858); unison, opt. second part, keyboard (2).

     "Ye Holy Angels Bright," R. Powell (Augsburg, 11-0329); unison, organ, and Orff instruments (2).

Reformation

H/D   "Salvation unto Us Has Come," arr. A. Strube in *The SSA Chorale Book,* ed. P. Thomas (Concordia, 97-7592); two different settings: (a) SSA a cappella, (b) SA a cappella; see entry under Epiphany 3 for another setting (3).

Additional choral settings on popular Reformation hymns:

"A Mighty Fortress Is Our God"

a. F. Tunder in *A Second Morning Star Choir Book,* ed. P. Thomas (Concordia, 97-4702); unison, keyboard (3).

b. Arr. C. Schalk in *Two-part Canons on Classic Hymns and Chorales,* Set I (Concordia, 98-1762); two equal voices, a cappella (2).

c. Arr. R. Hillert in *The Hymns of Martin Luther,* vol. 6 (Concordia, 97-5456), p. 16; for unison choir with varied accompaniment (2).

"Built on the Rock the Church Doth Stand," arr. J. Bender in *The Morning Star Choir Book,* ed. P. Thomas (Concordia, 97-6287; individual copy, 98-1646); unison, opt. alto, keyboard (3).

II (ABC)   "Reformation Day," N. Maeker (Augsburg, 11-3516); speech choir setting of John 8:31-32; uses finger cymbals, opt. gong (2).

All Saints

H/D   "For All the Saints Who from Their Labors Rest," arr. H. Ley (Oxford Univ. Press, 40.004); this SATB setting is readily adaptable for unison and keyboard, opt. descant and alto parts (2/3).

I (ABC)   "Thou Wilt Keep Him in Perfect Peace," R. Wienhorst (Concordia, 98-2427); unison, keyboard (2/3).

G (ABC)   "The Beatitudes," A. Lovelace (Augsburg, 11-1867); unison, keyboard, opt. congregation (3).

Sacraments
Baptism

While there are no specific pericopes for this, the following choral selections are offered in order to assist the participation of children's choirs in the context of the Sacrament wherever it is administered in a public service.

"Cradling Children in His Arm," arr. B. A. and M. Ramseth in *Take a Hymn . . .* (Augsburg, 11-2172); unison, keyboard, flute (2).

"You Have Put On Christ," H. Hughes (G.I.A. Publications, G-2283); unison, opt. canon, keyboard, opt. instruments (2).

"We Know That Christ Is Raised," R. Nelson (Augsburg, 11-0318); several stanzas specifically speak of baptism; soprano, opt. second part, Orff (2).

"The Lord Bless You and Keep You," P. Lutkin (Summy-

Birchard, 4128); soprano, alto, keyboard (4).

"A Cantata for Baptism," J. Bender (Chantry, COC 735); contains several settings for unison (solo) voice, keyboard, and descanting instrument using Mark 10:14-15 (from the baptismal liturgy) (3/4).

"Loving Jesus, Gentle Lamb," M. Ierley (Concordia, 98-2472); unison, opt. second part, keyboard (3).

"Children of the Heavenly Father," arr. D. Rotermund (Concordia, 98-2572); unison, opt. descant and second part, organ (2/3).

"Blessings" (I/II), N. Sleeth (Choristers Guild, A-145); I is unison, flute (or violin), keyboard (3); II is unison, keyboard (1).

"Little Children, Welcome," H. Hopson (Hope, JR 219); unison with keyboard, opt. C instrument, Orff, five handbells (2).

Consider also the hymns under Baptism in the hymnals.

Holy Communion

While there are no specific readings with which to correlate, the following choral selections are offered to assist the participation of children's choirs in the context of the Sacrament.

"Come, Let Us Eat," B. A. Ramseth in *Take a Hymn . . .* (Augsburg, 11-2172); unison, opt. canon, Orff instrument (2).

"O Taste and See"
a. Setting: R. Copley (Augsburg, 11-0681); unison, keyboard (2).
b. Setting: R. Vaughan Williams (Oxford, 44.415); SSA, keyboard introduction (3).

"Let All Mortal Flesh Keep Silence," T. Beck (Concordia, 98-2487); SA, keyboard, opt. flute (3).

"We Shall Approach the Altar of the Lord," G. Track (Augsburg, 11-0691); unison, keyboard (2).

"Art Thou Weary, Art Thou Laden," P. Gehring (Concordia, 98-1945); unison, keyboard (2).

"Songs for Holy Communion," B. Jacobson (Concordia, 98-5609); unison, keyboard; seven songs ranging in difficulty from 2 to 3; numbers 2 and 3 work well in alternation, singing st. 1 of no. 3 followed by st. 1 of no. 2, etc.

"At the Lamb's High Feast"—see suggested settings of this hymn under Easter Day.

Also consider settings of any of the following under Settings of Major Canticles:
a. Kyrie settings (especially during Lent).

b. Gloria in Excelsis settings (especially during the Christmas and Epiphany seasons).
c. Credo settings (especially on Holy Trinity or in the Pentecost season).
d. Sanctus settings (on Palm Sunday, Advent 1, Holy Trinity, and festival occasions).
e. Agnus Dei settings (especially during Lent or in services of a penitential character).
f. Magnificat settings (Advent 4 and the Christmas season).
g. Nunc Dimittis settings (Christmas season and for most services with Holy Communion).

These are also not to be overlooked:

a. Settings of the Hymn of the Day for the day (or service) in which these hymns reflect the focus of the worship.
b. Choral settings of the pericopes for the day, including the Psalms.
c. Hymns and choral settings of hymns of Holy Communion and of trust, also those reflecting praise that accent particularly the thoughts of God's loving concern for His flock.
d. Psalm settings with the trust/faith accents; for example, Psalms 23 and 90.
e. Penitential psalms; for use with children's choirs these may work best during the preparatory Lenten season where children can more immediately relate to the somber character of the texts and music.

Settings of Verses and Offertories

S. Owens. *This Is the Day Which the Lord Has Made* (Augsburg, 11-8472); 12 verses and 7 offertories for unison voices, opt. instruments (handbells and percussion), and organ, for selected days throughout the church year (3).

Verse and Offertories (Augsburg); a complete set (9 volumes) for the church year, with keyboard accompaniment; wide range of difficulty; some can be done effectively by children. Request sample copies on approval from the publisher.

Verse and Offertories (Concordia); a complete set (8 volumes) for the church year, with keyboard accompaniment; wide range of difficulty; some can be done effectively by children. Request sample copies on approval from the publisher.

Settings of Major Canticles

This list includes alternate choral arrangements, in addition to those contained in the various settings of the orders of service in the front of *Lutheran Worship* and *Lutheran Book of Worship,* of the major canticles, that is, those most frequently used in the services of Holy Communion, Matins/Morning Prayer, and Vespers/Evening Prayer.

Holy Communion Texts

Kyrie   Metrical paraphrases: *LW* 209; *LBW* 96, 168

Gloria in
Excelsis   Metrical paraphrases: *LW* 210, 215; *LBW* 166
                 Choir settings of the tune *Allein Gott in der Höh* (*LW* 215; *LBW* 166)
                 a. Arr. M. Rotermund (Concordia, 98-2231); unison, keyboard, opt. guitar (2).
                 b. Arr. M. Schlenker in *Settings of Chorales for Treble Voices,* ed. M. Egge (Augsburg, 11-9382); unison, opt. descant, Orff (2).
                 c. Arr. C. Schalk in *Two-part Canons on Classic Hymns and Chorales,* Set I (Concordia, 98-1762); two equal voices, a cappella (3).

Credo   Metrical paraphrases: *LW* 212, 213; *LBW* 374
                 Canticle setting: *LW* 4

Sanctus   Metrical paraphrases: *LW* 214; *LBW* 528
                 Canticle setting: *LW* 6
                 Choir settings on the tune *Jesaia, dem Propheten* (*LW* 214; *LBW* 528):
                 a. Arr. P. Bunjes in *Lift Up Your Hearts* (Concordia, 97-6219); unison, opt. descant, keyboard (2/3).
                 b. Arr. P. Bunjes in *The Hymns of Martin Luther* (Concordia, 97-5452); unison, opt. descant instruments, keyboard (2/3).
                 These two are different arrangements.
                 Choral settings of the Sanctus text:
                 "Holy, Holy, Holy," J. Bender in *A Second Morning Star Choir Book,* ed. P. Thomas (Concordia, 97-4702); unison, keyboard (2).
                 "Holy, Holy, Holy," H. Willan in *The Morning Star Choir Book,* ed. P. Thomas (Concordia, 97-6287); unison, keyboard (2).
                 "Holy, Holy, Holy," Sister C. Hager (Augsburg, 11-3002); unison, opt. canon, Orff instruments (2).

Agnus Dei   Metrical paraphrases: *LW* 208; *LBW* 103, 111
                 Canticle setting: *LW* 7
                 Choral settings on the tune *O Lamm Gottes, unschuldig* (*LW* 208; *LBW* 111):

a. Arr. C. Schalk in *Two-Part Canons on Classic Hymns and Chorales,* Set I (Concordia, 98-1762); two equal voices, a cappella (3).

b. Arr. M. Drischner in *Make a Joyful Noise* (Concordia, 97-4684); unison, keyboard, opt. descant instrument (2).

Choir setting on the tune *Christe, du Lamm Gottes* (*LW* 7; *LBW* 103):

Arr. H. Willan in *We Praise Thee* (Concordia, 97-1032), p. 30; unison, opt. alto, keyboard (2).

Choral setting of the Agnus Dei text:

"O Christ, Thou Lamb of God," J. Bender in *The Morning Star Choir Book,* ed. P. Thomas (Concordia, 97-6268); unison, keyboard (2).

Minor Services (Matins/Morning Prayer; Vespers/Evening Prayer)

Magnificat   Metrical paraphrases: *LW* 211; *LBW* 180
Choral settings of the Magnificat text (of the many settings available, these are especially attractive for children's voices and are relatively easy to learn):
"The Magnificat," P. Bouman (Concordia, 98-1689); unison, keyboard (suggests antiphonal groups) (2).
"Magnificat for Choir and Organ," J. Bonnet (Concordia); unison choir (simple chant), a cappella with organ versets (interludes) choir score: 98-2425 (1); organ score: 97-5483 (3).

Nunc Dimittis Metrical paraphrases: *LW* 185; *LBW* 349
Canticle setting: *LW* 11
Choir setting on the tune *Mit Fried und Freud* (*LW* 185; *LBW* 349):
Arr. C. Schalk in *A Second Crown Choir Book* (Concordia, 97-4882), p. 11; unison, opt. second part, keyboard, and descant instrument (3).
Choral settings of the Nunc Dimittis text:
"Magnificat and Nunc Dimittis," J. Arnold (Oxford, No. 485); SSA a cappella (4).
"The Nunc Dimittis," H. Willan in *We Praise Thee II* (Concordia, 97-7610); S(SA) keyboard (3).

Te Deum laudamus Metrical paraphrases: *LW* 171; *LBW* 535
Canticle setting: *LW* 8
Choral settings of the Te Deum laudamus text (of the many available, these are particularly successful arrangements for use with children's choirs):
"We Praise Thee, O God" (abbreviated text), H. Willan

in *We Praise Thee* (Concordia, 97-1032; available separately as 98-1059); unison, keyboard (3).

"We Praise You, O God," H. Rohlig in *Explode with Joy* (Concordia, 97-5165); unison, keyboard, opt. descant instrument (3).

Collections with Church Year Focus

The following are included for their pertinent texts and quality of music oriented to the church year.

Dreamer, P., R. V. Williams, and Martin Shaw. *Oxford Book of Carols*. London: Oxford University Press, 1928. Of particular value to the choir director is the list of carols arranged according to the church year, pp. 473—81 (1-3).

Drischner, M. *Make a Joyful Noise*. Concordia (97-4684). 25 carols and hymns for the church year for unison voices with treble descanting instrument, keyboard (1-3).

Kemp, Helen. *Hymns Plus*. Hinshaw Music (HMB-128). For grades 4—8. Includes Service of Dedication for Choirs and Choristers.(2).

Music for the Contemporary Choir. Book 1. Augsburg (11-9288). By eight contemporary composers. Several anthems on pericope texts; unison and two-part keyboard (3-4).

Music for the Contemporary Choir. Book 2. Augsburg (11-9285). By nine contemporary composers. Similar to Book 1 (2-3).

Pooler, M. *Children's Choir Book*. Augsburg (11-9125). Nine seasonal songs: Advent, Christmas, Easter, General. S(S), keyboard (2).

Ramseth, B. *Prepare Ye the Way*. Augsburg (11-9365). Ten short selections, all canons for the church year on Scripture texts; unison, two-part to five-part canons with Orff instruments, autoharp (guitar) (2).

Ramseth, B. A., and M. Ramseth. *Take a Hymn*. Augsburg (11-2172). Unison with instruments (keyboard or Orff). Some settings can be used for alternating hymn stanzas (2).

Rohlig, H. *Explode with Joy*. Concordia (97-5165). Settings of Psalms 9, 25, 33, 47, 96, 100, 146, and 150; several significant New Testament verses; and a Te Deum (abbrev.) (3-4).

Settings of Chorales for Treble Voices. Augsburg (11-9382). 18 unaccompanied, 10 with instruments (Orff, including recorders). All major seasons of church year represented (1-2).

Sleeth, N. *Sunday Songbook*. Hinshaw Music (HMB-102). Advent/Christmas, Easter, Thanksgiving, Benediction, and Praise selections; S(A), keyboard, Orff optional (2).

Thomas, P., ed. *The Morning Star Choir Book*. Concordia (97-1142). Unison and two-part music of church year selections of hymn tunes, Scripture texts (2-3).

Thomas, P., ed. *A Second Morning Star Choir Book*. Concordia (97-4702). Unison and two-part music based on church year Scripture texts and excellent hymn tunes (2-4).

Thomas, P., ed. *A Third Morning Star Choir Book*. Concordia (97-4972). Mostly unison with keyboard. Church year orientation (2-4).

Walker, David S. *He Justly Claims a Song from Me*. Concordia (97-5208). A collection of seasonal anthems, folk songs, hymns, and rounds with suggested teaching concepts accompanying each selection. Contents relate to all seasons of the church year (2).

We Come to Praise Him. Choristers Guild (BK-23). Intended for younger choirs (ages 5—8). Advent, Christmas, Palm Sunday, and Praise. Anthems are included by eight different contemporary composers. Unison, opt. second part, keyboard, opt. percussion (2).

Willan, H. *We Praise Thee*. Vol. 1. Concordia (97-5165). Numerous settings of Scripture texts for S(SA), keyboard. Some hymns and carol settings. Church year oriented (3-5).

Willan, H. *We Praise Thee*. Vol. 2. Concordia (97-7610). Similar to volume I. S(SA), keyboard. Strong church year orientation (3-5).

Orff and Handbell Resources

This section contains a starter list of music and materials. See pp. 125—26 for addresses of publishers.

Pedagogy

McRae, Shirley W. *Celebrate*. Augsburg Publishing House (11-5328), 1984. A practical guide for the use of Orff techniques and materials in the church.

Springer, Ronald. *Orff in the Church*. Chantry Music Press.

Wheeler, Lawrence, and Lois Raebeck. *Orff and Kodaly Adapted for the Elementary School*. Dubuque, Iowa: Wm. C. Brown Co., Pub., 1972.

Music

Scripture Texts (not hymn based)

McNair, M., and G. Nash. *Junior Choir with Orff Instruments*. Intermediate levels. Swartwout Enterprises, 1975 editions. Bible texts and speech ensembles that will have liturgical applications.

Ramseth, Betty Ann. *Open Thou My Lips*. Augsburg (11-9324). Twelve canons, most of which use psalm verses with simple rhythmic and melodic patterns for percussion instruments. Useful for serving in the fabric of the liturgy. Medium easy.

Ramseth, Betty Ann. *That I May Speak*. Augsburg (11-9490). Rhythmic speech ensembles to express brief Old and New Testament verses using canon, rondo, and ostinati treatments. Medium easy.

Hymn and Carol Collections

Martens, E. *Five Folk Hymns from Southern Harmony*. Concordia (97-5439). General and Christmas; unison voices. Easy.

———. *Seven Carols of Christmas*. Concordia (97-5720). Unison, opt. second part.

———. *Weihnachtszeit: Eight German Christmas Songs*. Concordia (97-5440). In English. Unison.

Thoren, Nancy. *Children's Carols for Improvisation*. Augsburg (11-9115). Seasonal carols. Unison, opt. second part.

Walker, David. *Christmas Spiritual Collection*. Concordia (97-5204). Four individual settings, plus a quodlibet. Orff plus other instruments.

Many single octavos are available, not only for Christmas but for other seasons as well. Concordia, Augsburg, and Magnamusic-Baton are among several publishers and suppliers of music for children's voices and Orff instrumentation designed for worship use.

Instrument Suppliers

Magnamusic-Baton, Inc. (STUDIO-49 Instrumentum)
Rhythm Band, Inc. (New Era instruments)
Suzuki Musical Instruments (Suzuki instruments)
Fortress Press (Sonor instruments)
Augsburg Publishing House (Sonor instruments)

Other brands can also be purchased. The above instruments have proven to be both durable and musically satisfying.

Handbell Resources

Booklets

These provide useful information on the rudiments of playing and the use of handbells in worship with children's voices.

Folkening, John. *Handbells in the Liturgical Service*. Concordia, 1984. Offers a variety of approaches for accompanying chanting and hymn singing.
Proulx, Richard. *Tintinnabulum*. G.I.A. Publications, 1980 (G-2358). The liturgical use of handbells with a commentary on performance and repertoire suggestions.
Thompson, Martha Lynn. *Bell, Book, and Ringer*. Harold Flammer, Inc., 1982. A manual for handbell ringers.

Hymn Accompaniments

Beck, Theodore. *12 Seasonal and Festival Hymns for Handbells and Organ*. Concordia (97-5312).
Bender, Jan. *Prelude, 10 Chorale Settings and Postlude for Unison Choir and Handbells*. Concordia (full score, 97-5387; handbell score, 97-5388; choir score, 98-2308).
———. *Prelude, 10 Christmas Chorales and Postlude for Unison Choir and Handbells*. Concordia (full score, 97-5401; handbell score, 97-5402; choir score, 98-2319). Contains Advent, Christmas, and Epiphany chorales.

Care must be exercised in selecting handbell arrangements because many that use the tune of the hymn are set in different keys from the hymnal in order to accommodate a better instrumental arrangement. Most of the above settings use the keys found in *Lutheran Worship* and the *Lutheran Book of Worship*. A number of the Hymns of the Day indicated in these hymnals are included in the above collections.

Representatives/Distributors of Handbells

Malmark, Inc. (Malmark Handbells/American)
Petit and Fritsen (Petit and Fritsen Handbells/Dutch)
Schulmerich Carillons, Inc. (Schulmerich Handbells/American)
Whitechapel (Whitechapel Handbells/English)

When you praise the Lord, exalt him as much as you can
for he will surpass even that. When you exalt him,
put forth all your strength, and do not grow weary,
for you cannot praise Him enough.

Ecclesiasticus 43:30

Appendix A

Sample Letters
to Parents

Written communication with parents strengthens the work of the choir and builds rapport between parents and choir director.

Notes highlighting vital facts and needs are usually the most effective for conveying messages to parents. Often these notes will serve to reinforce verbal messages shared with the choir members during rehearsals.

For the more adventurous choir director, a choir newsletter of one or two pages with announcements, humorous anecdotes, and promotional ideas can be an alternate form for communicating with both the children and the parents. Such a letter could be prepared for either monthly, bimonthly, or quarterly release. A choir parent or interested adult or teenager adept at writing could be the helping hand for this enterprise, thereby expanding the involvement and interest of others. An artistic touch, while optional, could provide the extra visual appeal that can gain the reader's attention and emphasize important messages. Personal interest stories related to the children in the choir might be included.

Other identifying hallmarks could be a specific symbol or visual, a choir letter title—for example, THE CHORISTERS NOTES—and/or a paper color other than white. Any or all of these could help accent the musical nature of the correspondence.

Any written communication benefits from neatness and a clarity of information. It is often desirable to include brief words of commendation to parents and children for their positive support, thereby sharing one's personal appreciation for the team effort.

Clear, written communication that is both informational and inspirational can strengthen the bond of ministry that is shared by the church and the triad of children, parents, and director.

The bond between the congregation and choir can also be aided by including brief articles in the church's weekly bulletin or newspaper. Photographs and articles featuring some aspect of the choir's ministry might be shared in an attractive display in the church's narthex or hallway. For very special events, seek to inform an even larger audience by means of an article or picture in the local newspaper.

Some directors have the children return some part of notes sent to the home, thereby ensuring that the information has reached the parents. If it is not overused, all who are involved benefit and feel more secure in their supporting colleagues.

The following samples will help to illustrate several of the above points.

A Motivational Letter to Choir Prospects

WHAT TEAM?—the team that takes a special trip every year (next year in May!)

WHAT TEAM?—the team that parties now and then to celebrate team spirit!

WHAT TEAM?—the team that takes on important work at (name of church or choir) and in other places to sing the good news of our Lord Jesus!

WHAT TEAM?—the team that will (describe a special future activity with a visual here)!

WHAT TEAM?—the team that has (describe an activity of interest that the choir has done in the recent past)!

CAROLING

WHAT TEAM?—THE TEAM THAT <u>NEEDS YOU</u> TO COMPLETE THE ROSTER!!
THE (name of choir in caps)—THE "VOCAL ATHLETES"

JOIN NOW! Don't miss the fun of the new season!

Please tear off and return immediately, so that we may plan for you.

....

YES—Count me in for the (name of choir) 198__/198__ season!

Name _____Grade _____ Phone _____

Address_____ZIP_____

Parent's Signature_____

Chorister's Signature_____

A Letter "Introducing" the New Choir Year

(date)

Dear Parents,

A new school year and a new choir season are here, and with them come new opportunities to help our children develop one of their most precious gifts—the singing voice. As parents we have a tremendous influence on our children, also on their decisions and what they tend to see as valuable and important. What we support, they are usually willing to pursue, and what we encourage and give priority to, they continue to be a part of— even when the luster at times temporarily wears thin.

For us at (name of church or school) the beginning of (name of choir) this fall brings extra excitement as we organize and anticipate these special events and activities: (name several to create interest).

As you would expect in any Christian choir, our foremost goal is to develop the children's singing voices in order that they can share a unique gift, something of their very own, in worship to the greater glory of God and to help proclaim His great love and Word to us through song. To assist them in doing this more nearly to their potential, we assure you and your child(ren) of our best effort as we seek to help them develop their singing voice more nearly to its potential.

Now is the time to "get started." The first rehearsal of the (name of choir) will be (give date, time, place, and concluding time). Thereafter regular weekly rehearsals will be on (day and time).

If you have any concerns or questions of any kind, please feel free to call me at (home and work phone numbers and times when you can be reached). We truly look forward to a <u>great</u> year of rewarding time, learning, and fulfillment. I hope your child(ren) will be part of this choir experience with us.

Cordially yours,

(director's name)

Children's Choir Commitment Pledge

PLEASE RETURN TO (choir director's name)

198__/8__

+ CHILDREN'S CHOIR COMMITMENT PLEDGE +

"Take my voice and let me sing
Always, only for my King;
Take my lips and let them be
Filled with messages from Thee."

We are pleased for the opportunity that

_____

(child's name)

has to participate in the (name of the choir) of (name of the church or school), for the 198__/8__ school year.

As God gives us strength, we will do our best to be dependable and cooperative and to be present for all appearances, unless emergencies or sickness make an absence necessary. In case of the latter, we will try to inform the director before the absence, if possible.

We recognize this commitment is for the duration of the current school year.

_____

(child's signature)

_____

(parent's signature)

He Who Sings Prays Twice

St. Augustine

"He Who Sings Prays Twice"   St. Augustine

A Letter Highlighting One Event

Note: Return of the attached form is requested from only those <u>unable</u> to participate.

(date)

To the Parents of Children's Choir Members:

We're off to a wonderful start this year, and another opportunity for service presents itself this coming (day) when the Children's Choir is scheduled to sing at the (time) service, (date).

If your child is <u>unable</u> to be present, please sign the attached form and return it to me by (day and date). It is important that I know how many to expect in order to arrange for seating and processional partners.

I would like to remind you that the children should be robed by (time). (An important factor like a time change in the fall or spring could be highlighted also.)

Thank you for your cooperation.

Sincerely yours,

Children's Choir Director

....

_____ is <u>not able</u>
to be present to sing with the choir on (day, month, date) at the (time) service.

_____
(Parent's signature)

"In choir everyone is on the first team."

A Schedule of Appearances for the Fall Season

Dear Parents,

This is the SCHEDULE OF APPEARANCES for the (name of choir) for the 1st semester—(first date through last date).

Sunday	September ____	(time) Service
Sunday	October ____	(time) Service
Sunday	November ____	(time) Service
Sunday	December ____	(time) Service
Sunday	January ____	(time) Service

At this time I would like to make you aware of (list a special rehearsal or deviation from the routine schedule times).

We request that your child be present 25 minutes before all services for rehearsing and robing. Cooperation on the part of everyone is necessary for our choir to sing at its optimum.

Your interest in and support of this activity of Christian ministry through music is sincerely appreciated. We hope the year will be rewarding for both you and your child(ren). Our continuing prayer is that God will richly bless our offerings of word and song.

In His Service,

Children's Choir
Director

(PLEASE RETAIN THIS SCHEDULE
FOR FAMILY PLANNING)

A Sample Letter Announcing and Inviting Choir Members and Parents to a Social Event

TO ALL (name of choir) AND FAMILIES:

COME TO OUR CHORISTER FAMILY POTLUCK—
(month, date, day) at (time) in (place).

FOR — FUN
          FELLOWSHIP and
      IMPORTANT DISCUSSION ABOUT PROJECTED PLANS

Bring your family

Bring a dish to feed 6—8 as follows:

> Last names A—H a SALAD
>
> Last names I—R a DESSERT
>
> Last names S—Z a HOT DISH

Beverage, rolls, plates, and silverware will be provided.
PLEASE R.S.V.P. by returning the slip below by (date).

(A choir rehearsal will precede the supper from _____
to _____ .)

. . . .

(name of choir) FAMILY POTLUCK

Please check and fill out appropriate response:

_____ YES, our family will attend. Number of people: _____

_____ SORRY, we cannot attend.

Chorister's Name: _____

Parent's Signature: _____

A Letter of Commendation

Dear Parents of our young choristers,

One of the ingredients of a successful choir year is the support you parents provide. With only a few exceptions, our children maintained a very fine attendance level, missing only when illness or emergencies necessitated. Faithfully fulfilling a commitment of this type has helped our choir more nearly reach its optimum in music development, and—also important—it has helped to teach the children responsibility, dedication, and character—qualities to be treasured.

Each year it becomes increasingly clear how much your support as parents contributes to the children's attitude toward their choir membership. I'm pleased to share with you that, with the exception of one child, all who started in September completed the year, many with 100% attendance!

For the priority you gave this activity in your family schedule in order to permit the strong attendance level, I personally thank you. With the complexity of family lives and the constant pressure to put spiritual and cultural things in a secondary position, you are to be commended for the generally high level of importance this received. Congratulations on your fine parenting.

All of us are indebted to (name choir parents who helped regularly) for the steady assistance they provided as choir parents each time the children sang. We could not function adequately without such dependable and capable help. To all of you who have been involved in our partnership, we thank you most sincerely. Guiding lives and voices in the high calling of praising their Lord has been a blessing to many.

Have a great summer with your child(ren) as you help them recognize God's blessings in their lives every day.

Cordially yours,

Children's Choir Director

A Letter to Parents of Baptized Children

This letter accompanies the recording "With Joyful Hearts and Voices" (additional information on page 123 of chapter 7), which is given to the family of a newly baptized infant.

LETTER FROM YOUR DIRECTOR OF MUSIC
TO: PARENTS OF BAPTIZED CHILDREN

Throughout the country our public schools are facing budget cuts. Likely targets seem to be programs in music and the arts, which many view as unessential "frills" in the educational process. BUT ARE THEY? I am becoming more and more convinced that the arts—which preceded the three Rs, after all, in mankind's civilization—are BASIC ingredients in an education that can be considered in any sense complete.

HYMNALS

Martin Luther—that great intellect who translated the entire Bible—placed music second only to theology in its importance to life.

What exposure to music and the arts does a "normal" environment give to your child? As you think of your own children's environment, whatever their ages, remember that psychologists are placing increasing emphasis on the preschool years—even stating that basic personality and attitudes are formed by age five!

Suzuki, the great Japanese music educator whose work inspired us to begin our preschool Choir School program, insists that <u>music education begins at birth.</u> This is the reason we are now placing our first record in your home after the baptism of your child. By the time you consider enrolling your three-year-old in Choir School these songs may have been a part of his (her) environment for nearly three years. Yes, Suzuki proved (read his fascinating book, <u>Nurtured by Love</u>, now in our church library) that even a baby of three months had learned to recognize not a nursery rhyme but a Vivaldi concerto her sister had worked on daily since the day the baby was born.

— 2 —

To be content in our homes with a "typical" musical environment that includes only the average TV fare, a few pop records, and a top-40 radio station is like feeding a child only candy from the day he is first introduced to it. Compare this environment with one that is filled with ALL kinds of music from the day the baby arrives—pop hits and TV, yes, but also symphony, opera, chamber music, art songs, <u>and the music of the church.</u> Infants are totally impartial in their musical taste. They don't even know that they are supposed to like nursery rhymes better than Bach cantatas! At a day care center with a wide variety of recorded music, the all-time favorite with those tiny children proved to be Beethoven's Fifth Symphony! The value of this environment may well surpass that of the music lessons offered later in their lives. More probably it will make them far more enthusiastic about those lessons than they could otherwise have been.

Another reason to play our Chorister records for your little child is that most children today have no <u>vocal models</u> to encourage them to use correctly the marvelous musical instrument God has given them—their voices! Hearing other children sing well may be the biggest help in teaching <u>them</u> to sing. No child is naturally a "nonsinger." But the earlier they have this exposure, the better!

In summary, then—how can you as parents use music and the arts to provide a richer life for your child? Here are just a few suggestions:

1. Put the sound of good music into your home through fine recordings of all kinds. For older children mealtime might be a time when <u>you</u> can choose the music—at least for some meals. (Later on <u>they</u> will be choosing what you would hope they'd choose—if you've caught them soon enough!) The child will gradually learn to understand the language of this music in the same way he/she learned to understand English—by repeated listening. <u>Repeat the same recording often at first.</u>

— 3 —

2. As your child grows older, let some of your family activities and outings be to concerts, museums, drama, etc. The seeds sown earlier at home will make this exciting and enriching for your children. If you—like me—grew up with no great appreciation for the visual arts, it will be exciting to grow WITH your children in that area.

3. Through our chorister records let your infants and toddlers be steeped in the sounds of Christian song used in Sunday worship. Then the worship hour is no longer so foreign; at least the music will be in a "familiar language."

4. In addition to our Chorister records, get some other fine records of the best children's choirs—European boy choirs are often fine examples, especially for boys who in our American culture sometimes get the strange notion that they can't sing "as well as girls." (Nonsense!)

Baptism is the beginning of your child's intimate relationship with God and with the church. Use the music of the church to help your child grow in faith—even from infancy!

Yours in Christ,

Ronald A. Nelson
Director of Music

P.S. <u>Your Children Need Music</u> by Marvin Greenberg, now in our church library, has a wealth of ideas—ways to stimulate interest in and <u>talent for</u> music in infants. That chapter is a <u>must</u> reading for all new parents. Don't miss it. Your child will never again be as receptive as right now!

Appendix B

Indexes from
Lutheran Worship

Index to the Three-Year Lectionary

* alternates

Ps. 27:1-6 (7-14) .... 4 Lent B
Ps. 27:1-9 .... 3 Epiphany A
                  18 Pentecost A
Ps. 28 .... 3 Pentecost B
                  12 Pentecost A
Ps. 28:1-2, 6-9 .... 3 Easter C
Ps. 28:1-3, 6-9 .... 5 Lent C
Ps. 32 .... 6 Epiphany B
                  4 Lent C
                  4 Pentecost C
Ps. 34 .... 23 Pentecost C
Ps. 34:1-8 .... 12 Pentecost B
Ps. 34:1-10 .... All Saints' Day A, B, C
Ps. 34:9-14 .... 13 Pentecost B
Ps. 34:15-22 .... 14 Pentecost B
Ps. 36 .... 4 Epiphany C
Ps. 36:5-10 .... 2 Epiphany C
                  Monday, Holy Week A, B, C
                  St. Philip and St. James A, B, C
Ps. 45 .... Annunciation of Our Lord A, B, C
Ps. 45:7-9 .... 1 Epiphany A, B, C
Ps. 45:10-15 .... St. Mary, Mother of Our Lord A, B, C
Ps. 46 .... Reformation Day A, B, C
Ps. 50 .... 12 Pentecost C
Ps. 50:1-6 .... Transfiguration B
Ps. 50:1-15 .... 1 Advent A
Ps. 51:1-13 .... Ash Wednesday A, B, C,
Ps. 51:1-17 .... 17 Pentecost C
Ps. 51:10-15 .... 5 Lent B
Ps. 62 .... 8 Epiphany A
                  20 Pentecost C
Ps. 62:5-12 .... 3 Epiphany B
Ps. 65 .... 8 Pentecost A
                  Harvest Festival A, B, C
                  Day of Special or National Thanksgiving A, B, C
Ps. 67 .... 2 Epiphany B
                  6 Easter C
                  13 Pentecost A
                  Conversion of St. Paul A, B, C
Ps. 72 .... Epiphany A, B, C
Ps. 72:1-14 (15-19) .... 2 Advent A
Ps. 73:23-28 .... St. Mary Magdalene A, B, C
Ps. 77 .... Transfiguration C
Ps. 84 .... St. Timothy and St. Titus A, B, C
                  Presentation of Our Lord A, B, C
                  Dedication of a Church and Anniversary of a Congregation A, B, C
Ps. 84:1-7 .... 24 Pentecost A
Ps. 90:1-12 .... Third-Last Sunday A
Ps. 90:13-17 .... 25 Pentecost A
Ps. 91 .... 1 Lent C
                  5 Pentecost A
Ps. 91:9-16 .... 22 Pentecost B
Ps. 92 .... 8 Epiphany C
                  Palm Sunday A, B, C
Ps. 92:1-5 .... 2 Epiphany A
Ps. 92:1-5 (6-11) 12-15 .... 4 Pentecost B
Ps. 92:1-8 .... Second-Last Sunday C
Ps. 96 .... 4 Advent C
                  Christmas Eve A, B, C

                  Holy Trinity B
                  22 Pentecost A
                  Mission Festival A, B, C
Ps. 98 .... 1 Advent B
                  4 Advent B
                  Christmas Day A, B, C
                  6 Easter A, B
                  Pentecost Eve A, B, C
                  Third-Last Sunday C
Ps. 98:1-5 .... Holy Cross Day A, B, C
Ps. 100 .... 2 Easter C
                  4 Pentecost A
                  11 Pentecost C
                  Last Sunday A*
Ps. 103:1-13 .... 7 Epiphany A, C
                  8 Epiphany B
                  17 Pentecost A
Ps. 103:1-5, 20-22 .... St. Michael and All Angels A, B, C
Ps. 103:19-22 .... St. James the Elder A, B, C
Ps. 105:1-7 .... 2 Easter A
                  Second-Last Sunday A
Ps. 105:4-11 .... 2 Lent A
Ps. 107:1-3, 23-32 .... 5 Pentecost B
Ps. 107:1-3, 33-43 .... 25 Pentecost B
Ps. 110 .... 5 Easter C
                  Ascension A, B, C
Ps. 111 .... 1 Christmas A, B, C
                  21 Pentecost C
                  Second-Last Sunday B
Ps. 116:1-9 .... 5 Lent A
                  3 Pentecost C
                  17 Pentecost B
Ps. 116:12-19 .... Maundy Thursday A, B, C
                  St. John A, B, C
Ps. 117 .... 2 Pentecost C
                  14 Pentecost C
Ps. 118:1-2, 15-24 .... Resurrection A, B, C
Ps. 118:14-24 .... Resurrection C*
Ps. 118:19-24 .... 20 Pentecost A
Ps. 119:1-16 .... 6 Epiphany A
Ps. 119:17-24 .... 5 Epiphany A
Ps. 119:25-32 .... 18 Pentecost B
Ps. 119:33-40 .... 18 Pentecost C
                  St. Matthew A, B, C
Ps. 119:41-48 .... 5 Pentecost C
Ps. 119:49-56 .... 20 Pentecost B
Ps. 119:57-64 .... 9 Pentecost A
Ps. 119:65-72 .... 3 Pentecost A
Ps. 119:73-80 .... 21 Pentecost B
                  St. Simon and St. Jude A, B, C
Ps. 119:81-88 .... 13 Pentecost C
                  St. Laurence A, B, C
Ps. 119:89-104 .... 11 Pentecost B
Ps. 119:105-112 .... 15 Pentecost A
Ps. 119:113-120 .... 16 Pentecost A
Ps. 119:121-128 .... 24 Pentecost B
Ps. 119:129-136 .... 10 Pentecost A
                  15 Pentecost B
Ps. 119:137-144 .... 7 Pentecost A
                  St. Stephen A, B, C
Ps. 119:145-152 .... 24 Pentecost C
Ps. 119:153-160 .... 6 Pentecost A
Ps. 119:161-168 .... 15 Pentecost C
Ps. 119:169-176 .... 16 Pentecost C
Ps. 121 .... 6 Pentecost B
                  22 Pentecost C
                  St. Bartholomew A, B, C
Ps. 126 .... 2 Advent C

Mark 10:2-16 . . . . .20 Pentecost B
Mark 10:17-27 (28-30) . . . . .21 Pentecost B
Mark 10:35-45 . . . . .22 Pentecost B
                                 St. James the Elder A, B, C
Mark 10:46-52 . . . . .23 Pentecost B
Mark 11:1-10 . . . . .1 Advent B*
Mark 12:28-34 (35-37) . . . .24 Pentecost B
Mark 12:41-44 . . . . .25 Pentecost B
Mark 13:1-13 . . . . .Third-Last Sunday B
Mark 13:24-31 . . . . .Second-Last Sunday B
Mark 13:32-37 . . . . .Last Sunday B
Mark 13:33-37 . . . . .1 Advent B
Mark 14:1—15:47 . . . . . . .Palm Sunday B
Mark 14:12-26 . . . . .Maundy Thursday B
Mark 15:1-39 . . . . .Palm Sunday B*
Mark 16:1-8 . . . . .Resurrection B
Luke 1:1-4; 24:44-53 . . . . . .St. Luke A, B, C
Luke 1:25-38 . . . . .Annunciation of Our Lord
                                 A, B, C
Luke 1:26-38 . . . . .4 Advent B
Luke 1:39-45 (46-55) . . . . . .4 Advent C
Luke 1:39-47 . . . . .Visitation A, B, C
Luke 1:46-55 . . . . .St. Mary, Mother of Our
                                 Lord A, B, C
Luke 1:46b-55 . . . . .3 Advent B
Luke 1:57-67 (68-80) . . . . . .Nativity of St. John the
                                 Baptist A, B, C
Luke 2:1-20 . . . . .Christmas Eve A, B, C
                                 Christmas Day A, B, C
Luke 2:21 . . . . .New Year's Day A, B, C
Luke 2:22-40 . . . . .Presentation of Our Lord
                                 A, B, C
Luke 2:25-40 . . . . .1 Christmas B
Luke 2:41-52 . . . . .1 Christmas C
Luke 3:1-6 . . . . .2 Advent C
Luke 3:7-18 . . . . .3 Advent C
Luke 3:15-17, 21-22 . . . . . .1 Epiphany C
Luke 4:1-13 . . . . .1 Lent C
Luke 4:14-21 . . . . .3 Epiphany C
Luke 4:21-32 . . . . .4 Epiphany C
Luke 5:1-11 . . . . .5 Epiphany C
Luke 6:12-16 . . . . .St. Matthias A, B, C
Luke 6:17-26 . . . . .6 Epiphany C
Luke 6:27-38 . . . . .7 Epiphany C
Luke 6:39-49 . . . . .8 Epiphany C
Luke 7:1-10 . . . . .2 Pentecost C
Luke 7:11-17 . . . . .3 Pentecost C
Luke 7:36-50 . . . . .4 Pentecost C
Luke 9:18-24 . . . . .5 Pentecost C
Luke 9:28-36 . . . . .Transfiguration C
Luke 9:51-62 . . . . .6 Pentecost C
Luke 10:1-12, 16 (17-20) . . .7 Pentecost C
Luke 10:17-20 . . . . .St. Michael and All Angels
                                 A, B, C
Luke 10:25-37 . . . . .8 Pentecost C
Luke 10:38-42 . . . . .9 Pentecost C
Luke 11:1-13 . . . . .10 Pentecost C
Luke 12:13-21 . . . . .11 Pentecost C
Luke 12:32-40 . . . . .12 Pentecost C
Luke 12:42-48 . . . . .Last Sunday C
Luke 12:49-53 . . . . .13 Pentecost C
Luke 13:1-9 . . . . .3 Lent C
Luke 13:22-30 . . . . .14 Pentecost C
Luke 13:31-35 . . . . .2 Lent C
Luke 14:1, 7-14 . . . . .15 Pentecost C
Luke 14:25-33 . . . . .16 Pentecost C
Luke 15:1-3, 11-32 . . . . . . .4 Lent C
Luke 15:1-10 . . . . .17 Pentecost C
Luke 15:11-32 . . . . .Day of Supplication and
                                 Prayer A, B, C

Luke 16:1-13 . . . . .18 Pentecost C
Luke 16:19-31 . . . . .19 Pentecost C
Luke 17:1-10 . . . . .20 Pentecost C
Luke 17:11-19 . . . . .21 Pentecost C
                                 Day of Special or National
                                 Thanksgiving A, B, C
Luke 17:20-30 . . . . .Third-Last Sunday C
Luke 18:1-8a . . . . .22 Pentecost C
Luke 18:9-14 . . . . .23 Pentecost C
Luke 19:1-10 . . . . .24 Pentecost C
Luke 19:11-27 . . . . .Second-Last Sunday C
Luke 19:28-40 . . . . .1 Advent C*
Luke 20:9-19 . . . . .5 Lent C
Luke 20:27-38 . . . . .25 Pentecost C
Luke 21:5-19 . . . . .Third-Last Sunday C*
Luke 21:10-19 . . . . .Conversion of St. Paul A,
                                 B, C
Luke 21:25-36 . . . . .1 Advent C
Luke 22:1—23:56 . . . . . . .Palm Sunday C
Luke 22:7-10 . . . . .Maundy Thursday C
Luke 23:1-49 . . . . .Palm Sunday C*
Luke 23:35-43 . . . . .Last Sunday C*
Luke 24:1-11 . . . . .Resurrection C
Luke 24:13-35 . . . . .3 Easter A
Luke 24:13-49 . . . . .Easter Evening A, B, C
Luke 24:36-49 . . . . .3 Easter B
Luke 24:44-54 . . . . .Ascension A, B, C
                                 Mission Festival A, B, C
John 1:1-14 . . . . .Christmas Dawn A, B, C
John 1:1-18 . . . . .2 Christmas A, B, C
John 1:6-8, 19-28 . . . . .3 Advent B
John 1:29-41 . . . . .2 Epiphany A
John 1:35-42 . . . . .St. Andrew A, B, C
John 1:43-51 . . . . .2 Epiphany B
                                 St. Bartholomew A, B, C
John 2:1-11 . . . . .2 Epiphany C
John 2:13-22 . . . . .3 Lent B
John 3:1-17 . . . . .Holy Trinity B
John 3:14-21 . . . . .4 Lent B
John 4:5-26
   (27-30, 39-42) . . . . .2 Lent A
John 6:1-15 . . . . .10 Pentecost B
John 6:24-35 . . . . .11 Pentecost B
John 6:41-51 . . . . .12 Pentecost B
John 6:51-58 . . . . .13 Pentecost B
John 6:60-69 . . . . .14 Pentecost B
John 7:37-39a . . . . .Pentecost Eve A, B, C
                                 Pentecost B
John 8:31-36 . . . . .Reformation Day A, B, C
John 9:1-41 . . . . .3 Lent A
John 9:13-17, 34-39 . . . . . . .3 Lent A*
John 10:1-10 . . . . .4 Easter A
John 10:11-18 . . . . .4 Easter B
John 10:22-30 . . . . .4 Easter C
                                 Dedication of a Church and
                                 Anniversary of a
                                 Congregation A, B, C
John 11:1-53 . . . . .5 Lent A
John 11:47-53 . . . . .5 Lent A*
John 12:1-11 . . . . .Monday, Holy Week A,
                                 B, C
John 12:20-33 . . . . .5 Lent B
                                 Holy Cross Day A, B, C
John 12:20-36 . . . . .Tuesday, Holy Week A,
                                 B, C
John 13:1-17, 34 . . . . .Maundy Thursday A
John 13:31-35 . . . . .5 Easter C
John 14:1-7 . . . . .St. Thomas A, B, C
John 14:1-12 . . . . .5 Easter A

1 Cor. 15:54-58 ....Second-Last Sunday C*
2 Cor. 1:18-22 ....7 Epiphany B
2 Cor. 3:1b-6 ....8 Epiphany B
2 Cor. 3:12—4:2 ....Transfiguration B
2 Cor. 4:1-6 ....St. Philip and St. James A, B, C
2 Cor. 4:3-6 ....Transfiguration C
2 Cor. 4:5-12 ....2 Pentecost B
2 Cor. 4:13-18 ....3 Pentecost B
2 Cor. 5:1-10 ....4 Pentecost B
                            Second-Last Sunday C
2 Cor. 5:14-21 ....5 Pentecost B
2 Cor. 5:20b—6:2 ....Ash Wednesday A, B, C
2 Cor. 8:1-9, 13-14 .....6 Pentecost B
2 Cor. 9:6-15 ....Harvest Festival A, B, C
2 Cor. 12:7-10 ....7 Pentecost B
2 Cor. 13:11-14 ....Holy Trinity A
Gal. 1:1-10 ....2 Pentecost C
Gal. 1:11-24 ....3 Pentecost C
                            Conversion of St. Paul A, B, C
Gal. 2:11-21 ....4 Pentecost C
Gal. 3:23-29 ....5 Pentecost C
Gal. 4:4-7 ....1 Christmas A
                            St. Mary, Mother of Our Lord A, B, C
Gal. 5:1, 13-25 ....6 Pentecost C
Gal. 6:1-10, 14-16 .....7 Pentecost C
Eph. 1:3-6, 15-18 ......2 Christmas A, B, C
Eph. 1:3-14 ....8 Pentecost B
Eph. 1:16-23 ....Ascension A, B, C
Eph. 2:4-10 ....4 Lent B
                            St. Matthew A, B, C
Eph. 2:13-22 ....9 Pentecost B
Eph. 3:2-12 ....Epiphany A, B, C
Eph. 3:14-21 ....St. Timothy and St. Titus A, B, C*
Eph. 4:1-7, 11-16 ......10 Pentecost B
Eph. 4:11-16 ....St. Thomas A, B, C
Eph. 4:17-24 ....11 Pentecost B
Eph. 4:30—5:2 ....12 Pentecost B
Eph. 5:8-14 ....3 Lent A
Eph. 5:15-20 ....13 Pentecost B
Eph. 5:21-31 ....14 Pentecost B
Eph. 6:10-20 ....15 Pentecost B
Phil. 1:1-5 (6-11), 19-27 ...18 Pentecost A
Phil. 1:3-11 ....2 Advent C
Phil. 2:1-5 (6-11) .....19 Pentecost A
Phil. 2:5-11 ....Palm Sunday A, B, C
Phil. 2:9-13 ....New Year's Day A, B, C*
Phil. 3:8-14 ....5 Lent C
Phil. 3:12-21 ....20 Pentecost A
Phil. 3:17—4:1 ....2 Lent C
Phil. 4:4-7 (8-9) ......3 Advent C
Phil. 4:4-13 ....21 Pentecost A
Phil. 4:6-20 ....Day of Special or National Thanksgiving A, B, C
Col. 1:1-14 ....8 Pentecost C
Col. 1:13-20 ....Last Sunday C*
Col. 1:21-28 ....9 Pentecost C
Col. 2:6-15 ....10 Pentecost C
Col. 3:1-4 ....Resurrection A
Col. 3:1-11 ....11 Pentecost C
Col. 3:12-17 ....1 Christmas B
1 Thess. 1:1-5a ....22 Pentecost A
1 Thess. 1:3-10 ....Second-Last Sunday A
1 Thess. 1:5b-10 ....23 Pentecost A
1 Thess. 2:8-13 ....Third-Last Sunday A*
1 Thess. 3:7-13 ....Second-Last Sunday A*
1 Thess. 3:9-13 ....1 Advent C

1 Thess. 3:11-13 ....Third-Last Sunday A
1 Thess. 4:13-14 (15-18) ...24 Pentecost A
1 Thess. 5:1-11 ....25 Pentecost A
1 Thess. 5:16-24 ....3 Advent B
2 Thess. 1:1-5, 11-12 .....24 Pentecost C
2 Thess. 2:13—3:5 ....25 Pentecost C
2 Thess. 3:1-5 ....Third-Last Sunday C
2 Thess. 3:6-13 ....Third-Last Sunday C*
1 Tim. 1:12-17 ....17 Pentecost C
1 Tim. 2:1-4 ....Day of Special or National Thanksgiving A, B, C*
1 Tim. 2:1-8 ....18 Pentecost C
1 Tim. 3:16 ....The Annunciation of Our Lord A, B, C
1 Tim. 6:6-16 ....19 Pentecost C
2 Tim. 1:3-14 ....20 Pentecost C
2 Tim. 2:8-13 ....21 Pentecost C
2 Tim. 3:14—4:5 ....22 Pentecost C
2 Tim. 4:5-11 ....St. Luke A, B, C
2 Tim. 4:6-8, 16-18 ....23 Pentecost C
2 Tim. 4:6-11, 18 ......St. Mark A, B, C
Titus 2:11-14 ....Christmas Eve A, B, C
Titus 3:4-7 ....Christmas Day A, B, C
Philemon 1 (2-9) 10-21 ....16 Pentecost C
Heb. 1:1-9 ....Christmas Dawn A, B, C
Heb. 2:9-11 (12-18) ....20 Pentecost B
Heb. 2:10-18 ....1 Christmas C
Heb. 2:14-18 ....Presentation of Our Lord A, B, C
Heb. 3:1-6 ....21 Pentecost B
Heb. 4:9-16 ....22 Pentecost B
Heb. 4:14-16; 5:7-9 ....Good Friday A, B, C
Heb. 5:1-10 ....23 Pentecost B
Heb. 5:7-9 ....5 Lent B
Heb. 7:23-28 ....24 Pentecost B
Heb. 9:11-15 ....Monday, Holy Week A, B, C
Heb. 9:24-28 ....25 Pentecost B
Heb. 10:5-10 ....4 Advent C
Heb. 10:11-18 ....Third-Last Sunday B*
Heb. 10:15-39 ....Maundy Thursday C
Heb. 11:1-3, 8-16 ......12 Pentecost C
Heb. 12:1-2 ....Second-Last Sunday B
Heb. 12:1-13 ....13 Pentecost C
Heb. 12:18-24 ....14 Pentecost C
Heb. 12:26-29 ....Third-Last Sunday B
Heb. 13:1-8 ....15 Pentecost C
Heb. 13:20-21 ....Second-Last Sunday B*
James 1:17-22 (23-25) 26-27 ....16 Pentecost B
James 2:1-5, 8-10, 14-18 ...17 Pentecost B
James 3:16—4:6 ....18 Pentecost B
James 4:7-12 (13—5:6) ....19 Pentecost B
James 5:7-10 ....3 Advent A
1 Peter 1:3-9 ....2 Easter A
1 Peter 1:17-21 ....3 Easter A
1 Peter 2:1-9 ....Dedication of a Church and Anniversary of a Congregation A, B, C
1 Peter 2:4-10 ....5 Easter A
1 Peter 2:19-25 ....4 Easter A
1 Peter 3:15-22 ....6 Easter A
1 Peter 4:12-17; 5:6-11 ...7 Easter A
1 Peter 4:12-19 ....Holy Innocents A, B, C
1 Peter 5:1-4 ....St. Timothy and St. Titus A, B, C
2 Peter 1:16-19 (20-21) ....Transfiguration A
2 Peter 3:3-4, 8-10a, 13 ....Last Sunday A
2 Peter 3:8-14 ....2 Advent B

1 John 1:1—2:2 . . . . 3 Easter B
                 St. John A, B, C
1 John 1:5—2:2 . . . . Day of Supplication and
                 Prayer A, B, C
1 John 3:1-2 . . . . 4 Easter B
1 John 3:18-24 . . . . 5 Easter B
1 John 4:1-6 . . . . St. Simon and St. Jude A,
                 B, C
1 John 4:1-11 . . . . 6 Easter B
1 John 4:13-21 . . . . 7 Easter B
1 John 5:1-6 . . . . 2 Easter B
Jude 20-25 . . . . Last Sunday B

Rev. 1:4-18 . . . . 2 Easter C
Rev. 1:4b-8 . . . . Last Sunday B*
Rev. 5:11-14 . . . . 3 Easter C
Rev. 6:9-11 . . . . St. Laurence A, B, C
Rev. 7:9-17 . . . . 4 Easter C
Rev. 12:7-12 . . . . St. Michael and All Angels
                 A, B, C
Rev. 21:1-5 . . . . 5 Easter C
Rev. 21:9-11, 22-27
  (22:1-5) . . . . All Saints' Day A, B, C
Rev. 21:10-14, 22-23 . . . . . . 6 Easter C
Rev. 22:6-13 . . . . Last Sunday C
Rev. 22:12-17, 20 . . . . 7 Easter C

Psalm Index

Ps. 1 . . . . 4 Epiphany (AB)**
         6 Epiphany (C)
         7 Epiphany
         9 Pentecost
         23 Pentecost (A)
Ps. 2 . . . . Christmas Dawn (ABC)
         Transfiguration (A)
         25 Pentecost
Ps. 4 . . . . 2 Lent (C)
         2 Pentecost (A)
         16 Pentecost
Ps. 6 . . . . 1 Lent (B)
         Day of Supplication and
         Prayer (ABC)
Ps. 8 . . . . Holy Innocents
         Holy Innocents (ABC)
         New Year's Eve
         New Year's Day (ABC)
         Easter Evening
         7 Easter
         Holy Trinity (C)
Ps. 16 . . . . St. Matthias
         2 Easter
         3 Easter (A)
         6 Pentecost (C)
         St. James the Elder
         Third-Last Sunday (B)
Ps. 18 . . . . Confession of St. Peter (ABC)
         3 Epiphany
         Tuesday, Holy Week (ABC)
         Wednesday, Holy Week (ABC)
         St. Peter and St. Paul (ABC)
Ps. 19 . . . . St. Andrew (ABC)
         2 Advent (B)
         4 Advent
         3 Lent (B)

         7 Pentecost (C)
Ps. 22 . . . . Good Friday
         Good Friday (ABC)
         3 Easter
         5 Easter (B)
Ps. 23 . . . . Confession of St. Peter
         4 Easter
         4 Easter (ABC)
         9 Pentecost (B)
         21 Pentecost (A)
Ps. 24 . . . . 4 Advent (A)
         Palm Sunday
Ps. 25 . . . . 1 Advent
         1 Advent (C)
         Wednesday, Holy Week
         St. Philip and St. James
         8 Pentecost (C)
         19 Pentecost (A)
Ps. 27 . . . . 3 Epiphany (A)
         2 Lent
         4 Lent (B)
         9 Pentecost (C)
         18 Pentecost (A)
Ps. 28 . . . . 5 Lent (C)
         Tuesday, Holy Week
         3 Easter (C)
         3 Pentecost (B)
         12 Pentecost (A)
Ps. 32 . . . . 6 Epiphany (B)
         4 Lent (C)
         4 Pentecost (C)
         20 Pentecost
Ps. 34 . . . . 8 Epiphany
         St. Mary, Mother of Our Lord
         12 Pentecost (B)
         13 Pentecost (B)
         14 Pentecost (B)
         21 Pentecost
         All Saints' Day (ABC)
         Commemoration of Faithful Departed
         23 Pentecost (C)

  * *Alternates*
  ** *The letters A, B, and C are references to the Three-Year Lectionary Series. Other entries refer to the One-Year Series.*

Metrical Paraphrases of Psalms

For hymns which relate to specific psalm verses, see Scripture References in Hymns and Spiritual Songs.

Scripture References in Hymns and Spiritual Songs

Appendix C

Indexes from *Lutheran Book of Worship*

Index to the Three-Year Lectionary

*alternates

Psalm Index

*alternates
**The letters A, B, and C are references to lectionary series.

Hymn Paraphrases of Psalms

Scripture References in Hymns

Appendix D

Hymn of the Day
Lists

Hymn of the Day
(from *Lutheran Worship*)

1 Advent
Savior of the nations, come 13

2 Advent
Lo, he comes with clouds descending* 15
On Jordan's bank the Baptist's cry.............. 14

3 Advent
O people, rise and labor 25

4 Advent
Oh, come, oh, come, Emmanuel 31

Nativity, Christmas Eve
From heaven above to earth I come 37, 38
or Once again my heart rejoices 39

Nativity, Christmas Dawn
We praise, O Christ, your holy name............. 35
or Of the Father's love begotten 36

Nativity, Christmas Day
We praise, O Christ, your holy name............. 35
or Of the Father's love begotten 36

1 Christmas
Let all together praise our God 44
or In peace and joy I now depart (BC) 185

New Year's Eve, Name of Jesus
O Savior of our fallen race 45

New Year's Day, Circumcision of our Lord
Greet now the swiftly changing year 183

2 Christmas
From east to west, from shore to shore 43

Epiphany
O Morning Star, how fair and bright 73

1 Epiphany, Baptism of our Lord
To Jordan came the Christ, our Lord 223

2 Epiphany
The only Son from heaven* (AB) 72
Jesus, priceless treasure (C)................... 270

3 Epiphany
Salvation unto us has come* 355
"Come, follow me," said Christ, the Lord (AB) 379
O Christ, our light, O Radiance true (C) 314

4 Epiphany
May God embrace us with his grace* 288
Seek where you may to find a way.............. 358

5 Epiphany
O Christ, our light, O Radiance true* 314
Thy strong word did cleave the darkness (A) 328
Hail to the Lord's anointed (BC) 82

6 Epiphany
Seek where you may to find a way* 358
O Christ, our hope, our hearts' desire 151

7 Epiphany
Lord Jesus Christ, will you not stay* 344
My soul, now praise your Maker (AC) 453

O God, O Lord of heaven and earth (B) 319

8 Epiphany
"Take up your cross," the Savior said* 382
Sing praise to God, the highest good 452

Transfiguration
Oh, wondrous type! Oh, vision fair 87

Ash Wednesday
From depths of woe I cry to you 230

1 Lent
A mighty fortress is our God 297, 298
or Triune God, oh, be our stay................... 170
(Substitute "Lord, have mercy" for "alleluia")

2 Lent
God loved the world so that he gave* 352
Lord, you I love with all my heart 413

3 Lent
Let us ever walk with Jesus* 381
May God embrace us with his grace 288

4 Lent
Jesus, priceless treasure* 270
I trust, O Christ, in you alone (AC) 357
God loved the world so that he gave (B) 352

5 Lent
My song is love unknown 91

Palm Sunday, Sunday of the Passion
Ride on, ride on in majesty.................... 105
or The royal banners forward go 103, 104

Maundy Thursday
Jesus Christ, our blessed Savior 236, 237
or O Lord, we praise you, bless you, and adore
you 238

Good Friday
A lamb alone bears willingly.................... 111
or Sing, my tongue, the glorious battle 117

Resurrection, Easter Eve
Christ is arisen 124

Resurrection, Easter Day
Christ Jesus lay in death's strong bands 123

Resurrection, Easter Evening
Good Christian friends, rejoice and sing 129

2 Easter
O sons and daughters of the King 130

3 Easter
The King of love my shepherd is* 412
With high delight let us unite 134

4 Easter
At the Lamb's high feast we sing* 126
The King of love my shepherd is 412

5 Easter
Dear Christians, one and all, rejoice* 353
(Complete, or sts. 1 and 5-10)
At the Lamb's high feast we sing 126

6 Easter
Our Father, who from heaven above* 430, 431
Dear Christians, one and all, rejoice 353
(Complete, or sts. 1 and 5-10)

---

* In instances where the selected hymn(s) varies for the two lectionaries, the asterisk (*) marks the hymn(s) appropriate to the one-year series. The letters A, B, and C are references to the three-year series.

27 Pentecost or Second Last Sunday
The day is surely drawing near* (AB) 462
Forth in your name, O Lord, I go (C) 380

Last Sunday, Sunday of the Fulfillment
Wake, awake, for night is flying 177

St. Michael and All Angels
Lord God, to you we all give praise 189
or Stars of the morning, so gloriously bright 190

Reformation Day
Salvation unto us has come 355

All Saints' Day
For all the saints who from their labors rest 191

Special or National Thanksgiving
Now thank we all our God 443
or I will sing my Maker's praises 439

Hymns for the Church Year
(from *Lutheran Book of Worship*)

1 Advent
Savior of the nations, come* 28
Fling wide the door, unbar the gate (ABC)** 32
Wake, awake, for night is flying 31

2 Advent
Comfort, comfort now my people 29
On Jordan's banks the Baptist's cry* (ABC) 36
Prepare the royal highway 26

3 Advent
The only Son from heaven 86
Hark! A thrilling voice is sounding!* (ABC) 37
Hark, the glad sound! The Savior comes 35

4 Advent
Savior of the nations, come 28
Oh, come, oh, come, Emmanuel* (ABC) 34
Come, thou long-expected Jesus 30

Christmas
Once again my heart rejoices 46
From heav'n above to earth I come* (ABC, Luke 2) 51
Of the Father's love begotten* (ABC, John 1) 42
All praise to you, eternal Lord 48

1 Christmas
Let all together praise our God* 47
All praise to you, eternal Lord (AB) 48
In a lowly manger born (C) 417
The only Son from heaven 86

2 Christmas
Of the Father's love begotten* 42
Let all together praise our God (ABC) 47
Let all mortal flesh keep silence 198

Epiphany
Brightest and best of the stars of the morning 84
O Morning Star, how fair and bright!* (ABC) 76
Bright and glorious is the sky 75

Baptism of Our Lord
From God the Father, virgin-born 83
To Jordan came the Christ, our Lord* (ABC) 79
When Christ's appearing was made known 85

2 Epiphany
The only Son from heaven* 86
Jesus calls us; o'er the tumult (AB) 494
All praise to you, O Lord (C) 78
Jesus, priceless treasure* 457, 458

3 Epiphany
O God of light, your Word, a lamp unfailing 237
"Come, follow me," the Savior spake (AB) 455
Hail to the Lord's anointed (C) 87
O Christ, our light, O Radiance true* 380

4 Epiphany
Hope of the world, thou Christ of great compassion* 493
Son of God, eternal Savior (A) 364
Dear Christians, one and all, rejoice (B) 299
God of grace and God of glory (C) 415
Songs of thankfulness and praise 90

5 Epiphany
Hail to the Lord's anointed* 87
May we your precepts, Lord, fulfill (A) 353
O Christ, the healer, we have come (B) 360
Lord, speak to us, that we may speak (C) 403
Your Word, O Lord, is gentle dew 232

6 Epiphany
O Christ, our hope, our heart's desire* 300
Lord Jesus, think on me (A) 309
O Jesus Christ, may grateful hymns be rising (BC) 427
Oh, that the Lord would guide my ways 480

---

* *Hymns which constitute a contemporary adaptation of the traditional Lutheran de tempore series.*
** *The letters A, B, and C are references to lectionary series.*

7 Epiphany
Oh, love, how deep, how broad, how high. 88
O God, O Lord of heav'n and earth* (ABC) 396
Lord, keep us steadfast in your Word. 230

8 Epiphany
Sing praise to God, the highest good* 542
Jesus, priceless treasure (A). 457, 458
Salvation unto us has come (B) .297
O God of mercy, God of might (C) 425
As with gladness men of old. 82

Transfiguration
How good, Lord, to be here! 89
Oh, wondrous type! Oh, vision fair* (ABC). 80
O God of God, O Light of light .536

Ash Wednesday
O Lord, throughout these forty days. 99
Out of the depths I cry to you* (ABC). 295
Savior, when in dust to you 91

1 Lent
God the Father, be our stay* 308
Who trusts in God, a strong abode (ABC). 450
A mighty fortress is our God* 228, 229

2 Lent
Lord, thee I love with all my heart* 325
O Jesus, joy of loving hearts (A) .356
"Take up your cross," the Savior said (B) 398
O Jesus Christ, may grateful hymns be rising (C). 427
Jesus, refuge of the weary 93

3 Lent
May God bestow on us his grace* 335
God, whose almighty word (A) .400
O God of earth and altar (B) 428
Jesus, the very thought of you (C). 316
In the cross of Christ I glory. 104

4 Lent
I trust, O Christ, in you alone* 395
Lord of glory, you have bought us (A). 424
God loved the world so that he gave* (B) 292
In Adam we have all been one (C) 372
On my heart imprint your image. 102

5 Lent
My song is love unknown* 94
Glory be to Jesus (ABC). 95
Christ, the life of all the living. 97

Sunday of the Passion
The royal banners forward go. 124, 125
A lamb goes uncomplaining forth* (ABC). 105
O sacred head, now wounded. 116, 117

Monday in Holy Week
Beneath the cross of Jesus. 107

Tuesday in Holy Week
O Christ, our king, creator, Lord 101

Wednesday in Holy Week
It happened on that fateful night. 127

Maundy Thursday
We who once were dead 207
Love consecrates the humblest act (A) 122
O Lord, we praise you, bless you, and adore you* (BC). . . .215
Thee we adore, O hidden Savior, thee 199

Good Friday
Deep were his wounds, and red. .100
Sing my tongue, the glorious battle* (ABC). 118
O sacred head, now wounded. 116, 117

Easter Day
Good Christian friends, rejoice and sing. 144
Christ Jesus lay in death's strong bands* (ABC). 134
At the Lamb's high feast we sing. 210

2 Easter
Come, you faithful, raise the strain 132
O sons and daughters of the King* (ABC) 139
That Easter day with joy was bright 154

3 Easter
With high delight let us unite* 140
Look, now he stands! Stones could not hold him down
 for long (ABC). 152
Now all the vault of heav'n resounds 143

4 Easter
O God of Jacob, by whose hand .477
The King of love my shepherd is* (A) 456
The Lord's my shepherd; I'll not want (B). 451
Savior, like a shepherd lead us (C) 481
I know that my Redeemer lives! .352

5 Easter
At the Lamb's high feast we sing* 210
You are the way; through you alone (A) 464
Amid the world's bleak wilderness (B) 378
Lord of all nations, grant me grace (C) 419
Jesus, thy boundless love to me .336

6 Easter
Dear Christians, one and all, rejoice* 299
Son of God, eternal Savior (ABC). 364
One there is, above all others. 298

Ascension
Up through endless ranks of angels* 159
Look, oh, look, the sight is glorious (A) 156
Lord, enthroned in heav'nly splendor (B). 172
Alleluia! Sing to Jesus (C). 158
A hymn of glory let us sing! 157

7 Easter
Oh, love, how deep, how broad, how high*. 88
Lord, teach us how to pray aright (A) 438
Have no fear, little flock (B) 476
Lord, receive this company (C) .255

Pentecost
To God the Holy Spirit let us pray 317
Come, Holy Ghost, our souls inspire (A). 472, 473
Come, Holy Ghost, God and Lord* (B). 163
Filled with the Spirit's pow'r, with one accord (C). 160
Lord God, the Holy Ghost 162

Holy Trinity
Creator Spirit, heav'nly dove* 284
Father most holy, merciful, and tender (ABC) 169
All glory be to God on high. 166

2 Pentecost
To God the Holy Spirit let us pray* 317
My hope is built on nothing less (A). 293, 294
Holy Spirit, truth divine (B) 257
Lord, whose love in humble service (C) 423

3 Pentecost
Jesus sinners will receive (A). 291
Oh, for a thousand tongues to sing (B). 559
When in the hour of deepest need* (C). 303

4 Pentecost
O God, O Lord of heav'n and earth* 396
Spread, oh, spread, almighty Word (A). 379
Almighty God, your Word is cast (B) 234
O Jesus, joy of loving hearts (C) .356

5 Pentecost

Lord of our life, and God of our salvation* 366
Let me be yours forever (A). 490
Who trusts in God, a strong abode* (B). 450
Christ is made the sure foundation (C). 367

6 Pentecost

Even as we live each day*. 350
O God, send heralds who will never falter (AC) 283
O God of mercy, God of light (B). 425

7 Pentecost

O Christ, our light, O Radiance true*. 380
Peace, to soothe our bitter woes (A) 338
God moves in a mysterious way (B). 483
Jesus shall reign where'er the sun (C). 530

8 Pentecost

Forth in thy name, O Lord, I go* 505
Almighty God, your Word is cast (A). 234
The Son of God, our Christ, the Word, the Way (B). 434
O God of mercy, God of light (C) 425

9 Pentecost

O Holy Spirit, enter in* 459
On what has now been sown (A). 261
O God of light, your Word, a lamp unfailing (B). 237
Lord, thee I love with all my heart (C) 325

10 Pentecost

From God can nothing move me*. 468
O God, O Lord of heav'n and earth (A) 396
Jesus, priceless treasure* (B). 457, 458
Lord, teach us how to pray aright (C) 438

11 Pentecost

Jesus, priceless treasure* 457, 458
Praise and thanksgiving (A) 409
O Bread of life from heaven (B) .222
Son of God, eternal Savior (C). .364

12 Pentecost

If God himself be for me* 454
Eternal Father, strong to save (A) 467
Guide me ever, great Redeemer (B) 343
Rise, my soul, to watch and pray (C) 443

13 Pentecost

When in the hour of deepest need* (A). 303
How blest are they who hear God's Word (B) 227
Lord, keep us steadfast in your Word* (C) 230

14 Pentecost

O Christ, our light, O Radiance true*. 380
Built on a rock the Church shall stand (A) 365
Hope of the world, thou Christ of great compassion (B). . .493
A multitude comes from the east and the west* (C) 313

15 Pentecost

Son of God, eternal Savior*. 364
If God himself be for me (A). 454
To you, omniscient Lord of all* (B) 310
O God of earth and altar (C). 428

16 Pentecost

Praise the Almighty, my soul, adore him! * 539
Lord of all nations, grant me grace* (A) 419
O Son of God, in Galilee (B). 426
Take my life, that I may be (C) 406

17 Pentecost

Forgive our sins as we forgive* (A). 307
Let me be yours forever (B) 490
Jesus sinners will receive* (C). 291

18 Pentecost

Salvation unto us has come* (A) .297
All depends on our possessing (B). 447
Father eternal, ruler of creation (C) 413

19 Pentecost

Lord, keep us steadfast in your Word*. 230
O Master, let me walk with you (A) 492
O Jesus, I have promised (B) 503
Oh, praise the Lord, my soul! (C) 538

20 Pentecost

The Church of Christ, in ev'ry age* (A). 433
Our Father, by whose name* (B). 357
O Jesus, I have promised* (C) 503

21 Pentecost

All who believe and are baptized*. 194
A multitude comes from the east and the west (A) 313
Thee will I love, my strength, my tow'r (B). 502
Your hand, O Lord, in days of old (C). 431

22 Pentecost

Forth in thy name, O Lord, I go* 505
Father eternal, ruler of creation (A) 413
God, who stretched the spangled heavens (B). 463
Out of the depths I cry to you (C) 295

23 Pentecost

Lord, teach us how to pray aright* 438
Oh, that the Lord would guide my ways (A). 480
Oh, praise the Lord, my soul! (B) 538
To you, omniscient Lord of all* (C) 310

24 Pentecost

Love divine, all loves excelling*. .315
Wake, awake, for night is flying* (A) 31
Lord of light, your name outshining (B). 405
If you but trust in God to guide you (C). 453

25 Pentecost

Rejoice, angelic choirs, rejoice! *. .146
Forth in thy name, O Lord, I go (A) 505
As saints of old their firstfruits brought (B). 404
I know that my Redeemer lives! (C). 352

26 Pentecost

O God of earth and altar* (A). 428
Through the night of doubt and sorrow* (B). 355
Fight the good fight with all your might* (C). 461

27 Pentecost

The day is surely drawing near* 321
Rise, O children of salvation (A) .182
Rejoice, rejoice, believers (B) 25
Lord Christ, when first you came to earth* 421

Christ the King

Rejoice, the Lord is king! 171
The day is surely drawing near* (A). 321
At the name of Jesus* (B). 179
O Jesus, king most wonderful! (C). 537
The head that once was crowned with thorns 173

See Topical Index to Hymns to make selections for Lesser Festivals, Commemorations, Occasions.